Ninja Foodi Cookbook UK for Beginners

600 Quick, Healthy, Crispy and Effortless Ninja Foodi Recipes to Impress Your Family and Friends with Metric Measurement On a Budget

Hobart Weimann

Copyright© 2022 By Hobart Weimann

All rights reserved worldwide.

No part of this book may be reproduced or transmitted in any form or by any means, electronic or mechanical, including photo- copying, recording or by any information storage and retrieval system, without written permission from the publisher, except for the inclusion of brief quotations in a review.

Warning-Disclaimer

The purpose of this book is to educate and entertain. The author or publisher does not guarantee that anyone following the techniques, suggestions, tips, ideas, or strategies will become successful. The author and publisher shall have neither liability or responsibility to anyone with respect to any loss or damage caused, or alleged to be caused, directly or indirectly by the information contained in this book.

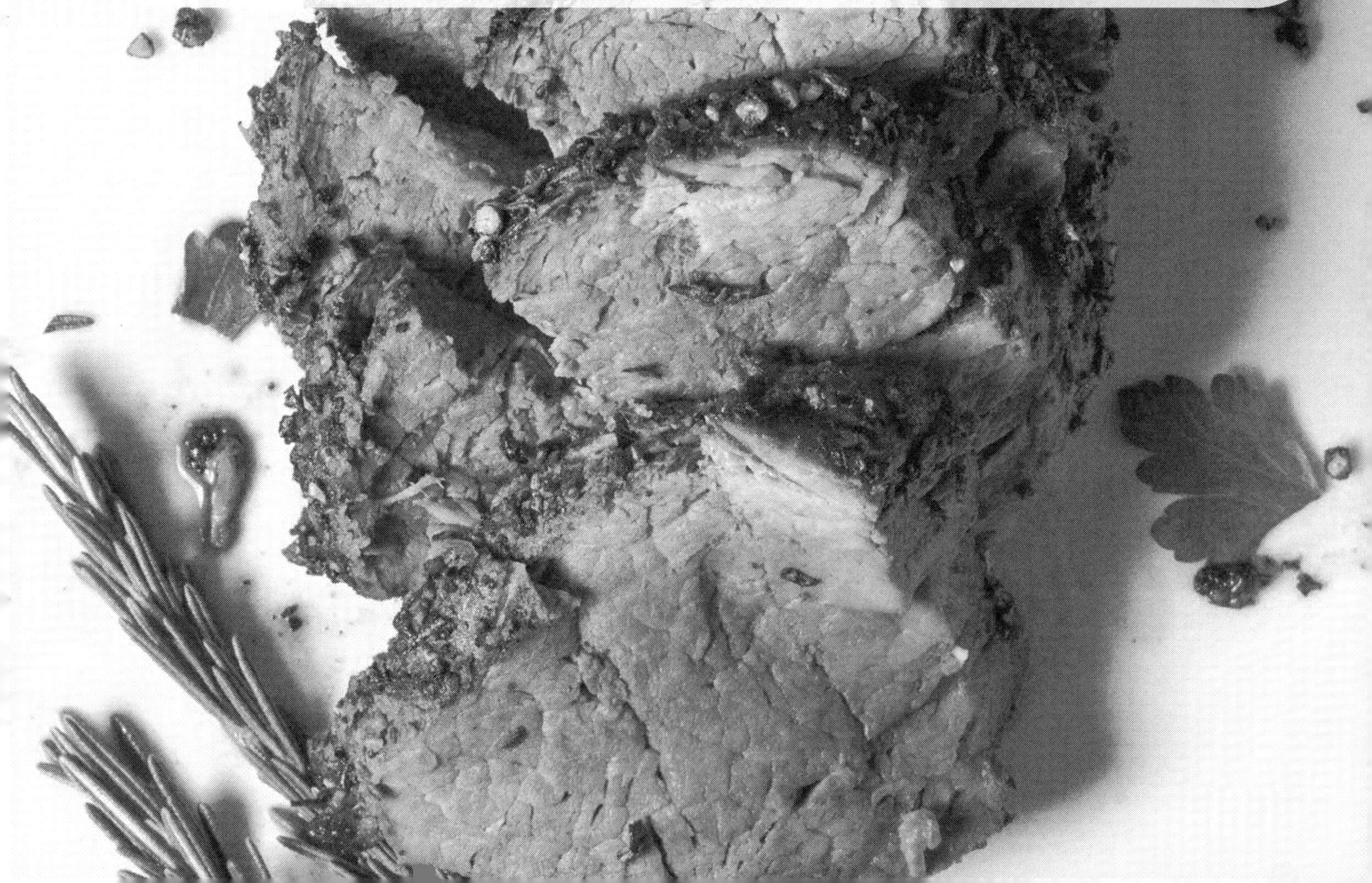

Table of Contents

Introduction	1
Chapter 1 The Beauty of the Ninja Foodi Max	**2**
How Can You Pressure Cook and Air Fry Recipes in a Single Appliance?	2
Exceptional Cooking and Meal Prep Versatility	2
Multifaceted Accessories to Help Prepare a Variety of Recipes	3
Cleaning the Ninja Foodi Is Simple	4
Chapter 2 Breakfasts	**5**
Parmesan Ranch Risotto	5
Spinach Omelet	5
Bacon and Mushroom Quiche Lorraine	5
Smoky Sausage Patties	5
Cauliflower and Cheese Quiche	5
Cheddar-Ham-Corn Muffins	6
Canadian Bacon Muffin Sandwiches	6
Cheddar Broccoli Egg Bites	6
Keto Cabbage Hash Browns	6
Pork and Quill Egg Cups	6
Drop Biscuits	6
Hard-Boiled Eggs	7
Fluffy Vanilla Pancake	7
Slow-Cooked Granola with Nuts	7
Traditional Porridge	7
Lettuce Wrapped Chicken Sandwich	7
Asparagus and Bell Pepper Strata	7
Mushroom-and-Tomato Stuffed Hash Browns	8
Oat and Chia Porridge	8
Blueberry Almond Cereal	8
Sausage Stuffed Peppers	8
Cajun Breakfast Sausage	8
Cheesy Vegetable Frittata	8
Poached Eggs on Whole Grain Avocado Toast	9
Egg and Bacon Muffins	9
Spinach and Swiss Frittata with Mushrooms	9
Buffalo Egg Cups	9
Vanilla Granola	9
Southwestern Ham Egg Cups	9
Butternut Squash and Ricotta Frittata	10
Denver Omelette	10
Bacon and Spinach Egg Muffins	10
Pecan and Walnut Granola	10
Western Frittata	10
Cheddar Soufflés	11
Cauliflower Nutty Porridge	11
Breakfast Calzone	11
Jalapeño Popper Egg Cups	11
Apple Rolls	11
Kale Omelet	12
Three-Cheese Quiche	12
Shredded Potato Omelet	12
Breakfast Pitta	12
Bacon Cheese Egg with Avocado	12
Cheesy Bell Pepper Eggs	12
Baked Egg and Mushroom Cups	13
Potato-Bacon Gratin	13
Baked Potato Breakfast Boats	13
Tropical Steel Cut Oats	13
Mini Chocolate Chip Muffins	13
Hard-boiled Eggs	14
Turkey Breakfast Sausage Patties	14
Chapter 3 Beef, Pork, and Lamb	**15**
Chicken-Fried Steak	15
Sausage and Courgette Lasagna	15
Beef Clod Vindaloo	15
Spice-Rubbed Pork Loin	15
Sirloin Steak with Honey-Mustard Butter	16
Bean and Beef Meatball Taco Pizza	16
Lemon Pork with Marjoram	16
Minute Steak Roll-Ups	16
Chicken-Fried Steak	16
Ginger Pork Meatballs	17
Filipino Pork Loin	17
Hawaiian Pulled Pork Roast with Cabbage	17
Romano-Crusted Pork Chops	17
Bacon Wrapped Pork with Apple Gravy	17
Kale and Beef Omelet	17
Barbecue Ribs	18
Italian Steak Rolls	18
Beef and Tomato Sauce Meatloaf	18
Baby Back Ribs	18
Beef Burgers with Kale and Cheese	18
Stuffed Beef Fillet with Feta Cheese	19
Lamb Sirloin Masala	19
Cider-Herb Pork Tenderloin	19
Mustard Herb Pork Tenderloin	19
Pork Meatballs with Thyme	19
Classic Pork and Cauliflower Keema	19
Cheddar Bacon Burst with Spinach	20
Greek-Style Meatloaf	20
Basil and Thyme Pork Loin	20
Beef Chili with Kale	20
Spicy Beef Stew with Butternut Squash	20
Sausage-Stuffed Peppers	21

Pork Schnitzels with Sour Cream and Dill Sauce	21
Beef Burger	21
Beef Steak Fingers	21
Italian Sausage Links	21
Roast Beef with Horseradish Cream	22
Buttery Pork Chops	22
Honey-Baked Pork Loin	22
Cantonese BBQ Pork	22
Beef and Red Cabbage Stew	22
Turmeric Pork Loin	23
Coconut Pork Muffins	23
Beef Steak with Cheese Mushroom Sauce	23
Cheesesteak Stuffed Peppers	23
Air Fried Beef Satay with Peanut Dipping Sauce	23
Beef Bavette Steak with Sage	24
Rosemary Ribeye Steaks	24
Korean Beef and Pickled Vegetable Bowls	24
Air Fried Crispy Venison	24
Pork Milanese	24
Egg Meatloaf	25
Garlic Beef Roast	25
Greek Pork with Tzatziki Sauce	25
Beef Masala Curry	25
Greek Lamb Rack	25

Chapter 4 Fish and Seafood 26

Prawn and Cherry Tomato Kebabs	26
Bacon Halibut Steak	26
Crab and Bell Pepper Cakes	26
Crab Cakes	26
Tuna Patties with Spicy Sriracha Sauce	26
Butter-Wine Baked Salmon	27
Paprika Prawns	27
Salade Niçoise with Oil-Packed Tuna	27
Louisiana Prawn Gumbo	27
Haddock and Veggie Foil Packets	27
Roasted Halibut Steaks with Parsley	28
Parmesan Salmon Loaf	28
Asian Marinated Salmon	28
Balsamic Tilapia	28
Clam Chowder with Bacon and Celery	28
Firecracker Prawns	28
Bacon-Wrapped Scallops	29
Roasted Fish with Almond-Lemon Crumbs	29
Scallops in Lemon-Butter Sauce	29
Prawn Kebabs	29
Italian Salmon	29
Fish Bake with Veggies	29
Lemony Prawns and Courgette	30
Asian Swordfish	30
Turmeric Salmon	30
Braised Striped Bass with Courgette and Tomatoes	30
Salmon Steaks with Garlicky yoghurt	30

Savory Prawns	31
Coconut Prawns with Pineapple-Lemon Sauce	31
Baked Flounder with Artichoke	31
Dill Salmon Cakes	31
Fish Gratin	31
Cajun Cod Fillet	32
Fish Sandwich with Tartar Sauce	32
Lemony Fish and Asparagus	32
Lemon Pepper Tilapia with Broccoli and Carrots	32
Coconut Prawns	32
Easy Scallops	33
Fried Prawns	33
Mediterranean Salmon with Whole-Wheat Couscous	33
Steamed Halibut with Lemon	33
Mackerel and Broccoli Casserole	33
Mahi-Mahi Fillets with Peppers	34
Rainbow Trout with Mixed Greens	34
Salmon with Dill Butter	34
Greek Prawn with Tomatoes and Feta	34
Cod with Warm Beetroot and Rocket Salad	34
Cod Fillets with Cherry Tomatoes	35
Tuna Fillets with Lemon Butter	35
Prawns Pasta with Basil and Mushrooms	35
Mussels with Fennel and Leeks	35
Aromatic Monkfish Stew	35
Snapper in Spicy Tomato Sauce	36
Creamy Haddock	36
Steamed Cod with Garlic and Swiss Chard	36
Tandoori Prawns	36
Prawn Caesar Salad	36
Sole and Cauliflower Fritters	37

Chapter 5 Poultry 38

Chicken and Mixed Greens Salad	38
Tuscan Chicken Drumsticks	38
Kung Pao Chicken	38
Curried Orange Honey Chicken	38
Sesame Chicken Breast	38
Chicken Casserole	39
Broccoli Chicken Divan	39
Mediterranean Stuffed Chicken Breasts	39
Apricot-Glazed Chicken Drumsticks	39
Chipotle Drumsticks	39
Bruschetta Chicken	40
Ann's Chicken Cacciatore	40
Sesame Chicken with Broccoli	40
Chicken Enchiladas	40
Classic Chicken Kebab	40
Chicken and Ham Meatballs with Dijon Sauce	41
Smoky Whole Chicken	41
Chicken Tagine	41
Chicken and Vegetable Fajitas	41
Ham Chicken with Cheese	42

Recipe	Page
Barbecue Shredded Chicken	42
Mexican Chicken with Red Salsa	42
Chicken Wings with Piri Piri Sauce	42
Mexican Turkey Tenderloin	42
Barbecued Chicken with Creamy Coleslaw	43
Lemon Garlic Chicken	43
Chicken Thighs with Coriander	43
Chili Lime Turkey Burgers	43
One-Dish Chicken and Rice	43
Crispy Duck with Cherry Sauce	44
Coconut Chicken Meatballs	44
Thai Coconut Chicken	44
Porchetta-Style Chicken Breasts	44
Chicken Reuben Bake	45
Hoisin Turkey Burgers	45
Thai Chicken with Cucumber and Chili Salad	45
Garlic Dill Wings	45
Gold Livers	45
Crack Chicken Breasts	46
African Chicken Peanut Stew	46
Brazilian Tempero Baiano Chicken Drumsticks	46
Harissa-Rubbed Chicken	46
Fajita Chicken Strips	46
BLT Chicken Salad	47
Buffalo Crispy Chicken Strips	47
Fried Chicken Breasts	47
Bruschetta and Cheese Stuffed Chicken	47
Gochujang Chicken Wings	48
Simple Chicken Masala	48
Chicken and Broccoli Casserole	48
Ninja Foodi cooker Crack Chicken	48
Spanish Chicken and Mini Sweet Pepper Baguette	48
Easy Cajun Chicken Drumsticks	49
African Merguez Meatballs	49
Garlic Parmesan Drumsticks	49
Chicken Piccata	49
Buttermilk Breaded Chicken	49
Chicken Enchilada Bowl	50
Barbecue Chicken and Coleslaw Tostadas	50
Chicken Tacos with Fried Cheese Shells	50
Parmesan Carbonara Chicken	50

Chapter 6 Snacks and Appetisers   51

Recipe	Page
Blackberry Baked Brie	51
Garlic-Roasted Tomatoes and Olives	51
Tangy Fried Pickle Spears	51
Browned Ricotta with Capers and Lemon	51
Stuffed Figs with Goat Cheese and Honey	51
Parmesan Artichoke	52
Fast Spring Kale Appetizer	52
Cheese Drops	52
Artichoke and Olive Pitta Flatbread	52
Mayo Chicken Celery	52
Taco Beef Bites	52
Parmesan Chicken Balls with Chives	53
Garlic Herb Butter	53
Chicken and Cabbage Salad	53
Garlic-Parmesan Croutons	53
Crispy Chilli Chickpeas	53
Rosemary-Garlic Shoestring Fries	53
Parmesan Courgette Fries	53
Cheesy Hash Brown Bruschetta	54
Polenta Fries with Chilli-Lime Mayo	54
Spinach and Crab Meat Cups	54
Dark Chocolate and Cranberry Granola Bars	54
Easy Roasted Chickpeas	54
Creole Pancetta and Cheese Balls	54
Bruschetta with Basil Pesto	55
Egg Roll Pizza Sticks	55
Stuffed Fried Mushrooms	55
Herbed Prawn	55
Sesame Mushrooms	55
Cabbage and Broccoli Slaw	55
Sweet Potato Fries with Mayonnaise	56
Red Wine Mushrooms	56
Curried Broccoli Skewers	56
Crispy Breaded Beef Cubes	56
Asparagus with Creamy Dip	56
String Bean Fries	56
Colby Cheese and Pepper Dip	57
Lemon-Cheese Cauliflower Bites	57
Instant Popcorn	57
Brussels Sprouts with Aioli Sauce	57
Oregano Sausage Balls	57
Onion Pakoras	57
Cauliflower Fritters with Cheese	58
Shrimp Pirogues	58
Parmesan French Fries	58
Cauliflower Cheese Balls	58
Broccoli with Garlic-Herb Cheese Sauce	58
Crispy Cajun Dill Pickle Chips	59
Goat Cheese and Garlic Crostini	59
Crunchy Basil White Beans	59
Vegetable Pot Stickers	59
Greek Potato Skins with Olives and Feta	59

Chapter 7 Vegetables and Sides   60

Recipe	Page
Seeds	60
Broccoli and Mushroom Bake	60
Spiced Honey-Walnut Carrots	60
Braised Fennel with radicchio, Pear, and Pecorino	60
Satarash with Eggs	61
Asparagus and Mushroom Soup	61
Thyme Cabbage	61
Mashed Sweet Potato Tots	61
Turnip Fries	61
Fig, Chickpea, and Rocket Salad	61

Falafel and Lettuce Salad	62
Roasted Salsa	62
Wild Rice Salad with Cranberries and Almonds	62
Courgette Balls	62
Buttery Mushrooms	62
Sweet and Crispy Roasted Pearl Onions	62
Gobi Masala	63
Mediterranean Courgette Boats	63
Lemon-Garlic Mushrooms	63
Cauliflower Rice Curry	63
Rosemary-Roasted Red Potatoes	63
Spicy Roasted Bok Choy	63
Lemony Broccoli	64
Ninja Foodi cooker Courgette Sticks	64
Garlic Cauliflower with Tahini	64
Cauliflower Steaks Gratin	64
Lemony Brussels Sprouts with Poppy Lemon Cabbage and Tempeh	64
Spicy Cauliflower Head	65
Savoury and Rich Creamed Kale	65
Potatoes with Parsley	65
Saltine Wax Beans	65
Asparagus Fries	65
Air Fried Potatoes with Olives	65
Garlicky Broccoli with Roasted Almonds	66
Buttery Green Beans	66
Roasted Radishes with Sea Salt	66
Spaghetti Squash	66
Parmesan Courgette Noodles	66
Chanterelle Mushrooms with Cheddar Cheese	66
Braised Radishes with Sugar Snap Peas and Dukkah	67
Green Peas with Mint	67
Fried Brussels Sprouts	67
Crispy Courgette Sticks	67
Herbed Shiitake Mushrooms	67
Corn on the Cob	68
Lemony Asparagus with Gremolata	68
Steamed Tomato with Halloumi Cheese	68
Perfect Sweet Potatoes	68
Dinner Rolls	68
Broccoli-Cheddar Twice-Baked Potatoes	68
Dijon Roast Cabbage	69
Chermoula-Roasted Beetroots	69
Parmesan-Thyme Butternut Squash	69
Parmesan-Topped Acorn Squash	69
Cauliflower Rice Balls	69

Chapter 8 Desserts 70

Vanilla Cookies with Hazelnuts	70
Lemon Poppy Seed Macaroons	70
Pumpkin Pie Spice Pots De Crème	70
Southern Almond Pie	70
Breaded Bananas with Chocolate Topping	71
Courgette Nut Muffins	71
Chocolate Peppermint Cheesecake	71
Double Chocolate Brownies	71
Hearty Crème Brûlée	71
Pecan Bars	72
Egg Custard Tarts	72
Cinnamon Cupcakes with Cream Cheese Frosting	72
Chocolate Macadamia Bark	72
Strawberry Cheesecake	72
Simple Apple Turnovers	73
Almond Butter Cookie Balls	73
Crispy Pineapple Rings	73
Spiced Pear Applesauce	73
Old-Fashioned Fudge Pie	73
Pine Nut Mousse	73
Chocolate Chip Brownies	74
Chocolate Croissants	74
Fried Oreos	74
Vanilla Cream Pie	74
Almond Butter Keto Fat Bombs	74
Cocoa Custard	74
Hazelnut Butter Cookies	75
Grilled Peaches	75
Apple Wedges with Apricots	75
Baked Peaches with Yogurt and Blueberries	75
Cocoa Cookies	75
Almond Pie with Coconut	75
Daikon and Almond Cake	76
Fried Cheesecake Bites	76
Maple-Pecan Tart with Sea Salt	76
Grilled Pineapple Dessert	76
Pecan Brownies	76
Goat Cheese–Stuffed Pears	77
Flourless Chocolate Tortes	77
Candied Mixed Nuts	77
New York Cheesecake	77
Butter Flax Cookies	77
Pumpkin Pudding with Vanilla Wafers	78
Thai Pandan Coconut Custard	78
Pumpkin Pie Pudding	78
Vanilla Crème Brûlée	78
Blackberry Cobbler	78
Coconut Lemon Squares	79
Cardamom Rolls with Cream Cheese	79
Apple Fries	79
Chocolate Fondue	79
Indian Toast and Milk	79
Nutmeg Cupcakes	80

INTRODUCTION

Even though I love cooking and have also worked as a professional chef at some fine dining restaurants, I do, at times, feel frustrated when I come back from work and realize that I need to cook lunch or dinner for my family. While I have always loved cooking from an early age, the only thing that sometimes gets to me is all meal preparation and the mess it can potentially cause if you're not careful. Overall, cooking, for me, at times, becomes a gigantic chore to overcome.

So, naturally, when someone told me that there's a godsent kitchen appliance that can do almost all the work for you, of course, I get curious as heck! This is essentially where the Ninja Food Pressure Cooker and Air Fryer comes into play. At first, I really couldn't believe that there was a cooking appliance that could do everything for you – and I also couldn't believe that I didn't know something like this existed.

But I quickly found out why the Ninja Foodi air fryer and pressure cooker became so exponentially popular. Well, first of all, the machine is designed to offer 3 cooking modes! It has 14 menu presets and cooking functions and comes with a flurry of essential cooking and meal prep accessories you'll quickly fall in love with. It is an absolute unit!

But perhaps one of the best things about the Ninja Foodi is the fact that you can cook almost anything in it. This is exactly why I was able to create a comprehensive cookbook featuring some pretty easy-to-understand air fryer and pressure cooker recipes anyone can prepare and enjoy. While my cookbook is for absolutely anyone who likes to cook or wants to learn how to cook, it is also specifically developed for working professionals who want nothing but to prepare their favourite meals with the utmost ease and simplicity.

Moreover, I have also strived and endeavoured to create recipes you can prepare using affordable and easily available ingredients at your local grocery store. All the recipes are featured in a digestible manner, with each detail, measurement, and ingredient usage outlined in a step-by-step manner so that you can considerably shorten your meal prep time. In addition, I have also focused on providing recipes that appeal to individuals with fitness goals or those who are on any sort of weight loss diet.

Chapter 1 The Beauty of the Ninja Foodi Max

Simply put, the Ninja Foodi Pressure Cooker and Air Fryer is a multifunctional cooking unit that is designed to function as a pressure cooker, air fryer, stovetop, and much more! I use it as an all-in-one kitchen appliance and I have got to say that it can significantly help cut down your meal prep and cooking time, allowing you to cook a variety of different recipes all at once.

Moreover, what I have also found interesting is that its pressure cooker mode potentially helps reduce the time to prepare some of my recipes by up to 70%! In addition, the Ninja Foodi comes with a plethora of menu presets and accessories – which is also one of the major reasons why (in my opinion) it is the best one-in-all cooking appliance.

How Can You Pressure Cook and Air Fry Recipes in a Single Appliance?

Now, I bet you're probably thinking how one kitchen appliance like the Ninja Foodi function as an electric pressure cooker and an efficient air fryer. That is a good question. The answer is simple. You see, the Ninja Foodi is designed with two separate lids. You can use one lid to steam cook your ingredients such as chicken, fish, and beef or you could use the other lid to air fry different recipes. The lids are conveniently designed with durable hinges so that you can use both or one lid(s) interchangeably without having them in your way.

Moreover, the all-in-one kitchen appliance also features the company's patented TenderCrisp Technology, which means you can cook your favourite recipes and achieve that delicious and savoury golden-brown texture. In addition, the Ninja Foodi can also help you prepare meals considerably faster (by up to 70%). You can select from 14 different cooking functionalities such as baking or roasting, grilling, rotisserie, and much more. Or you could also use the device to prepare slow-cook recipes or for braising.

Furthermore, this nifty cooking appliance provides 9 ways for you to cook different recipes. For example, you can make juicy chicken, steaks, pasta, steamed vegetables, steamed or grilled fish, sauté onions, bake brownies or cakes, defrost ingredients, and much more.

Exceptional Cooking and Meal Prep Versatility

Pressure Cook

You can pressure cook a variety of ingredients and proteins in the Ninja Foodi in a matter of minutes. Cook roast steak and chicken, steamed fish, chili, pasta, and more! Plus, you can also prepare a wide variety of delicious desserts.

Air Crisp

Thanks to Ninja Foodi's TenderCrisp Technology, you can cook recipes using up to 90% less oil and up to 75% less fat to make crispy and healthy recipes or other delicious things such as fried chicken, French fries, crispy vegetables, fried fish, etc.

Steam

You can also use the pressure cooker option to steam your ingredients and prepare things like smoked or steamed salmon, steamed roasted chicken or beef, steamed vegetables, and much more.

Slow Cook

You can use the Ninja Foodi to slow-cook recipes and make sure everything is nice and ready to eat as soon as you get home from work. For example, you can prepare risotto, pulled pork, and casseroles. The machine provides various features and adjustable time settings to slow-cook ingredients at high or low temperatures.

Yoghurt

The Ninja Foodi also comes with a built-in yoghurt-making feature. It's pretty simple to use and all you need to do is add the ingredients mentioned in my cookbook, push the start button, and voila! You have yoghurt!

Sear/Sauté

The product also comes with a sear/sauté feature using the appliance's stovetop. If you want to simmer the ingredients use the LO setting. To sauté, use the MED setting and for searing or boiling, use the HI setting. It's simple to use and pretty quick.

Bake/Roast

I often use the Ninja Foodi to roast dehydrated ingredients and prepare pulled pork recipes. The roasting function is simple to use, and you can prepare a variety of mouth-watering treats using different types of proteins.

Grill

Use the stove-top grill option to prepare your favourite grilled chicken, meat, or fish recipes. The appliance's Cook and Crisp plate is a wonderful feature you can use further add that golden-brown crispy texture to all your grilled recipes.

Dehydrate

You can use the dehydrating functionality of the Ninja Foodi to quickly dehydrate vegetables, fruits, and different proteins. Just be sure to use the lowest temperature setting so that ingredients dry out instead of slow cook. Dehydrating meats and vegetables can help provide you with that extra savoury and crispy texture.

Multifaceted Accessories to Help Prepare a Variety of Recipes

Another reason why I love the Ninja Food Pressure Cooker and Air Fryer is because the appliance comes with a slew of handy accessories. The accessories have helped me prepare a lot of recipes and dishes. Plus, you won't need any additional pots and pans except for maybe your favourite pans or whatnot. Otherwise, the Ninja Foodi is a complete cooking machine. In light of this, I have mentioned some pretty neat accessories that will come with your Ninja Foodi.

Pressure Lid

One of the best things about the Ninja Foodi Pressure Cooker and Air Fryer is that it is exceptionally designed for safe use. The product comes with a cleverly designed pressure-release valve that makes it easy for users to first release all the accumulated pressure with optimal safety. Just press the red button on the pressure lid and release all the steam and heat before completely opening the lid.

Crisping Lid

You can use the crisping lid to further air fry and add that golden-crispy texture to your roast chicken, fish, or beef after you have pressure cooked all the ingredients. It is pretty easy to use, just open the pressure-release lid and place the crisping lid on the stovetop.

Cooking PotCook and Crisp Basket

Along with pressure cooking and air frying your favourite ingredients and preparing mouth-watering recipes, the Ninja Foodi 9-in-1 cooker can also help you easily steam a large chicken. Using its PotCook, you can also dehydrate and defrost chicken, meat, or fish. The Ninja Foodi is designed with a streamlined airflow design, which can help make the process quicker.

Reversible Rack

The reversible rack is another thing that adds more versatility and functionality to the Ninja Foodi Pressure Cooker and Air Fryer. For example, I use the reversible rack not just to roast chicken or beef, but also use it to steam-cook vegetables. Plus, I also flip the rack to broil strip steaks.

Cleaning the Ninja Foodi Is Simple

For me, cleaning the Ninja Foodi has always been an easy task because you can disassemble the device and individually wash every part. However, I have outlined some cleaning tips you will find helpful.

Avoid soaking any part of your Ninja Foodi Max in water. This is because the product isn't designed like typical air fryers. It is better to wash and clean everything manually.

Stay away from harsh dishwashing agents and chemicals. Also, refrain from using oven cleaners. Harsh cleaning chemicals aren't food-grade and there is a chance the chemicals may leave some residue behind, mixing with your food. Another reason why I don't use strong cleaning chemicals is that the Ninja Foodi is prone to get discoloured. So, just use the simple soap and water solution.

Chapter 2 Breakfasts

Parmesan Ranch Risotto

Prep time: 10 minutes | Cook time: 30 minutes | Serves 2

1 tablespoon olive oil
1 clove garlic, minced
1 tablespoon unsalted butter
1 onion, diced
180 ml Arborio rice
475 ml chicken stock, boiling
120 ml Parmesan cheese, grated

1. Preheat the Ninja Foodi cooker to 200ºC. 2. Grease a round baking tin with olive oil and stir in the garlic, butter, and onion. 3. Transfer the tin to the Ninja Foodi cooker and bake for 4 minutes. Add the rice and bake for 4 more minutes. 4. Turn the Ninja Foodi cooker to 160ºC and pour in the chicken stock. Cover and bake for 22 minutes. 5. Scatter with cheese and serve.

Spinach Omelet

Prep time: 5 minutes | Cook time: 12 minutes | Serves 2

4 large eggs
350 ml chopped fresh spinach leaves
2 tablespoons peeled and chopped brown onion
2 tablespoons salted butter, melted
120 ml shredded mild Cheddar cheese
¼ teaspoon salt

1. In an ungreased round nonstick baking dish, whisk eggs. Stir in spinach, onion, butter, Cheddar, and salt. 2. Place dish into cook & crisp basket. Adjust the temperature to 160ºC and bake for 12 minutes. Omelet will be done when browned on the top and firm in the middle. 3. Slice in half and serve warm on two medium plates.

Bacon and Mushroom Quiche Lorraine

Prep time: 10 minutes | Cook time: 37 minutes | Serves 4

4 strips bacon, chopped
480 ml sliced button mushrooms
120 ml diced onions
8 large eggs
360 ml shredded Swiss cheese
240 ml unsweetened almond milk
60 ml sliced spring onions
½ teaspoon sea salt
¼ teaspoon ground black pepper
2 tablespoons coconut flour

1. Press the Sauté button on the Ninja Foodi cooker and add the bacon. Sauté for 4 minutes, or until crisp. Transfer the bacon to a plate lined with paper towel to drain, leaving the drippings in the pot. 2. Add the mushrooms and diced onions to the pot and sauté for 3 minutes, or until the onions are tender. Remove the mixture from the pot to a large bowl. Wipe the Ninja Foodi cooker clean. 3. Set a reversible rack in the Ninja Foodi cooker and pour in 240 ml water. 4. In a medium bowl, stir together the eggs, cheese, almond milk, spring onions, salt and pepper. Pour the egg mixture into the bowl with the mushrooms and onions. Stir to combine. Fold in the coconut flour. Pour the mixture into a greased round casserole dish. Spread the cooked bacon on top. 5. Place the casserole dish onto the reversible rack in the Ninja Foodi cooker. 6. Lock the lid, Set the cooking time for 30 minutes on High Pressure. When the timer goes off, do a natural pressure release for 15 minutes, then release any remaining pressure. Open the lid. 7. Remove the casserole dish from the Ninja Foodi cooker. 8. Let cool for 15 to 30 minutes before cutting into 4 pieces. Serve immediately.

Smoky Sausage Patties

Prep time: 30 minutes | Cook time: 9 minutes | Serves 8

450 g pork mince
1 tablespoon soy sauce or tamari
1 teaspoon smoked paprika
1 teaspoon dried sage
1 teaspoon sea salt
½ teaspoon fennel seeds
½ teaspoon dried thyme
½ teaspoon freshly ground black pepper
¼ teaspoon cayenne pepper

1. In a large bowl, combine the pork, soy sauce, smoked paprika, sage, salt, fennel seeds, thyme, black pepper, and cayenne pepper. Work the meat with your hands until the seasonings are fully incorporated. 2. Shape the mixture into 8 equal-size patties. Using your thumb, make a dent in the center of each patty. Place the patties on a plate and cover with plastic wrap. Refrigerate the patties for at least 30 minutes. 3. Working in batches if necessary, place the patties in a single layer in the Ninja Foodi cooker, being careful not to overcrowd them. 4. Set the Ninja Foodi cooker to 205ºC and air crisp for 5 minutes. Flip and cook for about 4 minutes more.

Cauliflower and Cheese Quiche

Prep time: 10 minutes | Cook time: 10 minutes | Serves 2

240 ml chopped cauliflower
60 ml shredded Cheddar cheese
5 eggs, beaten
1 teaspoon butter
1 teaspoon dried oregano
240 ml water

1. Grease the Ninja Foodi cooker baking pan with butter from inside. 2. Pour water in the Ninja Foodi cooker. 3. Sprinkle the cauliflower with dried oregano and put it in the prepared baking pan. Flatten the vegetables gently. 4. After this, add eggs and stir the vegetables. 5. Top the quiche with shredded cheese and transfer it in the Ninja Foodi cooker. Close and seal the lid. Cook the quiche on High Pressure for 10 minutes. Make a quick pressure release.

Cheddar-Ham-Corn Muffins

Prep time: 10 minutes | Cook time: 6 to 8 minutes per batch | Makes 8 muffins

180 ml cornmeal/polenta
60 ml flour
1½ teaspoons baking powder
¼ teaspoon salt
1 egg, beaten
2 tablespoons rapeseed oil
120 ml milk
120 ml shredded sharp Cheddar cheese
120 ml diced ham
8 foil muffin cups, liners removed and sprayed with cooking spray

1. Preheat the Ninja Foodi cooker to 200ºC. 2. In a medium bowl, stir together the cornmeal, flour, baking powder, and salt. 3. Add egg, oil, and milk to dry ingredients and mix well. 4. Stir in shredded cheese and diced ham. 5. Divide batter among the muffin cups. 6. Place 4 filled muffin cups in cook & crisp basket and bake for 5 minutes. 7. Reduce temperature to 165ºC and bake for 1 to 2 minutes or until toothpick inserted in center of muffin comes out clean. 8. Repeat steps 6 and 7 to cook remaining muffins.

Canadian Bacon Muffin Sandwiches

Prep time: 5 minutes | Cook time: 8 minutes | Serves 4

4 English muffins, split
8 slices back bacon
4 slices cheese
Cooking spray

1. Preheat the Ninja Foodi cooker to 190ºC. 2. Make the sandwiches: Top each of 4 muffin halves with 2 slices of bacon, 1 slice of cheese, and finish with the remaining muffin half. 3. Put the sandwiches in the cook & crisp basket and spritz the tops with cooking spray. 4. Bake for 4 minutes. Flip the sandwiches and bake for another 4 minutes. 5. Divide the sandwiches among four plates and serve warm.

Cheddar Broccoli Egg Bites

Prep time: 10 minutes | Cook time: 10 minutes | Serves 7

5 eggs, beaten
3 tablespoons double cream
⅛ teaspoon salt
⅛ teaspoon black pepper
30 g finely chopped broccoli
30 g shredded Cheddar cheese
120 ml water

1. In a blender, combine the eggs, double cream, salt and pepper and pulse until smooth. 2. Divide the chopped broccoli among the egg cups equally. Pour the egg mixture on top of the broccoli, filling the cups about three-fourths of the way full. Sprinkle the Cheddar cheese on top of each cup. 3. Cover the egg cups tightly with aluminium foil. 4. Pour the water and insert the reversible rack in the Ninja Foodi cooker. Put the egg cups on the reversible rack. 5. Lock the lid. Set the cooking time for 10 minutes on High Pressure. Once the timer goes off, perform a natural pressure release for 5 minutes, then release any remaining pressure. Carefully open the lid. 6. Serve immediately.

Keto Cabbage Hash Browns

Prep time: 5 minutes | Cook time: 8 minutes | Serves 3

240 ml shredded white cabbage
3 eggs, beaten
½ teaspoon ground nutmeg
½ teaspoon salt
½ teaspoon onion powder
½ courgette, grated
1 tablespoon coconut oil

1. In a bowl, stir together all the ingredients, except for the coconut oil. Form the cabbage mixture into medium hash browns. 2. Press the Sauté button on the Ninja Foodi cooker and heat the coconut oil. 3. Place the hash browns in the hot coconut oil. Cook for 4 minutes on each side, or until lightly browned. 4. Transfer the hash browns to a plate and serve warm.

Pork and Quill Egg Cups

Prep time: 15 minutes | Cook time: 15 minutes | Serves 4

280 g ground pork
1 jalapeño pepper, chopped
1 tablespoon butter, softened
1 teaspoon dried dill
½ teaspoon salt
240 ml water
4 quill eggs

1. In a bowl, stir together all the ingredients, except for the quill eggs and water. Transfer the meat mixture to the silicone muffin molds and press the surface gently. 2. Pour the water and insert the reversible rack in the Ninja Foodi cooker. Put the meat cups on the reversible rack. 3. Crack the eggs over the meat mixture. 4. Set the lid in place. Set the cooking time for 15 minutes on High Pressure. When the timer goes off, do a quick pressure release. Carefully open the lid. 5. Serve warm.

Drop Biscuits

Prep time: 10 minutes | Cook time: 9 to 10 minutes | Serves 5

1 L plain flour
1 tablespoon baking powder
1 tablespoon sugar (optional)
1 teaspoon salt
6 tablespoons butter, plus more
for brushing on the biscuits (optional)
180 ml buttermilk
1 to 2 tablespoons oil

1. In a large bowl, whisk the flour, baking powder, sugar (if using), and salt until blended. 2. Add the butter. Using a pastry cutter or 2 forks, work the dough until pea-size balls of the butter-flour mixture appear. Stir in the buttermilk until the mixture is sticky. 3. Preheat the Ninja Foodi cooker to 165ºC. Line the cook & crisp basket with parchment paper and spritz it with oil. 4. Drop the dough by the tablespoonful onto the prepared basket, leaving 1 inch between each, to form 10 biscuits. 5. Bake for 5 minutes. Flip the biscuits and cook for 4 minutes more for a light brown top, or 5 minutes more for a darker biscuit. Brush the tops with melted butter, if desired.

Hard-Boiled Eggs

Prep time: 10 minutes | Cook time: 5 minutes | Serves 7

240 ml water
6–8 eggs

1. Pour the water into the inner pot. Place the eggs in a steamer basket or rack that came with pot. 2. Close the lid and secure to the locking position. Be sure the vent is turned to sealing. Set for 5 minutes at high pressure. (It takes about 5 minutes for pressure to build and then 5 minutes to cook.) 3. Let pressure naturally release for 5 minutes, then do quick pressure release. 4. Place hot eggs into cool water to halt cooking process. You can peel cooled eggs immediately or refrigerate unpeeled.

Fluffy Vanilla Pancake

Prep time: 5 minutes | Cook time: 50 minutes | Serves 6

3 eggs, beaten
120 ml coconut flour
60 ml double cream
60 ml almond flour
3 tablespoons granulated sweetener
1 teaspoon vanilla extract
1 teaspoon baking powder
Cooking spray

1. In a bowl, stir together the eggs, coconut flour, double cream, almond flour, granulated sweetener and vanilla extract. Whisk in the baking powder until smooth. 2. Spritz the bottom and sides of Ninja Foodi cooker with cooking spray. Place the batter in the pot. 3. Set the lid in place. Set the cooking time for 50 minutes on Low Pressure. Once the timer goes off, perform a natural pressure release for 5 minutes, then release any remaining pressure. Carefully open the lid. 4. Let the pancake rest in the pot for 5 minutes before serving.

Slow-Cooked Granola with Nuts

Prep time: 5 minutes | Cook time: 2 hours 30 minutes | Serves 10

240 ml raw almonds
240 ml pumpkin seeds
240 ml raw walnuts
240 ml raw cashews
1 tablespoon coconut oil
60 ml unsweetened coconut chips
1 teaspoon sea salt
1 teaspoon cinnamon

1. In a large bowl, stir together the almonds, pumpkin seeds, walnuts, cashews and coconut oil. Make sure all the nuts are coated with the coconut oil. Place the nut mixture in the Ninja Foodi cooker and cover the pot with a paper towel. 2. Lock the lid. Select the Slow Cook mode and set the cooking time for 1 hour on More. When the timer goes off, stir the nuts. Set the timer for another hour. 3. Again, when the timer goes off, stir the nut mixture and add the coconut chips. Set the timer for another 30 minutes. The cashews should become a nice golden colour. 4. When the timer goes off, transfer the nut mixture to a baking pan to cool and sprinkle with the sea salt and cinnamon. Serve.

Traditional Porridge

Prep time: 5 minutes | Cook time: 4 minutes | Serves 4

2 tablespoons coconut oil
240 ml full-fat coconut milk
2 tablespoons blanched almond flour
2 tablespoons sugar-free chocolate chips
240 ml heavy whipping cream
120 ml chopped cashews
120 ml chopped pecans
½ teaspoon ground cinnamon
½ teaspoon sweetener, or more to taste
60 ml unsweetened coconut flakes

1. Set the Ninja Foodi cooker to Sauté and melt the coconut oil. 2. Pour in the coconut milk, 240 ml of filtered water, then combine and mix the flour, chocolate chips, whipping cream, cashews, pecans, cinnamon, sweetener, and coconut flakes, inside the Ninja Foodi cooker. 3. Close the lid, set the pressure release to sealing, and hit Start/Stop to stop the current program. Set the Ninja Foodi cooker to 4 minutes on High Pressure, and let cook. 4. Once cooked, perform a quick release by carefully switching the pressure valve to Venting. 5. Open the Ninja Foodi cooker, serve, and enjoy!

Lettuce Wrapped Chicken Sandwich

Prep time: 10 minutes | Cook time: 15 minutes | Serves 4

1 tablespoon butter
85 g scallions, chopped
480 ml ground chicken
½ teaspoon ground nutmeg
1 tablespoon coconut flour
1 teaspoon salt
240 ml lettuce

1. Press the Sauté button on the Ninja Foodi cooker and melt the butter. Add the chopped scallions, ground chicken and ground nutmeg to the pot and sauté for 4 minutes. Add the coconut flour and salt and continue to sauté for 10 minutes. 2. Fill the lettuce with the ground chicken and transfer it on the plate. Serve immediately.

Asparagus and Bell Pepper Strata

Prep time: 10 minutes | Cook time: 14 to 20 minutes | Serves 4

8 large asparagus spears, trimmed and cut into 2-inch pieces
80 ml shredded carrot
120 ml chopped red pepper
2 slices wholemeal bread, cut into ½-inch cubes
3 egg whites
1 egg
3 tablespoons 1% milk
½ teaspoon dried thyme

1. In a baking pan, combine the asparagus, carrot, red bell pepper, and 1 tablespoon of water. Bake in the Ninja Foodi cooker at 165ºC for 3 to 5 minutes, or until crisp-tender. Drain well. 2. Add the bread cubes to the vegetables and gently toss. 3. In a medium bowl, whisk the egg whites, egg, milk, and thyme until frothy. 4. Pour the egg mixture into the pan. Bake for 11 to 15 minutes, or until the strata is slightly puffy and set and the top starts to brown. Serve.

Mushroom-and-Tomato Stuffed Hash Browns

Prep time: 10 minutes | Cook time: 20 minutes | Serves 4

Olive oil cooking spray
1 tablespoon plus 2 teaspoons olive oil, divided
110 g baby mushrooms, diced
1 spring onion, white parts and green parts, diced
1 garlic clove, minced
475 ml shredded potatoes
½ teaspoon salt
¼ teaspoon black pepper
1 plum tomato, diced
120 ml shredded mozzarella

1. Preheat the Ninja Foodi cooker to 190ºC. Lightly coat the inside of a 6-inch cake pan with olive oil cooking spray. 2. In a small skillet, heat 2 teaspoons olive oil over medium heat. Add the mushrooms, spring onion, and garlic, and cook for 4 to 5 minutes, or until they have softened and are beginning to show some color. Remove from heat. 3. Meanwhile, in a large bowl, combine the potatoes, salt, pepper, and the remaining tablespoon olive oil. Toss until all potatoes are well coated. 4. Pour half of the potatoes into the bottom of the cake pan. Top with the mushroom mixture, tomato, and mozzarella. Spread the remaining potatoes over the top. 5. Bake in the Ninja Foodi cooker for 12 to 15 minutes, or until the top is golden brown. 6. Remove from the Ninja Foodi cooker and allow to cool for 5 minutes before slicing and serving.

Oat and Chia Porridge

Prep time: 10 minutes | Cook time: 5 minutes | Serves 4

2 tablespoons peanut butter
4 tablespoons honey
1 tablespoon butter, melted
1 L milk
475 ml oats
235 ml chia seeds

1. Preheat the Ninja Foodi cooker to 200ºC. 2. Put the peanut butter, honey, butter, and milk in a bowl and stir to mix. Add the oats and chia seeds and stir. 3. Transfer the mixture to a bowl and bake in the Ninja Foodi cooker for 5 minutes. Give another stir before serving.

Blueberry Almond Cereal

Prep time: 5 minutes | Cook time: 2 minutes | Serves 4

80 ml crushed roasted almonds
60 ml almond flour
60 ml unsalted butter, softened
60 ml vanilla-flavored egg white protein powder
2 tablespoons granulated sweetener
1 teaspoon blueberry extract
1 teaspoon ground cinnamon

1. Add all the ingredients to the Ninja Foodi cooker and stir to combine. 2. Lock the lid, Set the cooking time for 2 minutes on High Pressure. When the timer goes off, do a natural pressure release for 10 minutes, then release any remaining pressure. Open the lid. 3. Stir well and pour the mixture onto a sheet lined with baking paper to cool. It will be crispy when completely cool. 4. Serve the cereal in bowls.

Sausage Stuffed Peppers

Prep time: 15 minutes | Cook time: 15 minutes | Serves 4

230 g spicy pork sausage meat, removed from casings
4 large eggs
110 g full-fat cream cheese, softened
60 ml tinned diced tomatoes, drained
4 green peppers
8 tablespoons shredded chilli cheese
120 ml full-fat sour cream

1. In a medium skillet over medium heat, crumble and brown the sausage meat until no pink remains. Remove sausage and drain the fat from the pan. Crack eggs into the pan, scramble, and cook until no longer runny. 2. Place cooked sausage in a large bowl and fold in cream cheese. Mix in diced tomatoes. Gently fold in eggs. 3. Cut a 4-inch to 5-inch slit in the top of each pepper, removing the seeds and white membrane with a small knife. Separate the filling into four servings and spoon carefully into each pepper. Top each with 2 tablespoons cheese. 4. Place each pepper into the cook & crisp basket. 5. Adjust the temperature to 175ºC and set the timer for 15 minutes. 6. Peppers will be soft and cheese will be browned when ready. Serve immediately with sour cream on top.

Cajun Breakfast Sausage

Prep time: 10 minutes | Cook time: 15 to 20 minutes | Serves 8

680 g 85% lean turkey mince
3 cloves garlic, finely chopped
¼ onion, grated
1 teaspoon Tabasco sauce
1 teaspoon Cajun seasoning
1 teaspoon dried thyme
½ teaspoon paprika
½ teaspoon cayenne

1. Preheat the Ninja Foodi cooker to 190ºC. 2. In a large bowl, combine the turkey, garlic, onion, Tabasco, Cajun seasoning, thyme, paprika, and cayenne. Mix with clean hands until thoroughly combined. Shape into 16 patties, about ½ inch thick. (Wet your hands slightly if you find the sausage too sticky to handle.) 3. Working in batches if necessary, arrange the patties in a single layer in the cook & crisp basket. Pausing halfway through the cooking time to flip the patties, air crisp for 15 to 20 minutes until a thermometer inserted into the thickest portion registers 75ºC.

Cheesy Vegetable Frittata

Prep time: 10 minutes | Cook time: 10 minutes | Serves 4

4 eggs, beaten
60 g Pecorino cheese, grated
85 g okra, chopped
60 g radish, chopped
1 tablespoon cream cheese
1 teaspoon sesame oil

1. Heat up sesame oil in the Ninja Foodi cooker on Sauté mode. 2. Add chopped okra and radish and sauté the vegetables for 4 minutes. 3. Then stir them well and add cream cheese and beaten eggs. 4. Stir the mixture well and top with cheese. 5. Close the lid and cook the frittata on Sauté mode for 6 minutes more.

Poached Eggs on Whole Grain Avocado Toast

Prep time: 5 minutes | Cook time: 7 minutes | Serves 4

Olive oil cooking spray	4 pieces wholegrain bread
4 large eggs	1 avocado
Salt	Red pepper flakes (optional)
Black pepper	

1. Preheat the Ninja Foodi cooker to 160ºC. Lightly coat the inside of four small oven-safe ramekins with olive oil cooking spray. 2. Crack one egg into each ramekin, and season with salt and black pepper. 3. Place the ramekins into the cook & crisp basket. Close and set the timer to 7 minutes. 4. While the eggs are cooking, toast the bread in a toaster. 5. Slice the avocado in half lengthwise, remove the pit, and scoop the flesh into a small bowl. Season with salt, black pepper, and red pepper flakes, if desired. Using a fork, smash the avocado lightly. 6. Spread a quarter of the smashed avocado evenly over each slice of toast. 7. Remove the eggs from the Ninja Foodi cooker, and gently spoon one onto each slice of avocado toast before serving.

Egg and Bacon Muffins

Prep time: 5 minutes | Cook time: 15 minutes | Serves 1

2 eggs	85 g shredded Cheddar cheese
Salt and ground black pepper, to taste	140 g cooked bacon
1 tablespoon green pesto	1 spring onion, chopped

1. Preheat the Ninja Foodi cooker to 175ºC. Line a cupcake tin with parchment paper. 2. Beat the eggs with pepper, salt, and pesto in a bowl. Mix in the cheese. 3. Pour the eggs into the cupcake tin and top with the bacon and spring onion. 4. Bake in the preheated Ninja Foodi cooker for 15 minutes, or until the egg is set. 5. Serve immediately.

Spinach and Swiss Frittata with Mushrooms

Prep time: 10 minutes | Cook time: 20 minutes | Serves 4

Olive oil cooking spray	110 g baby mushrooms, sliced
8 large eggs	1 shallot, diced
½ teaspoon salt	120 ml shredded Swiss cheese, divided
½ teaspoon black pepper	
1 garlic clove, minced	Hot sauce, for serving (optional)
475 ml fresh baby spinach	

1. Preheat the Ninja Foodi cooker to 180ºC. Lightly coat the inside of a 6-inch round cake pan with olive oil cooking spray. 2. In a large bowl, beat the eggs, salt, pepper, and garlic for 1 to 2 minutes, or until well combined. 3. Fold in the spinach, mushrooms, shallot, and 60 ml the Swiss cheese. 4. Pour the egg mixture into the prepared cake pan, and sprinkle the remaining 60 ml Swiss over the top. 5. Place into the Ninja Foodi cooker and bake for 18 to 20 minutes, or until the eggs are set in the center. 6. Remove from the Ninja Foodi cooker and allow to cool for 5 minutes. Drizzle with hot sauce (if using) before serving.

Buffalo Egg Cups

Prep time: 10 minutes | Cook time: 15 minutes | Serves 2

4 large eggs	120 ml shredded sharp Cheddar cheese
60 g full-fat cream cheese	
2 tablespoons buffalo sauce	

1. Crack eggs into two ramekins. 2. In a small microwave-safe bowl, mix cream cheese, buffalo sauce, and Cheddar. Microwave for 20 seconds and then stir. Place a spoonful into each ramekin on top of the eggs. 3. Place ramekins into the cook & crisp basket. 4. Adjust the temperature to 160ºC and bake for 15 minutes. 5. Serve warm.

Vanilla Granola

Prep time: 5 minutes | Cook time: 40 minutes | Serves 4

235 ml rolled oats	¼ teaspoon vanilla
3 tablespoons maple syrup	¼ teaspoon cinnamon
1 tablespoon sunflower oil	¼ teaspoon sea salt
1 tablespoon coconut sugar	

1. Preheat the Ninja Foodi cooker to 120ºC. 2. Mix together the oats, maple syrup, sunflower oil, coconut sugar, vanilla, cinnamon, and sea salt in a medium bowl and stir to combine. Transfer the mixture to a baking pan. 3. Place the pan in the cook & crisp basket and bake for 40 minutes, or until the granola is mostly dry and lightly browned. Stir the granola four times during cooking. 4. Let the granola stand for 5 to 10 minutes before serving.

Southwestern Ham Egg Cups

Prep time: 5 minutes | Cook time: 12 minutes | Serves 2

4 (30 g) slices wafer-thin ham	2 tablespoons diced red pepper
4 large eggs	2 tablespoons diced brown onion
2 tablespoons full-fat sour cream	120 ml shredded medium Cheddar cheese
60 ml diced green pepper	

1. Place one slice of ham on the bottom of four baking cups. 2. In a large bowl, whisk eggs with sour cream. Stir in green pepper, red pepper, and onion. 3. Pour the egg mixture into the ham-lined baking cups. Top with Cheddar. Place cups into the cook & crisp basket. 4. Adjust the temperature to 160ºC and bake for 12 minutes or until the tops are browned. 5. Serve warm.

Butternut Squash and Ricotta Frittata

Prep time: 10 minutes | Cook time: 33 minutes | Serves 2 to 3

235 ml cubed (½-inch) butternut squash (160 g)
2 tablespoons olive oil
Coarse or flaky salt and freshly ground black pepper, to taste
4 fresh sage leaves, thinly sliced
6 large eggs, lightly beaten
120 ml ricotta cheese
Cayenne pepper

1. In a bowl, toss the squash with the olive oil and season with salt and black pepper until evenly coated. Sprinkle the sage on the bottom of a cake pan and place the squash on top. Place the pan in the Ninja Foodi cooker and bake at 205ºC for 10 minutes. Stir to incorporate the sage, then cook until the squash is tender and lightly caramelized at the edges, about 3 minutes more. 2. Pour the eggs over the squash, dollop the ricotta all over, and sprinkle with cayenne. Bake at 150ºC until the eggs are set and the frittata is golden brown on top, about 20 minutes. Remove the pan from the Ninja Foodi cooker and cut the frittata into wedges to serve.

Denver Omelette

Prep time: 5 minutes | Cook time: 8 minutes | Serves 1

2 large eggs
60 ml unsweetened, unflavoured almond milk
¼ teaspoon fine sea salt
⅛ teaspoon ground black pepper
60 ml diced ham (omit for vegetarian)
60 ml diced green and red peppers
2 tablespoons diced spring onions, plus more for garnish
60 ml shredded Cheddar cheese (about 30 g) (omit for dairy-free)
Quartered cherry tomatoes, for serving (optional)

1. Preheat the Ninja Foodi cooker to 175ºC. Grease a cake pan and set aside. 2. In a small bowl, use a fork to whisk together the eggs, almond milk, salt, and pepper. Add the ham, peppers, and spring onions. Pour the mixture into the greased pan. Add the cheese on top (if using). 3. Place the pan in the basket of the Ninja Foodi cooker. Bake for 8 minutes, or until the eggs are cooked to your liking. 4. Loosen the omelette from the sides of the pan with a spatula and place it on a serving plate. Garnish with spring onions and serve with cherry tomatoes, if desired. Best served fresh.

Bacon and Spinach Egg Muffins

Prep time: 7 minutes | Cook time: 12 to 14 minutes | Serves 6

6 large eggs
60 ml double (whipping) cream
½ teaspoon sea salt
¼ teaspoon freshly ground black pepper
¼ teaspoon cayenne pepper (optional)
180 ml frozen chopped spinach, thawed and drained
4 strips cooked bacon, crumbled
60 g shredded Cheddar cheese

1. In a large bowl (with a spout if you have one), whisk together the eggs, double cream, salt, black pepper, and cayenne pepper (if using). 2. Divide the spinach and bacon among 6 silicone muffin cups. Place the muffin cups in your cook & crisp basket. 3. Divide the egg mixture among the muffin cups. Top with the cheese. 4. Set the Ninja Foodi cooker to 150ºC. Bake for 12 to 14 minutes, until the eggs are set and cooked through.

Pecan and Walnut Granola

Prep time: 10 minutes | Cook time: 2 minutes | Serves 12

480 ml chopped raw pecans
420 ml vanilla-flavored egg white protein powder
300 ml unsalted butter, softened
240 ml sunflower seeds
120 ml chopped raw walnuts
120 ml slivered almonds
120 ml sesame seeds
120 ml granulated sweetener
1 teaspoon ground cinnamon
½ teaspoon sea salt

1. Add all the ingredients to the Ninja Foodi cooker and stir to combine. 2. Lock the lid, Set the cooking time for 2 minutes on High Pressure. When the timer goes off, do a natural pressure release for 10 minutes, then release any remaining pressure. Open the lid. 3. Stir well and pour the granola onto a sheet of baking paper to cool. It will become crispy when completely cool. Serve the granola in bowls.

Western Frittata

Prep time: 10 minutes | Cook time: 19 minutes | Serves 1 to 2

½ red or green pepper, cut into ½-inch chunks
1 teaspoon olive oil
3 eggs, beaten
60 ml grated Cheddar cheese
60 ml diced cooked ham
Salt and freshly ground black pepper, to taste
1 teaspoon butter
1 teaspoon chopped fresh parsley

1. Preheat the Ninja Foodi cooker to 205ºC. 2. Toss the peppers with the olive oil and air crisp for 6 minutes, shaking the basket once or twice during the cooking process to redistribute the ingredients. 3. While the vegetables are cooking, beat the eggs well in a bowl, stir in the Cheddar cheese and ham, and season with salt and freshly ground black pepper. Add the air-fried peppers to this bowl when they have finished cooking. 4. Place a cake pan into the cook & crisp basket with the butter using an aluminum sling to lower the pan into the basket. Air crisp for 1 minute at 190ºC to melt the butter. Remove the cake pan and rotate the pan to distribute the butter and grease the pan. Pour the egg mixture into the cake pan and return the pan to the Ninja Foodi cooker, using the aluminum sling. 5. Air crisp at 190ºC for 12 minutes, or until the frittata has puffed up and is lightly browned. Let the frittata sit in the Ninja Foodi cooker for 5 minutes to cool to an edible temperature and set up. Remove the cake pan from the Ninja Foodi cooker, sprinkle with parsley and serve immediately.

Cheddar Soufflés

Prep time: 15 minutes | Cook time: 12 minutes | Serves 4

3 large eggs, whites and yolks separated
¼ teaspoon cream of tartar
120 ml shredded sharp Cheddar cheese
85 g cream cheese, softened

1. In a large bowl, beat egg whites together with cream of tartar until soft peaks form, about 2 minutes. 2. In a separate medium bowl, beat egg yolks, Cheddar, and cream cheese together until frothy, about 1 minute. Add egg yolk mixture to whites, gently folding until combined. 3. Pour mixture evenly into four ramekins greased with cooking spray. Place ramekins into cook & crisp basket. Adjust the temperature to 175ºC and bake for 12 minutes. Eggs will be browned on the top and firm in the center when done. Serve warm.

Cauliflower Nutty Porridge

Prep time: 40 minutes | Cook time: 5 minutes | Serves 4

600 ml water, divided
120 ml raw cashews
120 ml almond slivers
60 ml raw pumpkin seeds
¼ head cauliflower, chopped
Sea salt, to taste
60 ml heavy whipping cream
Topping:
60 ml hemp seeds
60 ml chia seeds
1 tablespoon cinnamon

1. In a small bowl, add 480 ml of the water, the cashews, almonds and pumpkin seeds. Soak for 30 minutes. Drain the water and set aside. Reserve a few nuts and pumpkin seeds in a separate bowl to be used as garnish. 2. Pour the remaining 120 ml of the water into the Ninja Foodi cooker and add the soaked nuts mixture, cauliflower and sea salt. 3. Lock the lid. Set the cooking time for 5 minutes at High Pressure. When the timer goes off, use a natural pressure release for 10 minutes, then release any remaining pressure. Carefully open the lid. 4. Transfer the cauliflower and nuts mixture to a food processor, add the double cream and pulse until smooth. 5. Season with a pinch of sea salt. Garnish with the reserved nuts, pumpkin seeds, hemp seeds and chia seeds and sprinkle with the cinnamon. Serve immediately.

Breakfast Calzone

Prep time: 15 minutes | Cook time: 15 minutes | Serves 4

350 ml shredded Mozzarella cheese
120 ml blanched finely ground almond flour
30 g full-fat cream cheese
1 large whole egg
4 large eggs, scrambled
230 g cooked sausage meat, removed from casings and crumbled
8 tablespoons shredded mild Cheddar cheese

1. In a large microwave-safe bowl, add Mozzarella, almond flour, and cream cheese. Microwave for 1 minute. Stir until the mixture is smooth and forms a ball. Add the egg and stir until dough forms. 2. Place dough between two sheets of parchment and roll out to ¼-inch thickness. Cut the dough into four rectangles. 3. Mix scrambled eggs and cooked sausage together in a large bowl. Divide the mixture evenly among each piece of dough, placing it on the lower half of the rectangle. Sprinkle each with 2 tablespoons Cheddar. 4. Fold over the rectangle to cover the egg and meat mixture. Pinch, roll, or use a wet fork to close the edges completely. 5. Cut a piece of parchment to fit your cook & crisp basket and place the calzones onto the parchment. Place parchment into the cook & crisp basket. 6. Adjust the temperature to 190ºC and air crisp for 15 minutes. 7. Flip the calzones halfway through the cooking time. When done, calzones should be golden in color. Serve immediately.

Jalapeño Popper Egg Cups

Prep time: 10 minutes | Cook time: 10 minutes | Serves 2

4 large eggs
60 ml chopped pickled jalapeños
60 g full-fat cream cheese
120 ml shredded sharp Cheddar cheese

1. In a medium bowl, beat the eggs, then pour into four silicone muffin cups. 2. In a large microwave-safe bowl, place jalapeños, cream cheese, and Cheddar. Microwave for 30 seconds and stir. Take a spoonful, approximately ¼ of the mixture, and place it in the center of one of the egg cups. Repeat with remaining mixture. 3. Place egg cups into the cook & crisp basket. 4. Adjust the temperature to 160ºC and bake for 10 minutes. 5. Serve warm.

Apple Rolls

Prep time: 20 minutes | Cook time: 20 to 24 minutes | Makes 12 rolls

Apple Rolls:
475 ml plain flour, plus more for dusting
2 tablespoons granulated sugar
1 teaspoon salt
3 tablespoons butter, at room temperature
180 ml milk, whole or semi-skimmed
120 ml packed light brown sugar
1 teaspoon ground cinnamon
1 large Granny Smith apple, peeled and diced
1 to 2 tablespoons oil
Icing:
120 ml icing sugar
½ teaspoon vanilla extract
2 to 3 tablespoons milk, whole or semi-skimmed

Make the Apple Rolls 1. In a large bowl, whisk the flour, granulated sugar, and salt until blended. Stir in the butter and milk briefly until a sticky dough forms. 2. In a small bowl, stir together the brown sugar, cinnamon, and apple. 3. Place a piece of parchment paper on a work surface and dust it with flour. Roll the dough on the prepared surface to ¼ inch thickness. 4. Spread the apple mixture over the dough. Roll up the dough jelly roll-style, pinching the ends to seal. Cut the dough into 12 rolls. 5. Preheat the Ninja Foodi cooker to 160ºC. 6. Line the cook & crisp basket with parchment paper and spritz it with oil. Place 6 rolls on the prepared parchment. 7. Bake for 5 minutes. Flip the rolls and bake for 5 to 7 minutes more until lightly browned. Repeat with the remaining rolls. Make the Icing 8. In a medium bowl, whisk the icing sugar, vanilla, and milk until blended. 9. Drizzle over the warm rolls.

Kale Omelet

Prep time: 5 minutes | Cook time: 10 minutes | Serves 2

2 eggs
240 ml chopped kale
1 teaspoon double cream
⅔ teaspoon white pepper
½ teaspoon butter

1. Grease the Ninja Foodi cooker pan with butter. 2. Beat the eggs in the separated bowl and whisk them well. 3. After this, add double cream and white pepper. Stir it gently. 4. Place the chopped kale in the greased pan and add the whisked eggs. 5. Pour 240 ml of water in the Ninja Foodi cooker. 6. Place the reversible rack in the Ninja Foodi cooker and transfer the egg mixture pan on the reversible rack. 7. Close the Ninja Foodi cooker and cook the frittata on High Pressure for 5 minutes. Do a natural pressure release for 5 minutes.

Three-Cheese Quiche

Prep time: 10 minutes | Cook time: 6 minutes | Serves 6

6 eggs, beaten
2 tablespoon cream cheese
1 teaspoon Italian seasoning
60 ml shredded Cheddar cheese
85 g Monterey Jack cheese, shredded
60 g Mozzarella, shredded
240 ml water, for cooking

1. Pour water in the Ninja Foodi cooker. 2. In the mixing bowl, mix up eggs cream cheese, Italian seasoning, and all types of cheese. 3. Pour the mixture in the baking cups (molds) and place them in the Ninja Foodi cooker. 4. Close and seal the lid. 5. Cook the quiche cups for 6 minutes on High Pressure. 6. Make a quick pressure release.

Shredded Potato Omelet

Prep time: 15 minutes | Cook time: 20 minutes | Serves 6

3 slices bacon, cooked and crumbled
480 ml shredded cooked potatoes
60 ml minced onion
60 ml minced green bell pepper
240 ml egg substitute
60 ml fat-free milk
¼ teaspoon salt
⅛ teaspoon black pepper
240 ml 75%-less-fat shredded cheddar cheese
240 ml water

1. With nonstick cooking spray, spray the inside of a round baking dish that will fit in your Ninja Foodi cooker inner pot. 2. Sprinkle the bacon, potatoes, onion, and bell pepper around the bottom of the baking dish. 3. Mix together the egg substitute, milk, salt, and pepper in mixing bowl. Pour over potato mixture. 4. Top with cheese. 5. Add water, place the steaming rack into the bottom of the inner pot and then place the round baking dish on top. 6. Close the lid and secure to the locking position. Be sure the vent is turned to sealing. Set for 20 minutes at high pressure. 7. Let the pressure release naturally. 8. Carefully remove the baking dish with the handles of the steaming rack and allow to stand 10 minutes before cutting and serving.

Breakfast Pitta

Prep time: 5 minutes | Cook time: 6 minutes | Serves 2

1 wholemeal pitta
2 teaspoons olive oil
½ shallot, diced
¼ teaspoon garlic, minced
1 large egg
¼ teaspoon dried oregano
¼ teaspoon dried thyme
⅛ teaspoon salt
2 tablespoons shredded Parmesan cheese

1. Preheat the Ninja Foodi cooker to 190ºC. 2. Brush the top of the pitta with olive oil, then spread the diced shallot and minced garlic over the pitta. 3. Crack the egg into a small bowl or ramekin, and season it with oregano, thyme, and salt. 4. Place the pitta into the cook & crisp basket, and gently pour the egg onto the top of the pitta. Sprinkle with cheese over the top. 5. Bake for 6 minutes. 6. Allow to cool for 5 minutes before cutting into pieces for serving.

Bacon Cheese Egg with Avocado

Prep time: 15 minutes | Cook time: 20 minutes | Serves 4

6 large eggs
60 ml double cream
350 ml chopped cauliflower
235 ml shredded medium Cheddar cheese
1 medium avocado, peeled and pitted
8 tablespoons full-fat sour cream
2 spring onions, sliced on the bias
12 slices bacon, cooked and crumbled

1. In a medium bowl, whisk eggs and cream together. Pour into a round baking dish. 2. Add cauliflower and mix, then top with Cheddar. Place dish into the cook & crisp basket. 3. Adjust the temperature to 160ºC and set the timer for 20 minutes. 4. When completely cooked, eggs will be firm and cheese will be browned. Slice into four pieces. 5. Slice avocado and divide evenly among pieces. Top each piece with 2 tablespoons sour cream, sliced spring onions, and crumbled bacon.

Cheesy Bell Pepper Eggs

Prep time: 10 minutes | Cook time: 15 minutes | Serves 4

4 medium green peppers
85 g cooked ham, chopped
¼ medium onion, peeled and chopped
8 large eggs
235 ml mild Cheddar cheese

1. Cut the tops off each pepper. Remove the seeds and the white membranes with a small knife. Place ham and onion into each pepper. 2. Crack 2 eggs into each pepper. Top with 60 ml cheese per pepper. Place into the cook & crisp basket. 3. Adjust the temperature to 200ºC and air crisp for 15 minutes. 4. When fully cooked, peppers will be tender and eggs will be firm. Serve immediately.

Baked Egg and Mushroom Cups

Prep time: 5 minutes | Cook time: 15 minutes | Serves 6

Olive oil cooking spray
6 large eggs
1 garlic clove, minced
½ teaspoon salt
½ teaspoon black pepper
Pinch red pepper flakes
230 g baby mushrooms, sliced
235 ml fresh baby spinach
2 spring onions, white parts and green parts, diced

1. Preheat the Ninja Foodi cooker to 160ºC. Lightly coat the inside of six silicone muffin cups or a six-cup muffin tin with olive oil cooking spray. 2. In a large bowl, beat the eggs, garlic, salt, pepper, and red pepper flakes for 1 to 2 minutes, or until well combined. 3. Fold in the mushrooms, spinach, and spring onions. 4. Divide the mixture evenly among the muffin cups. 5. Place into the Ninja Foodi cooker and bake for 12 to 15 minutes, or until the eggs are set. 6. Remove and allow to cool for 5 minutes before serving.

Potato-Bacon Gratin

Prep time: 20 minutes | Cook time: 40 minutes | Serves 8

1 tablespoon olive oil
170 g bag fresh spinach
1 clove garlic, minced
4 large potatoes, peeled or unpeeled, divided
170 g Canadian bacon slices, divided
140 g reduced-fat grated Swiss cheddar, divided
240 ml lower-sodium, lower-fat chicken broth

1. Set the Ninja Foodi cooker to Sauté and pour in the olive oil. Cook the spinach and garlic in olive oil just until spinach is wilted (5 minutes or less). Turn off the Ninja Foodi cooker. 2. Cut potatoes into thin slices about ¼" thick. 3. In a springform pan that will fit into the inner pot of your Ninja Foodi cooker, spray it with nonstick spray then layer ⅓ the potatoes, half the bacon, ⅓ the cheese, and half the wilted spinach. 4. Repeat layers ending with potatoes. Reserve ⅓ cheese for later. 5. Pour chicken broth over all. 6. Wipe the bottom of your Ninja Foodi cooker to soak up any remaining oil, then add in 480 ml of water and the steaming rack. Place the springform pan on top. 7. Close the lid and secure to the locking position. Be sure the vent is turned to sealing. Set for 35 minutes at high pressure. 8. Perform a quick release. 9. Top with the remaining cheese, then allow to stand 10 minutes before removing from the Ninja Foodi cooker, cutting and serving.

Baked Potato Breakfast Boats

Prep time: 10 minutes | Cook time: 20 minutes | Serves 4

2 large white potatoes, scrubbed
Olive oil
Salt and freshly ground black pepper, to taste
4 eggs
2 tablespoons chopped, cooked bacon
235 ml shredded Cheddar cheese

1. Poke holes in the potatoes with a fork and microwave on full power for 5 minutes. 2. Turn potatoes over and cook an additional 3 to 5 minutes, or until the potatoes are fork-tender. 3. Cut the potatoes in half lengthwise and use a spoon to scoop out the inside of the potato. Be careful to leave a layer of potato so that it makes a sturdy "boat." 4. Preheat the Ninja Foodi cooker to 175ºC. 5. Lightly spray the cook & crisp basket with olive oil. Spray the skin side of the potatoes with oil and sprinkle with salt and pepper to taste. 6. Place the potato skins in the cook & crisp basket, skin-side down. Crack one egg into each potato skin. 7. Sprinkle ½ tablespoon of bacon pieces and 60 ml shredded cheese on top of each egg. Sprinkle with salt and pepper to taste. 8. Air crisp until the yolk is slightly runny, 5 to 6 minutes, or until the yolk is fully cooked, 7 to 10 minutes.

Tropical Steel Cut Oats

Prep time: 5 minutes | Cook time: 5 minutes | Serves 4

240 ml steel cut oats
240 ml unsweetened almond milk
480 ml coconut water or water
180 ml frozen chopped peaches
180 ml frozen mango chunks
1 (2-inch) vanilla bean, scraped (seeds and pod)
Ground cinnamon
60 ml chopped unsalted macadamia nuts

1. In the electric pressure cooker, combine the oats, almond milk, coconut water, peaches, mango chunks, and vanilla bean seeds and pod. Stir well. 2. Close and lock the lid of the pressure cooker. Set the valve to sealing. 3. Cook on high pressure for 5 minutes. 4. When the cooking is complete, allow the pressure to release naturally for 10 minutes, then quick release any remaining pressure. Hit Start/Stop. 5. Once the pin drops, unlock and remove the lid. 6. Discard the vanilla bean pod and stir well. 7. Spoon the oats into 4 bowls. Top each serving with a sprinkle of cinnamon and 1 tablespoon of the macadamia nuts.

Mini Chocolate Chip Muffins

Prep time: 5 minutes | Cook time: 20 minutes | Serves 7

240 ml blanched almond flour
2 eggs
180 ml sugar-free chocolate chips
1 tablespoon vanilla extract
120 ml granulated sweetener, or more to taste
2 tablespoons salted grass-fed butter, softened
½ teaspoon salt
¼ teaspoon bicarbonate of soda

1. Pour 240 ml of filtered water into the inner pot of the Ninja Foodi cooker, then insert the reversible rack. Using an electric mixer, combine flour, eggs, chocolate chips, vanilla, granulated sweetener, butter, salt, and bicarbonate of soda. Mix thoroughly. Transfer this mixture into a well-greased Ninja Foodi cooker-friendly muffin (or egg bites) mold. 2. Using a sling if desired, place the pan onto the reversible rack and cover loosely with aluminium foil. Close the lid, set the Ninja Foodi cooker to 20 minutes on High Pressure and let cook. 3. Once cooked, let the pressure naturally disperse from the Ninja Foodi cooker for about 10 minutes, then carefully switch the pressure release to Venting. 4. Open the Ninja Foodi cooker and remove the pan. Let cool, serve, and enjoy!

Hard-boiled Eggs

Prep time: 2 minutes | Cook time: 2 minutes | Serves 9

9 large eggs

1. Pour 240 ml of water into the electric pressure cooker and insert an egg rack. Gently stand the eggs in the rack, fat ends down. If you don't have an egg rack, place the eggs in a steamer basket or on a wire rack. 2. Close and lock the lid of the pressure cooker. Set the valve to sealing. 3. Cook on high pressure for 2 minutes. 4. When the cooking is complete, hit Start/Stop and allow the pressure to release naturally. 5. Once the pin drops, unlock and remove the lid. 6. Using tongs, carefully remove the eggs from the pressure cooker. Peel or refrigerate the eggs when they are cool enough to handle.

Turkey Breakfast Sausage Patties

Prep time: 5 minutes | Cook time: 10 minutes | Serves 4

1 tablespoon chopped fresh thyme
1 tablespoon chopped fresh sage
1¼ teaspoons coarse or flaky salt
1 teaspoon chopped fennel seeds
¾ teaspoon smoked paprika
½ teaspoon onion granules
½ teaspoon garlic powder
⅛ teaspoon crushed red pepper flakes
⅛ teaspoon freshly ground black pepper
450 g lean turkey mince
120 ml finely minced sweet apple (peeled)

1. Thoroughly combine the thyme, sage, salt, fennel seeds, paprika, onion granules, garlic powder, red pepper flakes, and black pepper in a medium bowl. 2. Add the turkey mince and apple and stir until well incorporated. Divide the mixture into 8 equal portions and shape into patties with your hands, each about ¼ inch thick and 3 inches in diameter. 3. Preheat the Ninja Foodi cooker to 205°C. 4. Place the patties in the cook & crisp basket in a single layer. You may need to work in batches to avoid overcrowding. 5. Air crisp for 5 minutes. Flip the patties and air crisp for 5 minutes, or until the patties are nicely browned and cooked through. 6. Remove from the basket to a plate and repeat with the remaining patties. 7. Serve warm.

Chapter 3 Beef, Pork, and Lamb

Chicken-Fried Steak

Prep time: 20 minutes | Cook time: 14 minutes | Serves 2

Steak:
Oil, for spraying
180 ml all-purpose flour
1 teaspoon salt
1 teaspoon freshly ground black pepper
½ teaspoon paprika
½ teaspoon onion granules
1 teaspoon granulated garlic
180 ml buttermilk
½ teaspoon hot sauce
2 (140 g) minute steaks
Gravy:
2 tablespoons unsalted butter
2 tablespoons all-purpose flour
235 ml milk
½ teaspoon salt
½ teaspoon freshly ground black pepper

Make the Steak 1. Line the cook & crisp basket with parchment and spray lightly with oil. 2. In a medium bowl, mix together the flour, salt, black pepper, paprika, onion granules, and garlic. 3. In another bowl, whisk together the buttermilk and hot sauce. 4. Dredge the steaks in the flour mixture, dip in the buttermilk mixture, and dredge again in the flour until completely coated. Shake off any excess flour. 5. Place the steaks in the prepared basket and spray liberally with oil. 6. Air crisp at 205ºC for 7 minutes, flip, spray with oil, and cook for another 6 to 7 minutes, or until crispy and browned. Make the Gravy 7. In a small saucepan, whisk together the butter and flour over medium heat until the butter is melted. Slowly add the milk, salt, and black pepper, increase the heat to medium-high, and continue to cook, stirring constantly, until the mixture thickens. Remove from the heat. 8. Transfer the steaks to plates and pour the gravy over the top. Serve immediately.

Sausage and Courgette Lasagna

Prep time: 25 minutes | Cook time: 56 minutes | Serves 4

1 courgette
Avocado oil spray
170 g hot Italian-seasoned sausage, casings removed
60 g mushrooms, stemmed and sliced
1 teaspoon minced garlic
235 ml keto-friendly marinara sauce
180 ml ricotta cheese
235 ml shredded gruyere cheese, divided
120 ml finely grated Parmesan cheese
Sea salt and freshly ground black pepper, to taste
Fresh basil, for garnish

1. Cut the courgette into long thin slices using a mandoline slicer or sharp knife. Spray both sides of the slices with oil. 2. Place the slices in a single layer in the cook & crisp basket, working in batches if necessary. Set the Ninja Foodi cooker to 165ºC and air crisp for 4 to 6 minutes, until most of the moisture has been released from the courgette. 3. Place a large skillet over medium-high heat. Crumble the sausage into the hot skillet and cook for 6 minutes, breaking apart the meat with the back of a spoon. Remove the sausage from the skillet, leaving any fats that remain. Add the mushrooms to the skillet and cook for 10 minutes, until the liquid nearly evaporates. Add the garlic and cook for 1 minute more. Stir in the marinara and cook for 2 more minutes. 4. In a medium bowl, combine the ricotta cheese, 120 ml of gruyere cheese, Parmesan cheese, and salt and pepper to taste. 5. Spread 60 ml of the meat sauce in the bottom of a deep pan (or other pan that fits inside your Ninja Foodi cooker). Top with half of the courgette slices. Add half of the cheese mixture. Top the cheese with half of the remaining meat sauce. Layer the remaining courgette over the meat sauce and top with the remaining cheese mixture. Top the lasagna with the remaining 120 ml of fontina cheese. 6. Cover the lasagna with aluminum foil or parchment paper and place it in the Ninja Foodi cooker. Bake for 25 minutes. Remove the foil and cook for 8 to 10 minutes more. 7. Allow the lasagna to rest for 15 minutes before cutting and serving. Garnish with basil.

Beef Clod Vindaloo

Prep time: 15 minutes | Cook time: 15 minutes | Serves 2

½ Serrano pepper, chopped
¼ teaspoon cumin seeds
¼ teaspoon minced ginger
¼ teaspoon cayenne pepper
¼ teaspoon salt
¼ teaspoon ground paprika
240 ml water
255 g beef clod, chopped

1. Put Serrano pepper, cumin seeds, minced ginger, cayenne pepper, salt, ground paprika, and water in a food processor. Blend the mixture until smooth. 2. Transfer the mixture in a bowl and add the chopped beef clod. Toss to coat well. 3. Transfer the beef clod and the mixture in the Ninja Foodi cooker and close the lid. 4. Set cooking time for 15 minutes on High Pressure. 5. When timer beeps, use a natural pressure release for 10 minutes, then release any remaining pressure. Open the lid. 6. Serve immediately.

Spice-Rubbed Pork Loin

Prep time: 5 minutes | Cook time: 20 minutes | Serves 6

1 teaspoon paprika
½ teaspoon ground cumin
½ teaspoon chili powder
½ teaspoon garlic powder
2 tablespoons coconut oil
1 (680 g) boneless pork loin
½ teaspoon salt
¼ teaspoon ground black pepper

1. In a small bowl, mix paprika, cumin, chili powder, and garlic powder. 2. Drizzle coconut oil over pork. Sprinkle pork loin with salt and pepper, then rub spice mixture evenly on all sides. 3. Place pork loin into ungreased cook & crisp basket. Adjust the temperature to 205ºC and air crisp for 20 minutes, turning pork halfway through cooking. Pork loin will be browned and have an internal temperature of at least 65ºC when done. Serve warm.

Sirloin Steak with Honey-Mustard Butter

Prep time: 5 minutes | Cook time: 14 minutes | Serves 4

900 g beef sirloin steak
1 teaspoon cayenne pepper
1 tablespoon honey
1 tablespoon Dijon mustard
½ stick butter, softened
Sea salt and freshly ground black pepper, to taste
Cooking spray

1. Preheat the Ninja Foodi cooker to 205ºC and spritz with cooking spray. 2. Sprinkle the steak with cayenne pepper, salt, and black pepper on a clean work surface. 3. Arrange the steak in the preheated Ninja Foodi cooker and spritz with cooking spray. 4. Air crisp for 14 minutes or until browned and reach your desired doneness. Flip the steak halfway through. 5. Meanwhile, combine the honey, mustard, and butter in a small bowl. Stir to mix well. 6. Transfer the air fried steak onto a plate and baste with the honey-mustard butter before serving.

Bean and Beef Meatball Taco Pizza

Prep time: 10 minutes | Cook time: 7 to 9 minutes per batch | Serves 4

180 ml refried beans (from a 450 g can)
120 ml salsa
10 frozen precooked beef meatballs, thawed and sliced
1 jalapeño pepper, sliced
4 whole-wheat pitta breads
235 ml shredded chilli cheese
120 ml shredded Monterey Jack or Cheddar cheese
Cooking oil spray
80 ml sour cream

1. In a medium bowl, stir together the refried beans, salsa, meatballs, and jalapeño. 2. Insert the crisper plate into the basket and the basket into the unit. Preheat the unit by selecting BAKE, setting the temperature to 190ºC, and setting the time to 3 minutes. Select START/STOP to begin. 3. Top the pittas with the refried bean mixture and sprinkle with the cheeses. 4. Once the unit is preheated, spray the crisper plate with cooking oil. Working in batches, place the pizzas into the basket. Select BAKE, set the temperature to 190ºC, and set the time to 9 minutes. Select START/STOP to begin. 5. After about 7 minutes, check the pizzas. They are done when the cheese is melted and starts to brown. If not ready, resume cooking. 6. When the cooking is complete, top each pizza with a dollop of sour cream and serve warm.

Lemon Pork with Marjoram

Prep time: 5 minutes | Cook time: 10 minutes | Serves 4

1 (450 g) pork tenderloin, cut into ½-inch-thick slices
1 tablespoon extra-virgin olive oil
1 tablespoon freshly squeezed lemon juice
1 tablespoon honey
½ teaspoon grated lemon zest
½ teaspoon dried marjoram leaves
Pinch salt
Freshly ground black pepper, to taste
Cooking oil spray

1. Put the pork slices in a medium bowl. 2. In a small bowl, whisk the olive oil, lemon juice, honey, lemon zest, marjoram, salt, and pepper until combined. Pour this marinade over the tenderloin slices and gently massage with your hands to work it into the pork. 3. Insert the crisper plate into the basket and the basket into the unit. Preheat the unit by selecting AIR ROAST, setting the temperature to 205ºC, and setting the time to 3 minutes. Select START/STOP to begin. 4. Once the unit is preheated, spray the crisper plate with cooking oil. Place the pork into the basket. 5. Select AIR ROAST, set the temperature to 205ºC, and set the time to 10 minutes. Select START/STOP to begin. 6. When the cooking is complete, a food thermometer inserted into the pork should register at least 65ºC. Let the pork stand for 5 minutes and serve.

Minute Steak Roll-Ups

Prep time: 30 minutes | Cook time: 8 to 10 minutes | Serves 4

4 minute steaks (170 g each)
1 (450 g) bottle Italian dressing
1 teaspoon salt
½ teaspoon freshly ground black pepper
120 ml finely chopped brown onion
120 ml finely chopped green pepper
120 ml finely chopped mushrooms
1 to 2 tablespoons oil

1. In a large resealable bag or airtight storage container, combine the steaks and Italian dressing. Seal the bag and refrigerate to marinate for 2 hours. 2. Remove the steaks from the marinade and place them on a cutting board. Discard the marinade. Evenly season the steaks with salt and pepper. 3. In a small bowl, stir together the onion, pepper, and mushrooms. Sprinkle the onion mixture evenly over the steaks. Roll up the steaks, jelly roll-style, and secure with toothpicks. 4. Preheat the Ninja Foodi cooker to 205ºC. 5. Place the steaks in the cook & crisp basket. 6. Cook for 4 minutes. Flip the steaks and spritz them with oil. Cook for 4 to 6 minutes more until the internal temperature reaches 65ºC. Let rest for 5 minutes before serving.

Chicken-Fried Steak

Prep time: 5 minutes | Cook time: 20 minutes | Serves 4

450 g beef braising steak
700 ml low-fat milk, divided
1 teaspoon dried thyme
1 teaspoon dried rosemary
2 medium egg whites
235 ml gluten-free breadcrumbs
120 ml coconut flour
1 tablespoon Cajun seasoning

1. In a bowl, marinate the steak in 475 ml of milk for 30 to 45 minutes. 2. Remove the steak from milk, shake off the excess liquid, and season with the thyme and rosemary. Discard the milk. 3. In a shallow bowl, beat the egg whites with the remaining 235 ml of milk. 4. In a separate shallow bowl, combine the breadcrumbs, coconut flour, and seasoning. 5. Dip the steak in the egg white mixture then dredge in the breadcrumb mixture, coating well. 6. Place the steak in the basket of an Ninja Foodi cooker. 7. Set the Ninja Foodi cooker to 200ºC, close, and cook for 10 minutes. 8. Open the Ninja Foodi cooker, turn the steaks, close, and cook for 10 minutes. Let rest for 5 minutes.

Ginger Pork Meatballs

Prep time: 10 minutes | Cook time: 7 minutes | Serves 3

310 g ground pork
1 teaspoon ginger paste
1 teaspoon lemon juice
¼ teaspoon chili flakes
1 tablespoon butter
60 ml water

1. Combine the ground pork and ginger paste in a large bowl. 2. Mix in the lemon juice and chili flakes. 3. Put the butter in the Ninja Foodi cooker and melt on Sauté mode. 4. Meanwhile, shape the mixture into small meatballs. 5. Place the meatballs in the Ninja Foodi cooker and cook for 2 minutes on each side. 6. Add water and lock the lid. 7. Set cooking time for 3 minutes on High Pressure. 8. When timer beeps, perform a quick pressure release. Open the lid. 9. Serve warm.

Filipino Pork Loin

Prep time: 10 minutes | Cook time: 40 minutes | Serves 4

450 g pork loin, chopped
120 ml apple cider vinegar
240 ml chicken broth
1 chili pepper, chopped
1 tablespoon coconut oil
1 teaspoon salt

1. Melt the coconut oil on Sauté mode. 2. When it is hot, and chili pepper and cook it for 2 minutes. Stir it. 3. Add chopped pork loin and salt. Cook the ingredients for 5 minutes. 4. After this, add apple cider vinegar and chicken broth. 5. Close and seal the lid and cook the Filipino pork for 30 minutes on High Pressure. Then make a quick pressure release.

Hawaiian Pulled Pork Roast with Cabbage

Prep time: 10 minutes | Cook time: 1 hour 2 minutes minutes | Serves 6

1½ tablespoons olive oil
1.4 kg pork shoulder roast, cut into 4 equal-sized pieces
3 cloves garlic, minced
1 tablespoon liquid smoke
480 ml water, divided
1 tablespoon sea salt
480 ml shredded cabbage

1. Select Sauté mode and add the olive oil to the Ninja Foodi cooker. Once the oil is hot, add the pork cuts and sear for 5 minutes per side or until browned. Once browned, transfer the pork to a platter and set aside. 2. Add the garlic, liquid smoke, and 360 ml water to the Ninja Foodi cooker. Stir to combine. 3. Return the pork to the pot and sprinkle the salt over top. 4. Lock the lid. Set cooking time for 1 hour on High Pressure. 5. When cooking is complete, allow the pressure to release naturally for 20 minutes, then release any remaining pressure. 6. Open the lid and transfer the pork to a large platter. Using two forks, shred the pork. Set aside. 7. Add the shredded cabbage and remaining water to the liquid in the pot. Stir. 8. Lock the lid. Set cooking time for 2 minutes on High Pressure. When cooking is complete, quick release the pressure. 9. Transfer the cabbage to the serving platter with the pork. Serve warm.

Romano-Crusted Pork Chops

Prep time: 10 minutes | Cook time: 18 minutes | Serves 3

3 pork chops
110 g Romano cheese, grated
½ teaspoon Cajun seasoning
1 egg, beaten
1 tablespoon cream cheese
80 ml almond flour
3 tablespoons avocado oil

1. Rub the pork chops with Cajun seasoning. 2. After this, in the mixing bowl mix up grated Romano cheese and almond flour. 3. In the separated bow mix up eggs and cream cheese. 4. Dip the pork chops in the egg mixture and then coat in the cheese mixture. 5. Repeat the step one more time. 6. Pour avocado oil in the Ninja Foodi cooker. Preheat it on Sauté mode for 2 minutes. 7. Add the pork chops and cook them for 8 minutes per side.

Bacon Wrapped Pork with Apple Gravy

Prep time: 10 minutes | Cook time: 25 minutes | Serves 4

Pork:
1 tablespoons Dijon mustard
1 pork tenderloin
3 strips bacon
Apple Gravy:
3 tablespoons ghee, divided
1 small shallot, chopped
2 apples
1 tablespoon almond flour
235 ml vegetable stock
½ teaspoon Dijon mustard

1. Preheat the Ninja Foodi cooker to 180ºC. 2. Spread Dijon mustard all over tenderloin and wrap with strips of bacon. 3. Put into Ninja Foodi cooker and air crisp for 12 minutes. Use a meat thermometer to check for doneness. 4. To make sauce, heat 1 tablespoons of ghee in a pan and add shallots. Cook for 1 minute. 5. Then add apples, cooking for 4 minutes until softened. 6. Add flour and 2 tablespoons of ghee to make a roux. Add stock and mustard, stirring well to combine. 7. When sauce starts to bubble, add 235 ml of sautéed apples, cooking until sauce thickens. 8. Once pork tenderloin is cooked, allow to sit 8 minutes to rest before slicing. 9. Serve topped with apple gravy.

Kale and Beef Omelet

Prep time: 15 minutes | Cook time: 16 minutes | Serves 4

230 g leftover beef, coarsely chopped
2 garlic cloves, pressed
235 ml kale, torn into pieces and wilted
1 tomato, chopped
¼ teaspoon sugar
4 eggs, beaten
4 tablespoons double cream
½ teaspoon turmeric powder
Salt and ground black pepper, to taste
⅛ teaspoon ground allspice
Cooking spray

1. Preheat the Ninja Foodi cooker to 180ºC. Spritz four ramekins with cooking spray. 2. Put equal amounts of each of the ingredients into each ramekin and mix well. 3. Air crisp for 16 minutes. Serve immediately.

Barbecue Ribs

Prep time: 5 minutes | Cook time: 30 minutes | Serves 4

1 (900 g) rack baby back ribs
1 teaspoon onion granules
1 teaspoon garlic powder
1 teaspoon light brown sugar
1 teaspoon dried oregano
Salt and freshly ground black pepper, to taste
Cooking oil spray
120 ml barbecue sauce

1. Use a sharp knife to remove the thin membrane from the back of the ribs. Cut the rack in half, or as needed, so the ribs fit in the cook & crisp basket. The best way to do this is to cut the ribs into 4- or 5-rib sections. 2. In a small bowl, stir together the onion granules, garlic powder, brown sugar, and oregano and season with salt and pepper. Rub the spice seasoning onto the front and back of the ribs. 3. Cover the ribs with plastic wrap or foil and let sit at room temperature for 30 minutes. 4. Insert the crisper plate into the basket and the basket into the unit. Preheat the unit by selecting AIR ROAST, setting the temperature to 180ºC, and setting the time to 3 minutes. Select START/STOP to begin. 5. Once the unit is preheated, spray the crisper plate with cooking oil. Place the ribs into the basket. It is okay to stack them. 6. Select AIR ROAST, set the temperature to 180ºC, and set the time to 30 minutes. Select START/STOP to begin. 7. After 15 minutes, flip the ribs. Resume cooking for 15 minutes, or until a food thermometer registers 88ºC. 8. When the cooking is complete, transfer the ribs to a serving dish. Drizzle the ribs with the barbecue sauce and serve.

Italian Steak Rolls

Prep time: 30 minutes | Cook time: 9 minutes | Serves 4

1 tablespoon vegetable oil
2 cloves garlic, minced
2 teaspoons dried Italian seasoning
1 teaspoon coarse or flaky salt
1 teaspoon black pepper
450 g bavette or skirt steak, ¼ to ½ inch thick
1 (280 g) package frozen spinach, thawed and squeezed dry
120 ml diced jarred roasted red pepper
235 ml shredded Mozzarella cheese

1. In a large bowl, combine the oil, garlic, Italian seasoning, salt, and pepper. Whisk to combine. Add the steak to the bowl, turning to ensure the entire steak is covered with the seasonings. Cover and marinate at room temperature for 30 minutes or in the refrigerator for up to 24 hours. 2. Lay the steak on a flat surface. Spread the spinach evenly over the steak, leaving a ¼-inch border at the edge. Evenly top each steak with the red pepper and cheese. 3. Starting at a long end, roll up the steak as tightly as possible, ending seam side down. Use 2 or 3 wooden toothpicks to hold the roll together. Using a sharp knife, cut the roll in half so that it better fits in the cook & crisp basket. 4. Place the steak roll, seam side down, in the cook & crisp basket. Set the Ninja Foodi cooker to 205ºC for 9 minutes. Use a meat thermometer to ensure the steak has reached an internal temperature of 65ºC. (It is critical to not overcook bavette steak, so as to not toughen the meat.) 5. Let the steak rest for 10 minutes before cutting into slices to serve.

Beef and Tomato Sauce Meatloaf

Prep time: 15 minutes | Cook time: 25 minutes | Serves 4

680 g beef mince
235 ml tomato sauce
120 ml breadcrumbs
2 egg whites
120 ml grated Parmesan cheese
1 diced onion
2 tablespoons chopped parsley
2 tablespoons minced ginger
2 garlic cloves, minced
½ teaspoon dried basil
1 teaspoon cayenne pepper
Salt and ground black pepper, to taste
Cooking spray

1. Preheat the Ninja Foodi cooker to 180ºC. Spritz a meatloaf pan with cooking spray. 2. Combine all the ingredients in a large bowl. Stir to mix well. 3. Pour the meat mixture in the prepared meatloaf pan and press with a spatula to make it firm. 4. Arrange the pan in the preheated Ninja Foodi cooker and bake for 25 minutes or until the beef is well browned. 5. Serve immediately.

Baby Back Ribs

Prep time: 5 minutes | Cook time: 25 minutes | Serves 4

900 g baby back ribs
2 teaspoons chili powder
1 teaspoon paprika
½ teaspoon onion granules
½ teaspoon garlic powder
¼ teaspoon ground cayenne pepper
120 ml low-carb, sugar-free barbecue sauce

1. Rub ribs with all ingredients except barbecue sauce. Place into the cook & crisp basket. 2. Adjust the temperature to 205ºC and roast for 25 minutes. 3. When done, ribs will be dark and charred with an internal temperature of at least 85ºC. Brush ribs with barbecue sauce and serve warm.

Beef Burgers with Kale and Cheese

Prep time: 6 minutes | Cook time: 6 minutes | Serves 6

450 g ground beef
230 g beef sausage, crumbled
360 ml chopped kale
60 ml chopped scallions
2 garlic cloves, minced
120 ml grated Romano cheese
80 ml crumbled blue cheese
Salt and ground black pepper, to taste
1 teaspoon crushed dried sage
½ teaspoon oregano
½ teaspoon dried basil
1 tablespoon olive oil

1. Place 360 ml of water and a steamer basket in your Ninja Foodi cooker. 2. Mix all ingredients until everything is well incorporated. 3. Shape the mixture into 6 equal sized patties. Place the burgers on the steamer basket. 4. Secure the lid. Choose High Pressure; cook for 6 minutes. Once cooking is complete, use a quick pressure release; carefully remove the lid. Bon appétit!

Stuffed Beef Fillet with Feta Cheese

Prep time: 10 minutes | Cook time: 10 minutes | Serves 4

680 g beef fillet, pounded to ¼ inch thick
3 teaspoons sea salt
1 teaspoon ground black pepper
60 g creamy goat cheese
120 ml crumbled feta cheese
60 ml finely chopped onions
2 cloves garlic, minced
Cooking spray

1. Preheat the Ninja Foodi cooker to 205°C. Spritz the cook & crisp basket with cooking spray. 2. Unfold the beef on a clean work surface. Rub the salt and pepper all over the beef to season. 3. Make the filling for the stuffed beef fillet: Combine the goat cheese, feta, onions, and garlic in a medium bowl. Stir until well blended. 4. Spoon the mixture in the center of the fillet. Roll the fillet up tightly like rolling a burrito and use some kitchen twine to tie the fillet. 5. Arrange the fillet in the cook & crisp basket and air crisp for 10 minutes, flipping the fillet halfway through to ensure even cooking, or until an instant-read thermometer inserted in the center of the fillet registers 57°C for medium-rare. 6. Transfer to a platter and serve immediately.

Lamb Sirloin Masala

Prep time: 10 minutes | Cook time: 25 minutes | Serves 3

340 g lamb sirloin, sliced
1 tablespoon garam masala
1 tablespoon lemon juice
1 tablespoon olive oil
60 ml coconut cream

1. Sprinkle the sliced lamb sirloin with garam masala, lemon juice, olive oil, and coconut cream in a large bowl. Toss to mix well. 2. Transfer the mixture in the Ninja Foodi cooker. Cook on Sauté mode for 25 minutes. Flip the lamb for every 5 minutes. 3. When cooking is complete, allow to cool for 10 minutes, then serve warm.

Cider-Herb Pork Tenderloin

Prep time: 15 minutes | Cook time: 18 minutes | Serves 4

¼ teaspoon ground cumin
½ teaspoon ground nutmeg
½ teaspoon dried thyme
½ teaspoon ground coriander
1 tablespoon sesame oil
450 g pork tenderloin
2 tablespoons apple cider vinegar
240 ml water

1. In the mixing bowl, mix up ground cumin, ground nutmeg, thyme, ground coriander, and apple cider vinegar. 2. Then rub the meat with the spice mixture. 3. Heat up sesame oil on Sauté mode for 2 minutes. 4. Put the pork tenderloin in the hot oil and cook it for 5 minutes from each side or until meat is light brown. 5. Add water. 6. Close and seal the lid. Cook the meat on High Pressure for 5 minutes. 7. When the time is finished, allow the natural pressure release for 15 minutes.

Mustard Herb Pork Tenderloin

Prep time: 5 minutes | Cook time: 20 minutes | Serves 6

60 ml mayonnaise
2 tablespoons Dijon mustard
½ teaspoon dried thyme
¼ teaspoon dried rosemary
1 (450 g) pork tenderloin
½ teaspoon salt
¼ teaspoon ground black pepper

1. In a small bowl, mix mayonnaise, mustard, thyme, and rosemary. Brush tenderloin with mixture on all sides, then sprinkle with salt and pepper on all sides. 2. Place tenderloin into ungreased cook & crisp basket. Adjust the temperature to 205°C and air crisp for 20 minutes, turning tenderloin halfway through cooking. Tenderloin will be golden and have an internal temperature of at least 65°C when done. Serve warm.

Pork Meatballs with Thyme

Prep time: 15 minutes | Cook time: 16 minutes | Serves 8

480 ml ground pork
1 teaspoon dried thyme
½ teaspoon chili flakes
½ teaspoon garlic powder
1 tablespoon coconut oil
¼ teaspoon ground ginger
3 tablespoons almond flour
60 ml water

1. In the mixing bowl, mix up ground pork, dried thyme, chili flakes, garlic powder, ground ginger, and almond flour. 2. Make the meatballs. 3. Melt the coconut oil in the Ninja Foodi cooker on Sauté mode. 4. Arrange the meatballs in the Ninja Foodi cooker in one layer and cook them for 3 minutes from each side. 5. Then add water and cook the meatballs for 10 minutes.

Classic Pork and Cauliflower Keema

Prep time: 15 minutes | Cook time: 8 minutes | Serves 6

1 tablespoon sesame oil
120 ml brown onion, chopped
1 garlic cloves, minced
1 (1-inch) piece fresh ginger, minced
680 g ground pork
240 ml cauliflower, chopped into small florets
1 ripe tomatoes, puréed
1 jalapeño pepper, seeded and minced
4 cloves, whole
1 teaspoon garam masala
½ teaspoon ground cumin
¼ teaspoon turmeric powder
1 teaspoon brown mustard seeds
½ teaspoon hot paprika
Sea salt and ground black pepper, to taste
240 ml wate

1. Press the Sauté button to heat up the Ninja Foodi cooker. Heat the sesame oil. Once hot, sauté brown onion for 3 minutes or until softened. 2. Stir in garlic and ginger; cook for an additional minute. Add the remaining ingredients. 3. Secure the lid. Set cooking time for 5 minutes on High pressure. 4. Once cooking is complete, use a quick pressure release. Carefully remove the lid. 5. Serve immediately.

Cheddar Bacon Burst with Spinach

Prep time: 5 minutes | Cook time: 60 minutes | Serves 8

30 slices bacon
1 tablespoon Chipotle chilli powder
2 teaspoons Italian seasoning
120 ml Cheddar cheese
1 L raw spinach

1. Preheat the Ninja Foodi cooker to 190°C. 2. Weave the bacon into 15 vertical pieces and 12 horizontal pieces. Cut the extra 3 in half to fill in the rest, horizontally. 3. Season the bacon with Chipotle chilli powder and Italian seasoning. 4. Add the cheese to the bacon. 5. Add the spinach and press down to compress. 6. Tightly roll up the woven bacon. 7. Line a baking sheet with kitchen foil and add plenty of salt to it. 8. Put the bacon on top of a cooling rack and put that on top of the baking sheet. 9. Bake for 60 minutes. 10. Let cool for 15 minutes before slicing and serving.

Greek-Style Meatloaf

Prep time: 5 minutes | Cook time: 25 minutes | Serves 6

450 g lean beef mince
2 eggs
2 plum tomatoes, diced
½ brown onion, diced
120 ml whole wheat bread crumbs
1 teaspoon garlic powder
1 teaspoon dried oregano
1 teaspoon dried thyme
1 teaspoon salt
1 teaspoon black pepper
60 g mozzarella cheese, shredded
1 tablespoon olive oil
Fresh chopped parsley, for garnish

1. Preheat the oven to 190°C. 2. In a large bowl, mix together the beef, eggs, tomatoes, onion, bread crumbs, garlic powder, oregano, thyme, salt, pepper, and cheese. 3. Form into a loaf, flattening to 1-inch thick. 4. Brush the top with olive oil, then place the meatloaf into the cook & crisp basket and cook for 25 minutes. 5. Remove from the Ninja Foodi cooker and allow to rest for 5 minutes, before slicing and serving with a sprinkle of parsley.

Basil and Thyme Pork Loin

Prep time: 10 minutes | Cook time: 17 minutes | Serves 4

450 g pork loin
1 teaspoon dried basil
1 tablespoon avocado oil
1 teaspoon dried thyme
½ teaspoon salt
2 tablespoons apple cider vinegar
240 ml water, for cooking

1. In the shallow bowl, mix up dried basil, avocado oil, thyme, salt, and apple cider vinegar. 2. Then rub the pork loin with the spice mixture and leave the meat for 10 minutes to marinate. 3. Wrap the meat in foil and put on the steamer rack. 4. Pour water and transfer the steamer rack with meat in the Ninja Foodi cooker. 5. Close and seal the lid. Cook the meat on High Pressure for 20 minutes. Allow the natural pressure release for 5 minutes. 6. Slice the cooked pork loin.

Beef Chili with Kale

Prep time: 10 minutes | Cook time: 10 minutes | Serves 6

2 tablespoons olive oil
680 g ground chuck
1 green bell pepper, chopped
1 red bell pepper, chopped
2 red chilies, minced
1 red onion
2 garlic cloves, smashed
1 teaspoon cumin
1 teaspoon Mexican oregano
1 teaspoon cayenne pepper
1 teaspoon smoked paprika
Salt and freshly ground black pepper, to taste
360 ml puréed tomatoes
1 L fresh kale

1. Press the Sauté button to heat up the Ninja Foodi cooker. Then, heat the oil; once hot, cook the ground chuck for 2 minutes, crumbling it with a fork or a wide spatula. 2. Add the pepper, onions, and garlic; cook an additional 2 minutes or until fragrant. Stir in the remaining ingredients, minus kale leaves. 3. Cook for 6 minutes at High Pressure. Once cooking is complete, use a natural pressure release; carefully remove the lid. 4. Add kale, cover with the lid and allow the kale leaves to wilt completely. Bon appétit!

Spicy Beef Stew with Butternut Squash

Prep time: 15 minutes | Cook time: 30 minutes | Serves 8

1½ tablespoons smoked paprika
2 teaspoons ground cinnamon
1½ teaspoons rock salt
1 teaspoon ground ginger
1 teaspoon red pepper flakes
½ teaspoon freshly ground black pepper
900 g beef shoulder roast, cut into 1-inch cubes
2 tablespoons avocado oil, divided
240 ml beef or vegetable broth
1 medium red onion, cut into wedges
8 garlic cloves, minced
1 (780 g) carton or can no-salt-added diced tomatoes
900 g butternut squash, peeled and cut into 1-inch pieces
Chopped fresh coriander or parsley, for serving

1. In a zip-top bag or medium bowl, combine the paprika, cinnamon, salt, ginger, red pepper, and black pepper. Add the beef and toss to coat. 2. Set the electric pressure cooker to the Sauté setting. When the pot is hot, pour in 1 tablespoon of avocado oil. 3. Add half of the beef to the pot and cook, stirring occasionally, for 3 to 5 minutes or until the beef is no longer pink. Transfer it to a plate, then add the remaining 1 tablespoon of avocado oil and brown the remaining beef. Transfer to the plate. Hit Start/Stop. 4. Stir in the broth and scrape up any brown bits from the bottom of the pot. Return the beef to the pot and add the onion, garlic, tomatoes and their juices, and squash. Stir well. 5. Close and lock lid of pressure cooker. Set the valve to sealing. 6. Cook on high pressure for 30 minutes. 7. When cooking is complete, hit Start/Stop. Allow the pressure to release naturally for 10 minutes, then quick release any remaining pressure. 8. Unlock and remove lid. 9. Spoon into serving bowls, sprinkle with coriander or parsley, and serve.

Sausage-Stuffed Peppers

Prep time: 15 minutes | Cook time: 28 to 30 minutes | Serves 6

Avocado oil spray
230 g Italian-seasoned sausage, casings removed
120 ml chopped mushrooms
60 ml diced onion
1 teaspoon Italian seasoning
Sea salt and freshly ground black pepper, to taste
235 ml keto-friendly marinara sauce
3 peppers, halved and seeded
85 g low-moisture Mozzarella or other melting cheese, shredded

1. Spray a large skillet with oil and place it over medium-high heat. Add the sausage and cook for 5 minutes, breaking up the meat with a wooden spoon. Add the mushrooms, onion, and Italian seasoning, and season with salt and pepper. Cook for 5 minutes more. Stir in the marinara sauce and cook until heated through. 2. Scoop the sausage filling into the pepper halves. 3. Set the Ninja Foodi cooker to 175°C. Arrange the peppers in a single layer in the cook & crisp basket, working in batches if necessary. Air crisp for 15 minutes. 4. Top the stuffed peppers with the cheese and air crisp for 3 to 5 minutes more, until the cheese is melted and the peppers are tender.

Pork Schnitzels with Sour Cream and Dill Sauce

Prep time: 5 minutes | Cook time: 24 minutes | Serves 4 to 6

120 ml flour
1½ teaspoons salt
Freshly ground black pepper, to taste
2 eggs
120 ml milk
355 ml toasted breadcrumbs
1 teaspoon paprika
6 boneless pork chops (about 680 g), fat trimmed, pound to ½-inch thick
2 tablespoons olive oil
3 tablespoons melted butter
Lemon wedges, for serving
Sour Cream and Dill Sauce:
235 ml chicken stock
1½ tablespoons cornflour
80 ml sour cream
1½ tablespoons chopped fresh dill
Salt and ground black pepper, to taste

1. Preheat the Ninja Foodi cooker to 205°C. 2. Combine the flour with salt and black pepper in a large bowl. Stir to mix well. Whisk the egg with milk in a second bowl. Stir the breadcrumbs and paprika in a third bowl. 3. Dredge the pork chops in the flour bowl, then in the egg milk, and then into the breadcrumbs bowl. Press to coat well. Shake the excess off. 4. Arrange one pork chop in the preheated Ninja Foodi cooker each time, then brush with olive oil and butter on all sides. 5. Air crisp each pork chop for 4 minutes or until golden brown and crispy. Flip the chop halfway through the cooking time. 6. Transfer the cooked pork chop (schnitzel) to a baking pan in the oven and keep warm over low heat while air frying the remaining pork chops. 7. Meanwhile, combine the chicken stock and cornflour in a small saucepan and bring to a boil over medium-high heat. Simmer for 2 more minutes. 8. Turn off the heat, then mix in the sour cream, fresh dill, salt, and black pepper. 9. Remove the schnitzels from the Ninja Foodi cooker to a plate and baste with sour cream and dill sauce. Squeeze the lemon wedges over and slice to serve.

Beef Burger

Prep time: 20 minutes | Cook time: 12 minutes | Serves 4

570 g lean beef mince
1 tablespoon soy sauce or tamari
1 teaspoon Dijon mustard
1/2 teaspoon smoked paprika
1 teaspoon shallot powder
1 clove garlic, minced
½ teaspoon cumin powder
60 ml spring onions, minced
⅓ teaspoon sea salt flakes
⅓ teaspoon freshly cracked mixed peppercorns
1 teaspoon celery salt
1 teaspoon dried parsley

1. Mix all of the above ingredients in a bowl; knead until everything is well incorporated. 2. Shape the mixture into four patties. Next, make a shallow dip in the center of each patty to prevent them puffing up during air frying. 3. Spritz the patties on all sides using nonstick cooking spray. Cook approximately 12 minutes at 180°C. 4. Check for doneness, an instant-read thermometer should read 70°C. Bon appétit!

Beef Steak Fingers

Prep time: 5 minutes | Cook time: 8 minutes | Serves 4

4 small beef minute steaks
Salt and ground black pepper, to taste
120 ml flour
Cooking spray

1. Preheat the Ninja Foodi cooker to 200°C. 2. Cut minute steaks into 1-inch-wide strips. 3. Sprinkle lightly with salt and pepper to taste. 4. Roll in flour to coat all sides. 5. Spritz cook & crisp basket with cooking spray. 6. Put steak strips in cook & crisp basket in a single layer. Spritz top of steak strips with cooking spray. 7. Air crisp for 4 minutes, turn strips over, and spritz with cooking spray. 8. Air crisp 4 more minutes and test with fork for doneness. Steak fingers should be crispy outside with no red juices inside. 9. Repeat steps 5 through 7 to air crisp remaining strips. 10. Serve immediately.

Italian Sausage Links

Prep time: 10 minutes | Cook time: 24 minutes | Serves 4

1 pepper (any color), sliced
1 medium onion, sliced
1 tablespoon avocado oil
1 teaspoon Italian seasoning
Sea salt and freshly ground black pepper, to taste
450 g Italian-seasoned sausage links

1. Place the pepper and onion in a medium bowl, and toss with the avocado oil, Italian seasoning, and salt and pepper to taste. 2. Set the Ninja Foodi cooker to 205°C. Put the vegetables in the cook & crisp basket and cook for 12 minutes. 3. Push the vegetables to the side of the basket and arrange the sausage links in the bottom of the basket in a single layer. Spoon the vegetables over the sausages. Cook for 12 minutes, tossing halfway through, until an instant-read thermometer inserted into the sausage reads 70°C.

Roast Beef with Horseradish Cream

Prep time: 5 minutes | Cook time: 35 to 45 minutes | Serves 6

900 g beef roasting joint
1 tablespoon salt
2 teaspoons garlic powder
1 teaspoon freshly ground black pepper
1 teaspoon dried thyme
Horseradish Cream:
80 ml double cream
80 ml sour cream
80 ml grated horseradish
2 teaspoons fresh lemon juice
Salt and freshly ground black pepper, to taste

1. Preheat the Ninja Foodi cooker to 205ºC. 2. Season the beef with the salt, garlic powder, black pepper, and thyme. Place the beef fat-side down in the basket of the Ninja Foodi cooker and lightly coat with olive oil. Pausing halfway through the cooking time to turn the meat, air crisp for 35 to 45 minutes, until a thermometer inserted into the thickest part indicates the desired doneness, 50ºC (rare) to 65ºC (medium). Let the beef rest for 10 minutes before slicing. 3. To make the horseradish cream: In a small bowl, combine the double cream, sour cream, horseradish, and lemon juice. Whisk until thoroughly combined. Season to taste with salt and freshly ground black pepper. Serve alongside the beef.

Buttery Pork Chops

Prep time: 5 minutes | Cook time: 12 minutes | Serves 4

4 (110 g) boneless pork chops
½ teaspoon salt
¼ teaspoon ground black pepper
2 tablespoons salted butter, softened

1. Sprinkle pork chops on all sides with salt and pepper. Place chops into ungreased cook & crisp basket in a single layer. Adjust the temperature to 205ºC and air crisp for 12 minutes. Pork chops will be golden and have an internal temperature of at least 65ºC when done. 2. Use tongs to remove cooked pork chops from Ninja Foodi cooker and place onto a large plate. Top each chop with ½ tablespoon butter and let sit 2 minutes to melt. Serve warm.

Honey-Baked Pork Loin

Prep time: 30 minutes | Cook time: 22 to 25 minutes | Serves 6

60 ml honey
60 ml freshly squeezed lemon juice
2 tablespoons soy sauce
1 teaspoon garlic powder
1 (900 g) pork loin
2 tablespoons vegetable oil

1. In a medium bowl, whisk together the honey, lemon juice, soy sauce, and garlic powder. Reserve half of the mixture for basting during cooking. 2. Cut 5 slits in the pork loin and transfer it to a resealable bag. Add the remaining honey mixture. Seal the bag and refrigerate to marinate for at least 2 hours. 3. Preheat the Ninja Foodi cooker to 205ºC. Line the cook & crisp basket with parchment paper. 4. Remove the pork from the marinade, and place it on the parchment. Spritz with oil, then baste with the reserved marinade. 5. Cook for 15 minutes. Flip the pork, baste with more marinade and spritz with oil again. Cook for 7 to 10 minutes more until the internal temperature reaches 65ºC. Let rest for 5 minutes before serving.

Cantonese BBQ Pork

Prep time: 30 minutes | Cook time: 15 minutes | Serves 4

60 ml honey
2 tablespoons dark soy sauce
1 tablespoon sugar
1 tablespoon Shaoxing wine (rice cooking wine)
1 tablespoon hoisin sauce
2 teaspoons minced garlic
2 teaspoons minced fresh ginger
1 teaspoon Chinese five-spice powder
450 g fatty pork shoulder, cut into long, 1-inch-thick pieces

1. In a small microwave-safe bowl, combine the honey, soy sauce, sugar, wine, hoisin, garlic, ginger, and five-spice powder. Microwave in 10-second intervals, stirring in between, until the honey has dissolved. 2. Use a fork to pierce the pork slices to allow the marinade to penetrate better. Place the pork in a large bowl or resealable plastic bag and pour in half the marinade; set aside the remaining marinade to use for the sauce. Toss to coat. Marinate the pork at room temperature for 30 minutes, or cover and refrigerate for up 24 hours. 3. Place the pork in a single layer in the cook & crisp basket. Set the Ninja Foodi cooker to 205ºC for 15 minutes, turning and basting the pork halfway through the cooking time. 4. While the pork is cooking, microwave the reserved marinade on high for 45 to 60 seconds, stirring every 15 seconds, to thicken it slightly to the consistency of a sauce. 5. Transfer the pork to a cutting board and let rest for 10 minutes. Brush with the sauce and serve.

Beef and Red Cabbage Stew

Prep time: 10 minutes | Cook time: 20 minutes | Serves 4

2 tablespoons butter, at room temperature
1 onion, chopped
2 garlic cloves, minced
680 g beef stew meat, cubed
600 ml beef stock
230 g sugar-free tomato sauce
480 ml shredded red cabbage
1 tablespoon coconut aminos
2 bay leaves
1 teaspoon dried parsley flakes
½ teaspoon crushed red pepper flakes
Sea salt and ground black pepper, to taste

1. Press the Sauté button to heat up the Ninja Foodi cooker. Then, melt the butter. Cook the onion and garlic until softened. 2. Add beef stew meat and cook an additional 3 minutes or until browned. Stir the remaining ingredients into the Ninja Foodi cooker. 3. Secure the lid. Choose High Pressure; cook for 15 minutes. Once cooking is complete, use a quick pressure release; carefully remove the lid. 4. Discard bay leaves and ladle into individual bowls. Enjoy!

Turmeric Pork Loin

Prep time: 10 minutes | Cook time: 22 minutes | Serves 4

450 g pork loin
1 teaspoon ground turmeric
1 teaspoon coconut oil
½ teaspoon salt
120 ml organic almond milk

1. Cut the pork loin into the strips and sprinkle with salt and ground turmeric. 2. Heat up the coconut oil on Sauté mode for 1 minute and add pork strips. 3. Sauté them for 6 minutes. Stir the meat from time to time. 4. After this, add almond milk and close the lid. 5. Sauté the pork for 15 minutes.

Coconut Pork Muffins

Prep time: 5 minutes | Cook time: 9 minutes | Serves 2

1 egg, beaten
2 tablespoons coconut flour
1 teaspoon parsley
¼ teaspoon salt
1 tablespoon coconut cream
110 g ground pork, fried
240 ml water

1. Whisk together the egg, coconut flour, parsley, salt, and coconut cream. Add the fried ground pork. Mix the the mixture until homogenous. 2. Pour the mixture into a muffin pan. 3. Pour the water in the Ninja Foodi cooker and place in the reversible rack. 4. Lower the muffin pan on the reversible rack and close the Ninja Foodi cooker lid. 5. Set cooking time for 4 minutes on High Pressure. 6. When timer beeps, perform a natural pressure release for 5 minutes, then release any remaining pressure. Open the lid. 7. Serve warm.

Beef Steak with Cheese Mushroom Sauce

Prep time: 6 minutes | Cook time: 30 minutes | Serves 6

1 tablespoon olive oil
680 g beef blade steak
240 ml stock
2 garlic cloves, minced
Sea salt and ground black pepper, to taste
½ teaspoon cayenne pepper
1 tablespoon coconut aminos
Sauce:
1 tablespoon butter, softened
480 ml sliced Porcini mushrooms
120 ml thinly sliced onions
120 ml sour cream
110 g goat cheese, crumbled

1. Press the Sauté button to heat up the Ninja Foodi cooker. Then, heat the olive oil until sizzling. Once hot, cook the blade steak approximately 3 minutes or until delicately browned. 2. Add the stock, garlic, salt, black pepper, cayenne pepper, and coconut aminos. 3. Secure the lid. Choose High Pressure; cook for 20 minutes. Once cooking is complete, use a quick pressure release; carefully remove the lid. 4. Take the meat out of the Ninja Foodi cooker. Allow it to cool slightly and then, slice it into strips. 5. Press the Sauté button again and add the butter, mushrooms and onions to the Ninja Foodi cooker. Let it cook for 5 minutes longer or until the mushrooms are fragrant and the onions are softened. 6. Add sour cream and goat cheese; continue to simmer for a couple of minutes more or until everything is thoroughly heated. 7. Return the meat to the Ninja Foodi cooker and serve. Bon appétit!

Cheesesteak Stuffed Peppers

Prep time: 10 minutes | Cook time: 8 minutes | Serves 4

1 tablespoon butter
450 g shaved beef
110 g mushrooms, coarsely chopped
70 g sliced onion
1 tablespoon Worcestershire sauce
1 teaspoon seasoned salt
¼ teaspoon salt
¼ teaspoon black pepper
4 large bell peppers (any colour)
120 ml water
4 slices provolone cheese

1. Heat the broiler. 2. Turn the pot to Sauté mode and add the butter. Once melted, add the beef, mushrooms, and onion. Sauté until softened, 2 to 3 minutes. Add the Worcestershire sauce, seasoned salt, salt, and black pepper. Stir to evenly combine. Press Start/Stop. 3. Slice the tops off the bell peppers and remove the cores and seeds. Fill each pepper with 120 g of the meat mixture. Rinse out the pot. 4. Place the pot back into the base. Add the water and the reversible rack. Place the peppers on top of the reversible rack. 5. Close the lid and seal the vent. Cook on High Pressure for 5 minutes. Quick release the steam. 6. Carefully remove the reversible rack from the pot. Transfer the peppers to a baking sheet. Place one slice of provolone cheese on top of each pepper and broil for about 1 minute to melt the cheese.

Air Fried Beef Satay with Peanut Dipping Sauce

Prep time: 30 minutes | Cook time: 5 to 7 minutes | Serves 4

230 g bavette or skirt steak, sliced into 8 strips
2 teaspoons curry powder
½ teaspoon coarse or flaky salt
Cooking spray
Peanut Dipping sauce:
2 tablespoons creamy peanut butter
1 tablespoon reduced-salt soy sauce
2 teaspoons rice vinegar
1 teaspoon honey
1 teaspoon grated ginger
Special Equipment:
4 bamboo skewers, cut into halves and soaked in water for 20 minutes to keep them from burning while cooking

1. Preheat the Ninja Foodi cooker to 180ºC. Spritz the cook & crisp basket with cooking spray. 2. In a bowl, place the steak strips and sprinkle with the curry powder and coarse or flaky salt to season. Thread the strips onto the soaked skewers. 3. Arrange the skewers in the prepared cook & crisp basket and spritz with cooking spray. Air crisp for 5 to 7 minutes, or until the beef is well browned, turning halfway through. 4. In the meantime, stir together the peanut butter, soy sauce, rice vinegar, honey, and ginger in a bowl to make the dipping sauce. 5. Transfer the beef to the serving dishes and let rest for 5 minutes. Serve with the peanut dipping sauce on the side.

Beef Bavette Steak with Sage

Prep time: 13 minutes | Cook time: 7 minutes | Serves 2

80 ml sour cream
120 ml spring onion, chopped
1 tablespoon mayonnaise
3 cloves garlic, smashed
450 g beef bavette or skirt steak, trimmed and cubed
2 tablespoons fresh sage, minced
½ teaspoon salt
⅓ teaspoon black pepper, or to taste

1. Season your meat with salt and pepper; arrange beef cubes on the bottom of a baking dish that fits in your Ninja Foodi cooker. 2. Stir in spring onions and garlic; air crisp for about 7 minutes at 195°C. 3. Once your beef starts to tender, add the cream, mayonnaise, and sage; air crisp an additional 8 minutes. Bon appétit!

Rosemary Ribeye Steaks

Prep time: 10 minutes | Cook time: 15 minutes | Serves 2

60 ml butter
1 clove garlic, minced
Salt and ground black pepper, to taste
1½ tablespoons balsamic vinegar
60 ml rosemary, chopped
2 ribeye steaks

1. Melt the butter in a skillet over medium heat. Add the garlic and fry until fragrant. 2. Remove the skillet from the heat and add the salt, pepper, and vinegar. Allow it to cool. 3. Add the rosemary, then pour the mixture into a Ziploc bag. 4. Put the ribeye steaks in the bag and shake well, coating the meat well. Refrigerate for an hour, then allow to sit for a further twenty minutes. 5. Preheat the Ninja Foodi cooker to 205°C. 6. Air crisp the ribeye steaks for 15 minutes. 7. Take care when removing the steaks from the Ninja Foodi cooker and plate up. 8. Serve immediately.

Korean Beef and Pickled Vegetable Bowls

Prep time: 15 minutes | Cook time: 10 minutes | Serves 6

1 tablespoon vegetable oil
5 garlic cloves, thinly sliced
1 tablespoon julienned fresh ginger
2 dried red chiles
240 ml sliced onions
450 g 80% lean ground beef
1 tablespoon gochujang, adjusted to taste
240 ml fresh basil leaves, divided
1 tablespoon coconut aminos
1 teaspoon granulated sweetener
2 tablespoons freshly squeezed lime juice
1 teaspoon salt
1 teaspoon freshly ground pepper
60 ml water
1 teaspoon sesame oil
For the Pickled Vegetables:
1 cucumber, peeled, coarsely grated
1 turnip, coarsely grated
60 ml white vinegar
½ teaspoon salt
½ teaspoon granulated sweetener

1. Select Sauté mode of the Ninja Foodi cooker. When the pot is hot, add the oil and heat until it is shimmering. 2. Add the garlic, ginger, and chiles and sauté for 1 minute. 3. Add the onions and sauté for 1 minute. 4. Add the ground beef and cooking for 4 minutes.. 5. Add the gochujang, 120 ml of basil, coconut aminos, sweetener, lime juice, salt, pepper, water, and sesame oil, and stir to combine. 6. Lock the lid. Set the time for 4 minutes on High Pressure. 7. When cooking is complete, let the pressure release naturally for 5 minutes, then release any remaining pressure. Unlock the lid and stir in the remaining 120 ml of basil. 8. Meanwhile, put the cucumber and turnip in a medium bowl and mix with the vinegar, salt, and sweetener. To serve, portion the basil beef into individual bowls and serve with the pickled salad.

Air Fried Crispy Venison

Prep time: 10 minutes | Cook time: 20 minutes | Serves 4

2 eggs
60 ml milk
235 ml whole wheat flour
½ teaspoon salt
¼ teaspoon ground black pepper
450 g venison backstrap/striploin, sliced
Cooking spray

1. Preheat the Ninja Foodi cooker to 180°C and spritz with cooking spray. 2. Whisk the eggs with milk in a large bowl. Combine the flour with salt and ground black pepper in a shallow dish. 3. Dredge the venison in the flour first, then into the egg mixture. Shake the excess off and roll the venison back over the flour to coat well. 4. Arrange half of the venison in the preheated Ninja Foodi cooker and spritz with cooking spray. 5. Air crisp for 10 minutes or until the internal temperature of the venison reaches at least 65°C for medium rare. Flip the venison halfway through. Repeat with remaining venison. 6. Serve immediately.

Pork Milanese

Prep time: 10 minutes | Cook time: 12 minutes | Serves 4

4 (1-inch) boneless pork chops
Fine sea salt and ground black pepper, to taste
2 large eggs
180 ml pre-grated Parmesan cheese
Chopped fresh parsley, for garnish
Lemon slices, for serving

1. Spray the cook & crisp basket with avocado oil. Preheat the Ninja Foodi cooker to 205°C. 2. Place the pork chops between 2 sheets of plastic wrap and pound them with the flat side of a meat tenderizer until they're ¼ inch thick. Lightly season both sides of the chops with salt and pepper. 3. Lightly beat the eggs in a shallow bowl. Divide the Parmesan cheese evenly between 2 bowls and set the bowls in this order: Parmesan, eggs, Parmesan. Dredge a chop in the first bowl of Parmesan, then dip it in the eggs, and then dredge it again in the second bowl of Parmesan, making sure both sides and all edges are well coated. Repeat with the remaining chops. 4. Place the chops in the cook & crisp basket and air crisp for 12 minutes, or until the internal temperature reaches 65°C, flipping halfway through. 5. Garnish with fresh parsley and serve immediately with lemon slices. Store leftovers in an airtight container in the refrigerator for up to 3 days. Reheat in a preheated 200°C Ninja Foodi cooker for 5 minutes, or until warmed through.

Egg Meatloaf

Prep time: 20 minutes | Cook time: 25 minutes | Serves 6

1 tablespoon avocado oil
1120 ml ground pork
1 teaspoon chives
1 teaspoon salt
½ teaspoon ground black pepper
2 tablespoons coconut flour
3 eggs, hard-boiled, peeled
240 ml water

1. Brush a loaf pan with avocado oil. 2. In the mixing bowl, mix the ground pork, chives, salt, ground black pepper, and coconut flour. 3. Transfer the mixture in the loaf pan and flatten with a spatula. 4. Fill the meatloaf with hard-boiled eggs. 5. Pour water and insert the reversible rack in the Ninja Foodi cooker. 6. Lower the loaf pan over the reversible rack in the Ninja Foodi cooker. Close the lid. 7. Set cooking time for 25 minutes on High Pressure. 8. When timer beeps, use a natural pressure release for 10 minutes, then release any remaining pressure. Open the lid. 9. Serve immediately.

Garlic Beef Roast

Prep time: 2 minutes | Cook time: 70 minutes | Serves 6

900 g top round roast
120 ml beef broth
2 teaspoons salt
1 teaspoon black pepper
3 whole cloves garlic
1 bay leaf

1. Add the roast, broth, salt, pepper, garlic, and bay leaf to the pot. 2. Close the lid and seal the vent. Cook on High Pressure for 15 minutes. Let the steam naturally release for 15 minutes before Manually releasing. 3. Remove the beef from the pot and slice or shred it. Store it in an airtight container in the fridge or freezer.

Greek Pork with Tzatziki Sauce

Prep time: 30 minutes | Cook time: 50 minutes | Serves 4

Greek Pork:
900 g pork loin roasting joint
Salt and black pepper, to taste
1 teaspoon smoked paprika
½ teaspoon mustard seeds
½ teaspoon celery salt
1 teaspoon fennel seeds
1 teaspoon chili powder
1 teaspoon turmeric powder
½ teaspoon ground ginger
2 tablespoons olive oil
2 cloves garlic, finely chopped
Tzatziki:
½ cucumber, finely chopped and squeezed
235 ml full-fat Greek yogurt
1 garlic clove, minced
1 tablespoon extra-virgin olive oil
1 teaspoon balsamic vinegar
1 teaspoon minced fresh dill
A pinch of salt

1. Toss all ingredients for Greek pork in a large mixing bowl. Toss until the meat is well coated. 2. Cook in the preheated Ninja Foodi cooker at 180°C for 30 minutes; turn over and cook another 20 minutes. 3. Meanwhile, prepare the tzatziki by mixing all the tzatziki ingredients. Place in your refrigerator until ready to use. 4. Serve the pork sirloin roast with the chilled tzatziki on the side. Enjoy!

Beef Masala Curry

Prep time: 10 minutes | Cook time: 20 minutes | Serves 4

2 tomatoes, quartered
1 small onion, quartered
4 garlic cloves, chopped
120 ml fresh coriander leaves
1 teaspoon garam masala
½ teaspoon ground coriander
1 teaspoon ground cumin
½ teaspoon cayenne
1 teaspoon salt
450 g beef chuck roast, cut into 1-inch cubes

1. In a blender, combine the tomatoes, onion, garlic, and coriander. 2. Process until the vegetables are puréed. Add the garam masala, coriander, cumin, cayenne, and salt. Process for several more seconds. 3. To the Ninja Foodi cooker, add the beef and pour the vegetable purée on top. 4. Lock the lid. Set cooking time for 20 minutes on High Pressure. 5. When timer beeps, let the pressure release naturally for 10 minutes, then release any remaining pressure. Unlock the lid. 6. Stir and serve immediately.

Greek Lamb Rack

Prep time: 5 minutes | Cook time: 10 minutes | Serves 4

60 ml freshly squeezed lemon juice
1 teaspoon oregano
2 teaspoons minced fresh rosemary
1 teaspoon minced fresh thyme
2 tablespoons minced garlic
Salt and freshly ground black pepper, to taste
2 to 4 tablespoons olive oil
1 lamb rib rack (7 to 8 ribs)

1. Preheat the Ninja Foodi cooker to 180°C. 2. In a small mixing bowl, combine the lemon juice, oregano, rosemary, thyme, garlic, salt, pepper, and olive oil and mix well. 3. Rub the mixture over the lamb, covering all the meat. Put the rack of lamb in the Ninja Foodi cooker. Roast for 10 minutes. Flip the rack halfway through. 4. After 10 minutes, measure the internal temperature of the rack of lamb reaches at least 65°C. 5. Serve immediately.

Chapter 4 Fish and Seafood

Prawn and Cherry Tomato Kebabs

Prep time: 15 minutes | Cook time: 5 minutes | Serves 4

680 g jumbo prawns, cleaned, peeled and deveined
455 g cherry tomatoes
2 tablespoons butter, melted
1 tablespoons Sriracha sauce
Sea salt and ground black pepper, to taste
1 teaspoon dried parsley flakes
½ teaspoon dried basil
½ teaspoon dried oregano
½ teaspoon mustard seeds
½ teaspoon marjoram
Special Equipment:
4 to 6 wooden skewers, soaked in water for 30 minutes

1. Preheat the Ninja Foodi cooker to 205ºC. 2. Put all the ingredients in a large bowl and toss to coat well. 3. Make the kebabs: Thread, alternating jumbo prawns and cherry tomatoes, onto the wooden skewers that fit into the Ninja Foodi cooker. 4. Arrange the kebabs in the cook & crisp basket. You may need to cook in batches depending on the size of your cook & crisp basket. 5. Air crisp for 5 minutes, or until the prawns are pink and the cherry tomatoes are softened. Repeat with the remaining kebabs. Let the prawns and cherry tomato kebabs cool for 5 minutes and serve hot.

Bacon Halibut Steak

Prep time: 15 minutes | Cook time: 10 minutes | Serves 4

680 g halibut steaks (170 g each fillet)
1 teaspoon avocado oil
1 teaspoon ground black pepper
110 g bacon, sliced

1. Sprinkle the halibut steaks with avocado oil and ground black pepper. 2. Then wrap the fish in the bacon slices and put in the Ninja Foodi cooker. 3. Cook the fish at 200ºC for 5 minutes per side.

Crab and Bell Pepper Cakes

Prep time: 5 minutes | Cook time: 10 minutes | Serves 4

230 g jumbo lump crabmeat
1 tablespoon Old Bay seasoning
40 g bread crumbs
40 g diced red bell pepper
40 g diced green bell pepper
1 egg
60 g mayonnaise
Juice of ½ lemon
1 teaspoon plain flour
Cooking oil spray

1. Sort through the crabmeat, picking out any bits of shell or cartilage. 2. In a large bowl, stir together the Old Bay seasoning, bread crumbs, red and green bell peppers, egg, mayonnaise, and lemon juice. Gently stir in the crabmeat. 3. Insert the crisper plate into the basket and the basket into the unit. Preheat the unit to 190ºC. 4. Form the mixture into 4 patties. Sprinkle ¼ teaspoon of flour on top of each patty. 5. Once the unit is preheated, spray the crisper plate with cooking oil. Place the crab cakes into the basket and spray them with cooking oil. 6. Cook for 10 minutes. 7. When the cooking is complete, the crab cakes will be golden brown and firm.

Crab Cakes

Prep time: 10 minutes | Cook time: 10 minutes | Serves 4

2 cans lump crab meat, 170 g each
¼ cup blanched finely ground almond flour
1 large egg
2 tablespoons full-fat mayonnaise
½ teaspoon Dijon mustard
½ tablespoon lemon juice
½ medium green bell pepper, seeded and chopped
235 g chopped spring onion
½ teaspoon Old Bay seasoning

1. In a large bowl, combine all ingredients. Form into four balls and flatten into patties. Place patties into the cook & crisp basket. 2. Adjust the temperature to 175ºC and air crisp for 10 minutes. 3. Flip patties halfway through the cooking time. Serve warm.

Tuna Patties with Spicy Sriracha Sauce

Prep time: 10 minutes | Cook time: 10 minutes | Serves 4

2 (170 g) cans tuna packed in oil, drained
3 tablespoons almond flour
2 tablespoons mayonnaise
1 teaspoon dried dill
½ teaspoon onion powder
Pinch of salt and pepper
Spicy Sriracha Sauce:
60 g mayonnaise
1 tablespoon Sriracha sauce
1 teaspoon garlic powder

1. Preheat the Ninja Foodi cooker to 190ºC. Line the basket with baking paper. 2. In a large bowl, combine the tuna, almond flour, mayonnaise, dill, and onion powder. Season to taste with salt and freshly ground black pepper. Use a fork to stir, mashing with the back of the fork as necessary, until thoroughly combined. 3. Use an ice cream scoop to form the tuna mixture patties. Place the patties in a single layer on the baking paper in the cook & crisp basket. Press lightly with the bottom of the scoop to flatten into a circle about ½ inch thick. Pausing halfway through the cooking time to turn the patties, air crisp for 10 minutes until lightly browned. 4. To make the Sriracha sauce: In a small bowl, combine the mayonnaise, Sriracha, and garlic powder. Serve the tuna patties topped with the Sriracha sauce.

Butter-Wine Baked Salmon

Prep time: 5 minutes | Cook time: 10 minutes | Serves 4

4 tablespoons butter, melted
2 cloves garlic, minced
Sea salt and ground black pepper, to taste
60 ml dry white wine or apple cider vinegar
1 tablespoon lime juice
1 teaspoon smoked paprika
½ teaspoon onion powder
4 salmon steaks
Cooking spray

1. Place all the ingredients except the salmon and oil in a shallow dish and stir to mix well. 2. Add the salmon steaks, turning to coat well on both sides. Transfer the salmon to the refrigerator to marinate for 30 minutes. 3. Preheat the Ninja Foodi cooker to 180°C. 4. Place the salmon steaks in the cook & crisp basket, discarding any excess marinade. Spray the salmon steaks with cooking spray. 5. Air crisp for about 10 minutes, flipping the salmon steaks halfway through, or until cooked to your preferred doneness. 6. Divide the salmon steaks among four plates and serve.

Paprika Prawns

Prep time: 5 minutes | Cook time: 6 minutes | Serves 2

230 g medium prawns, peeled and deveined
2 tablespoons salted butter, melted
1 teaspoon paprika
½ teaspoon garlic powder
¼ teaspoon onion powder
½ teaspoon Old Bay seasoning

1. Toss all ingredients together in a large bowl. Place prawns into the cook & crisp basket. 2. Adjust the temperature to 205°C and set the timer for 6 minutes. 3. Turn the prawns halfway through the cooking time to ensure even cooking. Serve immediately.

Salade Niçoise with Oil-Packed Tuna

Prep time: 5 minutes | Cook time: 20 minutes | Serves 4

230 g small red potatoes, quartered
230 g green beans, trimmed
4 large eggs
french vinaigrette
2 tablespoons extra-virgin olive oil
2 tablespoons cold-pressed avocado oil
2 tablespoons white wine vinegar
1 tablespoon water
1 teaspoon Dijon mustard
½ teaspoon dried oregano
¼ teaspoon fine sea salt
1 tablespoon minced shallot
2 hearts romaine lettuce, leaves separated and torn into bite-size pieces
120 ml grape tomatoes, halved
60 ml pitted Niçoise or Greek olives
1 can (200 g) oil-packed tuna, drained and flaked
Freshly ground black pepper
1 tablespoon chopped fresh flat-leaf parsley

1. Pour 240 ml water into the Ninja Foodi cooker and place a steamer basket into the pot. Add the potatoes, green beans, and eggs to the basket. 2. Secure the lid and set the pressure release to sealing. Select the Steam setting and set the cooking time for 3 minutes at high pressure. (The pot will take about 15 minutes to come up to pressure before the cooking program begins.) 3. To make the vinaigrette: While the vegetables and eggs are steaming, in a small jar or other small container with a tight-fitting lid, combine the olive oil, avocado oil, vinegar, water, mustard, oregano, salt, and shallot and shake vigorously to emulsify. Set aside. 4. Prepare an ice bath. 5. When the cooking program ends, perform a quick release by moving the Pressure Release to Venting. Open the pot and, wearing heat-resistant mitts, lift out the steamer basket. Using tongs, transfer the eggs and green beans to the ice bath, leaving the potatoes in the steamer basket. 6. While the eggs and green beans are cooling, divide the lettuce, tomatoes, olives, and tuna among four shallow individual bowls. Drain the eggs and green beans. Peel and halve the eggs lengthwise, then arrange them on the salads along with the green beans and potatoes. 7. Spoon the vinaigrette over the salads and sprinkle with the pepper and parsley. Serve right away.

Louisiana Prawn Gumbo

Prep time: 10 minutes | Cook time: 4 minutes | Serves 6

450 g prawn
60 ml chopped celery stalk
1 chili pepper, chopped
60 ml chopped okra
1 tablespoon coconut oil
480 ml chicken broth
1 teaspoon sugar-free tomato paste

1. Put all ingredients in the Ninja Foodi cooker and stir until you get a light red colour. 2. Then close and seal the lid. 3. Cook the meal on High Pressure for 4 minutes. 4. When the time is finished, allow the natural pressure release for 10 minutes.

Haddock and Veggie Foil Packets

Prep time: 5 minutes | Cook time: 10 minutes | Serves 4

360 ml water
1 lemon, sliced
2 bell peppers, sliced
1 brown onion, sliced into rings
4 sprigs parsley
2 sprigs thyme
2 sprigs rosemary
4 haddock fillets
Sea salt, to taste
⅓ teaspoon ground black pepper, or more to taste
2 tablespoons extra-virgin olive oil

1. Pour the water and lemon into your Ninja Foodi cooker and insert a steamer basket. 2. Assemble the packets with large sheets of heavy-duty foil. 3. Place the peppers, onion rings, parsley, thyme, and rosemary in the centre of each foil. Place the fish fillets on top of the veggies. 4. Sprinkle with the salt and black pepper and drizzle the olive oil over the fillets. Place the packets in the steamer basket. 5. Lock the lid. Set the cooking time for 10 minutes at Low Pressure. 6. When the timer beeps, perform a quick pressure release. Carefully remove the lid. 7. Serve warm.

Roasted Halibut Steaks with Parsley

Prep time: 5 minutes | Cook time: 10 minutes | Serves 4

455 g halibut steaks
60 ml vegetable oil
2½ tablespoons Worcester sauce
2 tablespoons honey
2 tablespoons vermouth or white wine vinegar
1 tablespoon freshly squeezed lemon juice
1 tablespoon fresh parsley leaves, coarsely chopped
Salt and pepper, to taste
1 teaspoon dried basil

1. Preheat the Ninja Foodi cooker to 200ºC. 2. Put all the ingredients in a large mixing dish and gently stir until the fish is coated evenly. 3. Transfer the fish to the cook & crisp basket and roast for 10 minutes, flipping the fish halfway through, or until the fish reaches an internal temperature of at least 65ºC on a meat thermometer. 4. Let the fish cool for 5 minutes and serve.

Parmesan Salmon Loaf

Prep time: 15 minutes | Cook time: 25 minutes | Serves 6

340 g salmon, boiled and shredded
3 eggs, beaten
120 ml almond flour
1 teaspoon garlic powder
60 ml grated Parmesan
1 teaspoon butter, softened
240 ml water, for cooking

1. Pour water in the Ninja Foodi cooker. 2. Mix up the rest of the ingredients in the mixing bowl and stir until smooth. 3. After this, transfer the salmon mixture in the loaf pan and flatten; insert the pan in the Ninja Foodi cooker. Close and seal the lid. 4. Cook the meal on High Pressure for 25 minutes. 5. When the cooking time is finished, make a quick pressure release and cool the loaf well before serving.

Asian Marinated Salmon

Prep time: 30 minutes | Cook time: 6 minutes | Serves 2

Marinade:
60 ml wheat-free tamari or coconut aminos
2 tablespoons lime or lemon juice
2 tablespoons sesame oil
2 tablespoons powdered sweetener
2 teaspoons grated fresh ginger
2 cloves garlic, minced
½ teaspoon ground black pepper
2 (110 g) salmon fillets (about 1¼ inches thick)
Sliced spring onions, for garnish
Sauce (Optional):
60 ml beef stock
60 ml wheat-free tamari
3 tablespoons powdered sweetener
1 tablespoon tomato sauce
⅛ teaspoon guar gum or xanthan gum (optional, for thickening)

1. Make the marinade: In a medium-sized shallow dish, stir together all the ingredients for the marinade until well combined. Place the salmon in the marinade. Cover and refrigerate for at least 2 hours or overnight. 2. Preheat the Ninja Foodi cooker to 205ºC. 3. Remove the salmon fillets from the marinade and place them in the Ninja Foodi cooker, leaving space between them. Air crisp for 6 minutes, or until the salmon is cooked through and flakes easily with a fork. 4. While the salmon cooks, make the sauce, if using: Place all the sauce ingredients except the guar gum in a medium-sized bowl and stir until well combined. Taste and adjust the sweetness to your liking. While whisking slowly, add the guar gum. Allow the sauce to thicken for 3 to 5 minutes. (The sauce can be made up to 3 days ahead and stored in an airtight container in the fridge.) Drizzle the sauce over the salmon before serving. 5. Garnish the salmon with sliced spring onions before serving. Store leftovers in an airtight container in the fridge for up to 3 days. Reheat in a preheated 175ºC Ninja Foodi cooker for 3 minutes, or until heated through.

Balsamic Tilapia

Prep time: 5 minutes | Cook time: 15 minutes | Serves 4

4 tilapia fillets, boneless
2 tablespoons balsamic vinegar
1 teaspoon avocado oil
1 teaspoon dried basil

1. Sprinkle the tilapia fillets with balsamic vinegar, avocado oil, and dried basil. 2. Then put the fillets in the cook & crisp basket and cook at 185ºC for 15 minutes.

Clam Chowder with Bacon and Celery

Prep time: 10 minutes | Cook time: 4 minutes | Serves 2

140 g clams
30 g bacon, chopped
85 g celery, chopped
120 ml water
120 ml double cream

1. Cook the bacon on Sauté mode for 1 minute. 2. Then add clams, celery, water, and double cream. 3. Close and seal the lid. 4. Cook the seafood on steam mode (High Pressure) for 3 minutes. Make a quick pressure release. 5. Ladle the clams with the double cream mixture in the bowls.

Firecracker Prawns

Prep time: 10 minutes | Cook time: 7 minutes | Serves 4

455 g medium prawns, peeled and deveined
2 tablespoons salted butter, melted
½ teaspoon Old Bay seasoning
¼ teaspoon garlic powder
2 tablespoons Sriracha
¼ teaspoon powdered sweetener
60 ml full-fat mayonnaise
⅛ teaspoon ground black pepper

1. In a large bowl, toss prawns in butter, Old Bay seasoning, and garlic powder. Place prawns into the cook & crisp basket. 2. Adjust the temperature to 205ºC and set the timer for 7 minutes. 3. Flip the prawns halfway through the cooking time. Prawns will be bright pink when fully cooked. 4. In another large bowl, mix Sriracha, sweetener, mayonnaise, and pepper. Toss prawns in the spicy mixture and serve immediately.

Bacon-Wrapped Scallops

Prep time: 5 minutes | Cook time: 10 minutes | Serves 4

8 sea scallops, 30 g each, cleaned and patted dry
8 slices bacon
¼ teaspoon salt
¼ teaspoon ground black pepper

1. Wrap each scallop in 1 slice bacon and secure with a toothpick. Sprinkle with salt and pepper. 2. Place scallops into ungreased cook & crisp basket. Adjust the temperature to 180°C and air crisp for 10 minutes. Scallops will be opaque and firm, and have an internal temperature of 55°C when done. Serve warm.

Roasted Fish with Almond-Lemon Crumbs

Prep time: 10 minutes | Cook time: 7 to 8 minutes | Serves 4

70 g raw whole almonds
1 spring onion, finely chopped
Grated zest and juice of 1 lemon
½ tablespoon extra-virgin olive oil
¾ teaspoon kosher or coarse sea salt, divided
Freshly ground black pepper, to taste
4 skinless fish fillets, 170 g each
Cooking spray
1 teaspoon Dijon mustard

1. In a food processor, pulse the almonds to coarsely chop. Transfer to a small bowl and add the scallion, lemon zest, and olive oil. Season with ¼ teaspoon of the salt and pepper to taste and mix to combine. 2. Spray the top of the fish with oil and squeeze the lemon juice over the fish. Season with the remaining ½ teaspoon salt and pepper to taste. Spread the mustard on top of the fish. Dividing evenly, press the almond mixture onto the top of the fillets to adhere. 3. Preheat the Ninja Foodi cooker to 190°C. 4. Working in batches, place the fillets in the cook & crisp basket in a single layer. Air crisp for 7 to 8 minutes, until the crumbs start to brown and the fish is cooked through. 5. Serve immediately.

Scallops in Lemon-Butter Sauce

Prep time: 10 minutes | Cook time: 6 minutes | Serves 2

8 large dry sea scallops (about 340 g)
Salt and freshly ground black pepper, to taste
2 tablespoons olive oil
2 tablespoons unsalted butter, melted
2 tablespoons chopped flat-leaf parsley
1 tablespoon fresh lemon juice
2 teaspoons capers, drained and chopped
1 teaspoon grated lemon zest
1 clove garlic, minced

1. Preheat the Ninja Foodi cooker to 205°C. 2. Use a paper towel to pat the scallops dry. Sprinkle lightly with salt and pepper. Brush with the olive oil. Arrange the scallops in a single layer in the cook & crisp basket. Pausing halfway through the cooking time to turn the scallops, air crisp for about 6 minutes until firm and opaque. 3. Meanwhile, in a small bowl, combine the oil, butter, parsley, lemon juice, capers, lemon zest, and garlic. Drizzle over the scallops just before serving.

Prawn Kebabs

Prep time: 15 minutes | Cook time: 6 minutes | Serves 4

Olive or vegetable oil, for spraying
455 g medium raw prawns, peeled and deveined
4 tablespoons unsalted butter, melted
1 tablespoon Old Bay seasoning
1 tablespoon packed light brown sugar
1 teaspoon granulated garlic
1 teaspoon onion powder
½ teaspoon freshly ground black pepper

1. Line the cook & crisp basket with baking paper and spray lightly with oil. 2. Thread the prawns onto the skewers and place them in the prepared basket. 3. In a small bowl, mix together the butter, Old Bay, brown sugar, garlic, onion powder, and black pepper. Brush the sauce on the prawns. 4. Air crisp at 205°C for 5 to 6 minutes, or until pink and firm. Serve immediately.

Italian Salmon

Prep time: 10 minutes | Cook time: 4 minutes | Serves 2

280 g salmon fillet
1 teaspoon Italian seasoning
240 ml water

1. Pour water and insert the reversible rack in the Ninja Foodi cooker. 2. Then rub the salmon fillet with Italian seasoning and wrap in the foil. 3. Place the wrapped fish on the reversible rack and close the lid. 4. Cook the meal on High Pressure for 4 minutes. 5. Make a quick pressure release and remove the fish from the foil. 6. Cut it into servings.

Fish Bake with Veggies

Prep time: 10 minutes | Cook time: 5 minutes | Serves 4

360 ml water
Cooking spray
2 ripe tomatoes, sliced
2 cloves garlic, minced
1 teaspoon dried oregano
1 teaspoon dried basil
½ teaspoon dried rosemary
1 red onion, sliced
1 head cauliflower, cut into florets
450 g tilapia fillets, sliced
Sea salt, to taste
1 tablespoon olive oil
240 ml crumbled feta cheese
80 ml Kalamata olives, pitted and halved

1. Pour the water into your Ninja Foodi cooker and insert a reversible rack. 2. Spritz a casserole dish with cooking spray. Add the tomato slices to the dish. Scatter the top with the garlic, oregano, basil, and rosemary. 3. Mix in the onion and cauliflower. Arrange the fish fillets on top. Sprinkle with the salt and drizzle with the olive oil. 4. Place the feta cheese and Kalamata olives on top. Lower the dish onto the reversible rack. 5. Lock the lid. Set the cooking time for 5 minutes at High Pressure. 6. When the timer beeps, perform a quick pressure release. Carefully remove the lid. 7. Allow to cool for 5 minutes before serving.

Lemony Prawns and Courgette

Prep time: 15 minutes | Cook time: 7 to 8 minutes | Serves 4

570 g extra-large raw prawns, peeled and deveined
2 medium courgettes (about 230 g each), halved lengthwise and cut into ½-inch-thick slices
1½ tablespoons olive oil
½ teaspoon garlic salt
1½ teaspoons dried oregano
⅛ teaspoon crushed red pepper flakes (optional)
Juice of ½ lemon
1 tablespoon chopped fresh mint
1 tablespoon chopped fresh dill

1. Preheat the Ninja Foodi cooker to 175°C. 2. In a large bowl, combine the prawns, courgette, oil, garlic salt, oregano, and pepper flakes (if using) and toss to coat. 3. Working in batches, arrange a single layer of the prawns and courgette in the cook & crisp basket. Air crisp for 7 to 8 minutes, shaking the basket halfway, until the courgette is golden and the prawns are cooked through. 4. Transfer to a serving dish and tent with foil while you air crisp the remaining prawns and courgette. 5. Top with the lemon juice, mint, and dill and serve.

Asian Swordfish

Prep time: 10 minutes | Cook time: 6 to 11 minutes | Serves 4

4 swordfish steaks, 100 g each
½ teaspoon toasted sesame oil
1 jalapeño pepper, finely minced
2 garlic cloves, grated
1 tablespoon grated fresh ginger
½ teaspoon Chinese five-spice powder
⅛ teaspoon freshly ground black pepper
2 tablespoons freshly squeezed lemon juice

1. Place the swordfish steaks on a work surface and drizzle with the sesame oil. 2. In a small bowl, mix the jalapeño, garlic, ginger, five-spice powder, pepper, and lemon juice. Rub this mixture into the fish and let it stand for 10 minutes. 3. Roast the swordfish in the Ninja Foodi cooker at 190°C for 6 to 11 minutes, or until the swordfish reaches an internal temperature of at least 60°C on a meat thermometer. Serve immediately.

Turmeric Salmon

Prep time: 10 minutes | Cook time: 4 minutes | Serves 3

450 g salmon fillet
1 teaspoon ground black pepper
½ teaspoon salt
1 teaspoon ground turmeric
1 teaspoon lemon juice
240 ml water

1. In the shallow bowl, mix up salt, ground black pepper, and ground turmeric. 2. Sprinkle the salmon fillet with lemon juice and rub with the spice mixture. 3. Then pour water in the Ninja Foodi cooker and insert the steamer rack. 4. Wrap the salmon fillet in the foil and place it on the rack. 5. Close and seal the lid. 6. Cook the fish on High Pressure for 4 minutes. 7. Make a quick pressure release and cut the fish on servings.

Braised Striped Bass with Courgette and Tomatoes

Prep time: 20 minutes | Cook time: 16 minutes | Serves 4

2 tablespoons extra-virgin olive oil, divided, plus extra for drizzling
3 courgette (230 g each), halved lengthwise and sliced ¼ inch thick
1 onion, chopped
¾ teaspoon table salt, divided
3 garlic cloves, minced
1 teaspoon minced fresh oregano or ¼ teaspoon dried
¼ teaspoon red pepper flakes
1 (800 g) can whole peeled tomatoes, drained with juice reserved, halved
680 g skinless striped bass, 1½ inches thick, cut into 2-inch pieces
¼ teaspoon pepper
2 tablespoons chopped pitted kalamata olives
2 tablespoons shredded fresh mint

1. Using highest sauté function, heat 1 tablespoon oil in Ninja Foodi cooker for 5 minutes (or until just smoking). Add courgette and cook until tender, about 5 minutes; transfer to bowl and set aside. 2. Add remaining 1 tablespoon oil, onion, and ¼ teaspoon salt to now-empty pot and cook, using highest sauté function, until onion is softened, about 5 minutes. Stir in garlic, oregano, and pepper flakes and cook until fragrant, about 30 seconds. Stir in tomatoes and reserved juice. 3. Sprinkle bass with remaining ½ teaspoon salt and pepper. Nestle bass into tomato mixture and spoon some of cooking liquid on top of pieces. Lock lid in place and close pressure release valve. Select high pressure and set cook time for 0 minutes. Once Ninja Foodi cooker has reached pressure, immediately turn off pot and quick-release pressure. Carefully remove lid, allowing steam to escape away from you. 4. Transfer bass to plate, tent with aluminium foil, and let rest while finishing vegetables. Stir courgette into pot and let sit until heated through, about 5 minutes. Stir in olives and season with salt and pepper to taste. Serve bass with vegetables, sprinkling individual portions with mint and drizzling with extra oil.

Salmon Steaks with Garlicky yoghurt

Prep time: 2 minutes | Cook time: 4 minutes | Serves 4

240 ml water
2 tablespoons olive oil
4 salmon steaks
Coarse sea salt and ground black pepper, to taste
Garlicky yoghurt:
1 (230 g) container full-fat Greek yoghurt
2 cloves garlic, minced
2 tablespoons mayonnaise
⅓ teaspoon Dijon mustard

1. Pour the water into the Ninja Foodi cooker and insert a reversible rack. 2. Rub the olive oil into the fish and sprinkle with the salt and black pepper on all sides. Put the fish on the reversible rack. 3. Lock the lid. Set the cooking time for 4 minutes at High Pressure. 4. When the timer beeps, perform a quick pressure release. Carefully remove the lid. 5. Meanwhile, stir together all the ingredients for the garlicky yoghurt in a bowl. 6. Serve the salmon steaks alongside the garlicky yoghurt.

Savory Prawns

Prep time: 5 minutes | Cook time: 8 to 10 minutes | Serves 4

455 g fresh large prawns, peeled and deveined	Sea salt and freshly ground black pepper, to taste
1 tablespoon avocado oil	2 tablespoons unsalted butter, melted
2 teaspoons minced garlic, divided	2 tablespoons chopped fresh parsley
½ teaspoon red pepper flakes	

1. Place the prawns in a large bowl and toss with the avocado oil, 1 teaspoon of minced garlic, and red pepper flakes. Season with salt and pepper. 2. Set the Ninja Foodi cooker to 175°C. Arrange the prawns in a single layer in the cook & crisp basket, working in batches if necessary. Cook for 6 minutes. Flip the prawns and cook for 2 to 4 minutes more, until the internal temperature of the prawns reaches 50°C. (The time it takes to cook will depend on the size of the prawns.) 3. While the prawns are cooking, melt the butter in a small saucepan over medium heat and stir in the remaining 1 teaspoon of garlic. 4. Transfer the cooked prawns to a large bowl, add the garlic butter, and toss well. Top with the parsley and serve warm.

Coconut Prawns with Pineapple-Lemon Sauce

Prep time: 10 minutes | Cook time: 18 minutes | Serves 4

100 g light brown sugar	680 g raw large prawns, peeled and deveined
2 teaspoons cornflour	2 eggs
⅛ teaspoon plus ½ teaspoon salt, divided	60 g plain flour
110 g crushed pineapple with syrup	95 g desiccated, unsweetened coconut
2 tablespoons freshly squeezed lemon juice	¼ teaspoon garlic granules
1 tablespoon yellow mustard	Olive oil spray

1. In a medium saucepan over medium heat, combine the brown sugar, cornflour, and ⅛ teaspoon of salt. 2. As the brown sugar mixture melts into a sauce, stir in the crushed pineapple with syrup, lemon juice, and mustard. Cook for about 4 minutes until the mixture thickens and begins to boil. Boil for 1 minute. Remove the pan from the heat, set aside, and let cool while you make the prawns. 3. Put the prawns on a plate and pat them dry with paper towels. 4. In a small bowl, whisk the eggs. 5. In a medium bowl, stir together the flour, desiccated coconut, remaining ½ teaspoon of salt, and garlic granules. 6. Insert the crisper plate into the basket and the basket into the unit. Preheat the unit to 205°C. 7. Dip the prawns into the egg and into the coconut mixture to coat. 8. Once the unit is preheated, place a baking paper liner into the basket. Place the coated prawns on the liner in a single layer and spray them with olive oil. 9. After 6 minutes, remove the basket, flip the prawns, and spray them with more olive oil. Reinsert the basket to resume cooking. Check the prawns after 3 minutes more. If browned, they are done; if not, resume cooking. 10. When the cooking is complete, serve with the prepared pineapple sauce.

Baked Flounder with Artichoke

Prep time: 10 minutes | Cook time: 10 minutes | Serves 2

230 g flounder fillet	½ large artichoke, chopped
1 lemon slice, chopped	1 tablespoon sesame oil
1 teaspoon ground black pepper	240 ml water, for cooking
¼ teaspoon salt	

1. Brush the round baking pan with sesame oil. 2. Then place the chopped artichoke in the baking pan and flatten it. 3. Sprinkle the flounder fillet with ground black pepper and salt and put over the artichoke. 4. Add chopped lemon. 5. Pour water and insert the steamer rack in the Ninja Foodi cooker. 6. Place the pan with fish in the steamer. Close and seal the lid. 7. Cook the meal on High Pressure for 10 minutes. Make a quick pressure release.

Dill Salmon Cakes

Prep time: 15 minutes | Cook time: 10 minutes | Serves 4

450 g salmon fillet, chopped	120 ml almond flour
1 tablespoon chopped dill	1 tablespoon coconut oil
2 eggs, beaten	

1. Put the chopped salmon, dill, eggs, and almond flour in the food processor. 2. Blend the mixture until it is smooth. 3. Then make the small balls (cakes) from the salmon mixture. 4. After this, heat up the coconut oil on Sauté mode for 3 minutes. 5. Put the salmon cakes in the Ninja Foodi cooker in one layer and cook them on Sauté mode for 2 minutes from each side or until they are light brown.

Fish Gratin

Prep time: 30 minutes | Cook time: 17 minutes | Serves 4

1 tablespoon avocado oil	chopped
455 g hake fillets	110 g cottage cheese
1 teaspoon garlic powder	120 ml sour cream
Sea salt and ground white pepper, to taste	1 egg, well whisked
2 tablespoons shallots, chopped	1 teaspoon yellow mustard
1 bell pepper, seeded and	1 tablespoon lime juice
	60 g Swiss cheese, shredded

1. Brush the bottom and sides of a casserole dish with avocado oil. Add the hake fillets to the casserole dish and sprinkle with garlic powder, salt, and pepper. 2. Add the chopped shallots and bell peppers. 3. In a mixing bowl, thoroughly combine the Cottage cheese, sour cream, egg, mustard, and lime juice. Pour the mixture over fish and spread evenly. 4. Cook in the preheated Ninja Foodi cooker at 190°C for 10 minutes. 5. Top with the Swiss cheese and cook an additional 7 minutes. Let it rest for 10 minutes before slicing and serving. Bon appétit!

Cajun Cod Fillet

Prep time: 10 minutes | Cook time: 4 minutes | Serves 2

280 g cod fillet
1 tablespoon olive oil
1 teaspoon Cajun seasoning
2 tablespoons coconut aminos

1. Sprinkle the cod fillet with coconut aminos and Cajun seasoning. 2. Then heat up olive oil in the Ninja Foodi cooker on Sauté mode. 3. Add the spiced cod fillet and cook it for 4 minutes from each side. 4. Then cut it into halves and sprinkle with the oily liquid from the Ninja Foodi cooker.

Fish Sandwich with Tartar Sauce

Prep time: 10 minutes | Cook time: 17 minutes | Serves 2

Tartar Sauce:
115 g mayonnaise
2 tablespoons onion granules
1 dill pickle spear, finely chopped
2 teaspoons pickle juice
¼ teaspoon salt
⅛ teaspoon ground black pepper

Fish:
2 tablespoons plain flour
1 egg, lightly beaten
120 g panko
2 teaspoons lemon pepper
2 tilapia fillets
Cooking spray
2 soft sub rolls

1. Preheat the Ninja Foodi cooker to 205°C. 2. In a small bowl, combine the mayonnaise, onion granules, pickle, pickle juice, salt, and pepper. 3. Whisk to combine and chill in the refrigerator while you make the fish. 4. Place a baking paper liner in the cook & crisp basket. 5. Scoop the flour out onto a plate; set aside. 6. Put the beaten egg in a medium shallow bowl. 7. On another plate, mix to combine the panko and lemon pepper. 8. Dredge the tilapia fillets in the flour, then dip in the egg, and then press into the panko mixture. 9. Place the prepared fillets on the liner in the Ninja Foodi cooker in a single layer. 10. Spray lightly with cooking spray and air crisp for 8 minutes. Carefully flip the fillets, spray with more cooking spray, and air crisp for an additional 9 minutes, until golden and crispy. 11. Place each cooked fillet in a sub roll, top with a little bit of tartar sauce, and serve.

Lemony Fish and Asparagus

Prep time: 5 minutes | Cook time: 3 minutes | Serves 4

2 lemons
480 ml cold water
2 tablespoons extra-virgin olive oil
4 (113 g) white fish fillets, such as cod or haddock
1 teaspoon fine sea salt
1 teaspoon ground black pepper
1 bundle asparagus, ends trimmed
2 tablespoons lemon juice
Fresh dill, for garnish

1. Grate the zest off the lemons until you have about 1 tablespoon and set the zest aside. Slice the lemons into ⅛-inch slices. 2. Pour the water into the Ninja Foodi cooker. Add 1 tablespoon of the olive oil to each of two stackable steamer pans. 3. Sprinkle the fish on all sides with the lemon zest, salt, and pepper. 4. Arrange two fillets in each steamer pan and top each with the lemon slices and then the asparagus. Sprinkle the asparagus with the salt and drizzle the lemon juice over the top. 5. Stack the steamer pans in the Ninja Foodi cooker. Cover the top steamer pan with its lid. 6. Lock the lid. Set the cooking time for 3 minutes at High Pressure. 7. Once cooking is complete, do a natural pressure release for 7 minutes, then release any remaining pressure. Carefully open the lid. 8. Lift the steamer pans out of the Ninja Foodi cooker. 9. Transfer the fish and asparagus to a serving plate. Garnish with the lemon slices and dill. 10. Serve immediately.

Lemon Pepper Tilapia with Broccoli and Carrots

Prep time: 0 minutes | Cook time: 15 minutes | Serves 4

450 g tilapia fillets
1 teaspoon lemon pepper seasoning
¼ teaspoon fine sea salt
2 tablespoons extra-virgin olive oil
2 garlic cloves, minced
1 small brown onion, sliced
120 ml vegetable broth
2 tablespoons fresh lemon juice
450 g broccoli crowns, cut into bite-size florets
230 g carrots, cut into ¼-inch thick rounds

1. Sprinkle the tilapia fillets all over with the lemon pepper seasoning and salt. 2. Select the Sauté setting on the Ninja Foodi cooker and heat the oil and garlic for 2 minutes, until the garlic is bubbling but not browned. Add the onion and sauté for about 3 minutes more, until it begins to soften. 3. Pour in the broth and lemon juice, then use a wooden spoon to nudge any browned bits from the bottom of the pot. Using tongs, add the fish fillets to the pot in a single layer; it's fine if they overlap slightly. Place the broccoli and carrots on top. 4. Secure the lid and set the pressure release to sealing. Press the Start/Stop button to reset the cooking program, then select the Pressure and set the cooking time for 1 minute at low pressure. (The pot will take about 10 minutes to come up to pressure before the cooking program begins.) 5. When the cooking program ends, let the pressure release naturally for 10 minutes (don't open the pot before the 10 minutes are up, even if the float valve has gone down), then move the Pressure Release to Venting to release any remaining steam. Open the pot. Use a fish spatula to transfer the vegetables and fillets to plates. Serve right away.

Coconut Prawns

Prep time: 5 minutes | Cook time: 6 minutes | Serves 2

230 g medium prawns, peeled and deveined
2 tablespoons salted butter, melted
½ teaspoon Old Bay seasoning
25 g desiccated, unsweetened coconut

1. In a large bowl, toss the prawns in butter and Old Bay seasoning. 2. Place shredded coconut in bowl. Coat each piece of prawns in the coconut and place into the cook & crisp basket. 3. Adjust the temperature to 205°C and air crisp for 6 minutes. 4. Gently turn the prawns halfway through the cooking time. Serve immediately.

Easy Scallops

Prep time: 5 minutes | Cook time: 4 minutes | Serves 2

12 medium sea scallops, rinsed and patted dry
1 teaspoon fine sea salt
¾ teaspoon ground black pepper, plus more for garnish
Fresh thyme leaves, for garnish (optional)
Avocado oil spray

1. Preheat the Ninja Foodi cooker to 200°C. Coat the cook & crisp basket with avocado oil spray. 2. Place the scallops in a medium bowl and spritz with avocado oil spray. Sprinkle the salt and pepper to season. 3. Transfer the seasoned scallops to the cook & crisp basket, spacing them apart. You may need to work in batches to avoid overcrowding. 4. Air crisp for 4 minutes, flipping the scallops halfway through, or until the scallops are firm and reach an internal temperature of just 65°C on a meat thermometer. 5. Remove from the basket and repeat with the remaining scallops. 6. Sprinkle the pepper and thyme leaves on top for garnish, if desired. Serve immediately.

Fried Prawns

Prep time: 15 minutes | Cook time: 5 minutes | Serves 4

70 g self-raising flour
1 teaspoon paprika
1 teaspoon salt
½ teaspoon freshly ground black pepper
1 large egg, beaten
120 g finely crushed panko bread crumbs
20 frozen large prawns (about 900 g), peeled and deveined
Cooking spray

1. In a shallow bowl, whisk the flour, paprika, salt, and pepper until blended. Add the beaten egg to a second shallow bowl and the bread crumbs to a third. 2. One at a time, dip the prawns into the flour, the egg, and the bread crumbs, coating thoroughly. 3. Preheat the Ninja Foodi cooker to 205°C. Line the cook & crisp basket with baking paper. 4. Place the prawns on the baking paper and spritz with oil. 5. Air crisp for 2 minutes. Shake the basket, spritz the prawns with oil, and air crisp for 3 minutes more until lightly browned and crispy. Serve hot.

Mediterranean Salmon with Whole-Wheat Couscous

Prep time: 5 minutes | Cook time: 30 minutes | Serves 4

Couscous
240 ml whole-wheat couscous
240 ml water
1 tablespoon extra-virgin olive oil
1 teaspoon dried basil
¼ teaspoon fine sea salt
1 pint cherry or grape tomatoes, halved
230 g courgette, halved lengthwise, then sliced crosswise ¼ inch thick
Salmon
450 g skinless salmon fillet
2 teaspoons extra-virgin olive oil
1 tablespoon fresh lemon juice
1 garlic clove, minced
¼ teaspoon dried oregano
¼ teaspoon fine sea salt
¼ teaspoon freshly ground black pepper
1 tablespoon capers, drained
Lemon wedges for serving

1. Pour 240 ml water into the Ninja Foodi cooker. Have ready two-tier stackable stainless-steel containers. 2. To make the couscous: In one of the containers, stir together the couscous, water, oil, basil, and salt. Sprinkle the tomatoes and courgette over the top. 3. To make the salmon: Place the salmon fillet in the second container. In a small bowl, whisk together the oil, lemon juice, garlic, oregano, salt, pepper, and capers. Spoon the oil mixture over the top of the salmon. 4. Place the container with the couscous and vegetables on the bottom and the salmon container on top. Cover the top container with its lid and then latch the containers together. Grasping the handle, lower the containers into the Ninja Foodi cooker. 5. Secure the lid and set the pressure release to sealing. Select the Pressure and set the cooking time for 20 minutes at high pressure. (The pot will take about 10 minutes to come up to pressure before the cooking program begins.) 6. When the cooking program ends, let the pressure release naturally for 5 minutes, then move the Pressure Release to Venting to release any remaining steam. Open the pot and, wearing heat-resistant mitts, lift out the stacked containers. Unlatch, unstack, and open the containers, taking care not to get burned by the steam. 7. Using a fork, fluff the couscous and mix in the vegetables. Spoon the couscous onto plates, then use a spatula to cut the salmon into four pieces and place a piece on top of each couscous serving. Serve right away, with lemon wedges on the side.

Steamed Halibut with Lemon

Prep time: 10 minutes | Cook time: 9 minutes | Serves 3
3 halibut fillet
½ lemon, sliced
½ teaspoon white pepper
½ teaspoon ground coriander
1 tablespoon avocado oil
240 ml water, for cooking

1. Pour water and insert the steamer rack in the Ninja Foodi cooker. 2. Rub the fish fillets with white pepper, ground coriander, and avocado oil. 3. Place the fillets in the steamer rack. 4. Then top the halibut with sliced lemon. Close and seal the lid. 5. Cook the meal on High Pressure for 9 minutes. Make a quick pressure release.

Mackerel and Broccoli Casserole

Prep time: 15 minutes | Cook time: 15 minutes | Serves 5

240 ml shredded broccoli
280 g mackerel, chopped
120 ml shredded Cheddar cheese
240 ml coconut milk
1 teaspoon ground cumin
1 teaspoon salt

1. Sprinkle the chopped mackerel with ground cumin and salt and transfer in the Ninja Foodi cooker. 2. Top the fish with shredded broccoli and Cheddar cheese, 3. Then add coconut milk. Close and seal the lid. 4. Cook the casserole on High Pressure for 15 minutes. 5. Allow the natural pressure release for 10 minutes and open the lid.

Mahi-Mahi Fillets with Peppers

Prep time: 10 minutes | Cook time: 3 minutes | Serves 3

2 sprigs fresh rosemary
2 sprigs dill, tarragon
1 sprig fresh thyme
240 ml water
1 lemon, sliced
3 mahi-mahi fillets
2 tablespoons coconut oil, melted
Sea salt and ground black pepper, to taste
1 serrano pepper, seeded and sliced
1 green bell pepper, sliced
1 red bell pepper, sliced

1. Add the herbs, water, and lemon slices to the Ninja Foodi cooker and insert a steamer basket. 2. Arrange the mahi-mahi fillets in the steamer basket. 3. Drizzle the melted coconut oil over the top and season with the salt and black pepper. 4. Lock the lid. Set the cooking time for 3 minutes at Low Pressure. 5. When the timer beeps, perform a natural pressure release for 10 minutes, then release any remaining pressure. Carefully remove the lid. 6. Place the peppers on top. Select the Sauté mode and let it simmer for another 1 minute. 7. Serve immediately.

Rainbow Trout with Mixed Greens

Prep time: 5 minutes | Cook time: 12 minutes | Serves 4

240 ml water
680 g rainbow trout fillets
4 tablespoons melted butter, divided
Sea salt and ground black pepper, to taste
450 g mixed greens, trimmed and torn into pieces
1 bunch of spring onions
120 ml chicken broth
1 tablespoon apple cider vinegar
1 teaspoon cayenne pepper

1. Pour the water into your Ninja Foodi cooker and insert a steamer basket. 2. Add the fish to the basket. Drizzle with 1 tablespoon of the melted butter and season with the salt and black pepper. 3. Lock the lid. Set the cooking time for 12 minutes at Low pressure. 4. When the timer beeps, perform a quick pressure release. Carefully remove the lid. 5. Wipe down the Ninja Foodi cooker with a damp cloth. 6. Add and warm the remaining 3 tablespoons of butter. Once hot, add the greens, scallions, broth, vinegar, and cayenne pepper and cook until the greens are wilted, stirring occasionally. 7. Serve the prepared trout fillets with the greens on the side.

Salmon with Dill Butter

Prep time: 7 minutes | Cook time: 8 minutes | Serves 2

1 teaspoon salt
2 tablespoons chopped fresh dill
280 g salmon fillet
60 ml butter
120 ml water

1. Put butter and salt in the baking pan. 2. Add salmon fillet and dill. Cover the pan with foil. 3. Pour water in the Ninja Foodi cooker and insert the baking pan with fish inside. 4. Set the Steam mode and cook the salmon for 8 minutes. 5. Unwrap the cooked salmon and serve!

Greek Prawn with Tomatoes and Feta

Prep time: 10 minutes | Cook time: 2 minutes | Serves 6

3 tablespoons unsalted butter
1 tablespoon garlic
½ teaspoon red pepper flakes, or more as needed
360 ml chopped onion
1 (410 g) can diced tomatoes, undrained
1 teaspoon dried oregano
1 teaspoon salt
450 g frozen prawn, peeled
240 ml crumbled feta cheese
120 ml sliced black olives
60 ml chopped parsley

1. Preheat the Ninja Foodi cooker by selecting Sauté and adjusting to high heat. When the inner cooking pot is hot, add the butter and heat until it foams. Add the garlic and red pepper flakes, and cook just until fragrant, about 1 minute. 2. Add the onion, tomatoes, oregano, and salt, and stir to combine. 3. Add the frozen prawn. 4. Lock the lid into place. Adjust the pressure to Low. Cook for 1 minute. When the cooking is complete, quick-release the pressure. Unlock the lid. 5. Mix the prawn in with the lovely tomato broth. 6. Allow the mixture to cool slightly. Right before serving, sprinkle with the feta cheese, olives, and parsley. This dish makes a soupy broth, so it's great over mashed cauliflower.

Cod with Warm Beetroot and Rocket Salad

Prep time: 15 minutes | Cook time: 8 minutes | Serves 4

60 ml extra-virgin olive oil, divided, plus extra for drizzling
1 shallot, sliced thin
2 garlic cloves, minced
680 g small Beetroots, scrubbed, trimmed, and cut into ½-inch wedges
120 ml chicken or vegetable broth
1 tablespoon dukkah, plus extra for sprinkling
¼ teaspoon table salt
4 (170 g) skinless cod fillets, 1½ inches thick
1 tablespoon lemon juice
60 g baby rocket

1. Using highest sauté function, heat 1 tablespoon oil in Ninja Foodi cooker until shimmering. Add shallot and cook until softened, about 2 minutes. Stir in garlic and cook until fragrant, about 30 seconds. Stir in Beetroots and broth. Lock lid in place and close pressure release valve. Select high pressure and cook for 3 minutes. Turn off Ninja Foodi cooker and quick-release pressure. Carefully remove lid, allowing steam to escape away from you. 2. Fold sheet of aluminium foil into 16 by 6-inch sling. Combine 2 tablespoons oil, dukkah, and salt in bowl, then brush cod with oil mixture. Arrange cod skinned side down in centre of sling. Using sling, lower cod into Ninja Foodi cooker; allow narrow edges of sling to rest along sides of insert. Lock lid in place and close pressure release valve. Select high pressure and cook for 2 minutes. 3. Turn off Ninja Foodi cooker and quick-release pressure. Carefully remove lid, allowing steam to escape away from you. Using sling, transfer cod to large plate. Tent with foil and let rest while finishing Beetroot salad. 4. Combine lemon juice and remaining 1 tablespoon oil in large bowl. Using slotted spoon, transfer Beetroots to bowl with oil mixture. Add rocket and gently toss to combine. Season with salt and pepper to taste. 5 Serve cod with salad, sprinkling individual portions with extra dukkah and drizzling with extra oil.

Cod Fillets with Cherry Tomatoes

Prep time: 2 minutes | Cook time: 15 minutes | Serves 4

2 tablespoons butter
60 ml diced onion
1 clove garlic, minced
240 ml cherry tomatoes, halved
60 ml chicken broth
¼ teaspoon dried thyme
¼ teaspoon salt
⅛ teaspoon pepper
4 (110 g) cod fillets
240 ml water
60 ml fresh chopped Italian parsley

1. Set your Ninja Foodi cooker to Sauté. Add and melt the butter. Once hot, add the onions and cook until softened. Add the garlic and cook for another 30 seconds. 2. Add the tomatoes, chicken broth, thyme, salt, and pepper. Continue to cook for 5 to 7 minutes, or until the tomatoes start to soften. 3. Pour the sauce into a glass bowl. Add the fish fillets. Cover with foil. 4. Pour the water into the Ninja Foodi cooker and insert a reversible rack. Place the bowl on top. 5. Lock the lid. Set the cooking time for 3 minutes at Low Pressure. 6. Once cooking is complete, do a quick pressure release. Carefully open the lid. 7. Sprinkle with the fresh parsley and serve.

Tuna Fillets with Lemon Butter

Prep time: 5 minutes | Cook time: 3 minutes | Serves 4

240 ml water
80 ml lemon juice
2 sprigs fresh thyme
2 sprigs fresh parsley
2 sprigs fresh rosemary
450 g tuna fillets
4 cloves garlic, pressed
Sea salt, to taste
¼ teaspoon black pepper, or more to taste
2 tablespoons butter, melted
1 lemon, sliced

1. Pour the water into your Ninja Foodi cooker. Add the lemon juice, thyme, parsley, and rosemary and insert a steamer basket. 2. Put the tuna fillets in the basket. Top with the garlic and season with the salt and black pepper. 3. Drizzle the melted butter over the fish fillets and place the lemon slices on top. 4. Lock the lid. Set the cooking time for 3 minutes at Low Pressure. 5. When the timer beeps, perform a quick pressure release. Carefully remove the lid. Serve immediately.

Prawns Pasta with Basil and Mushrooms

Prep time: 10 minutes | Cook time: 10 minutes | Serves 6

455 g small prawns, peeled and deveined
120 ml olive oil plus 1 tablespoon, divided
¼ teaspoon garlic powder
¼ teaspoon cayenne
455 g whole grain pasta
5 garlic cloves, minced
230 g baby mushrooms, sliced
45 g Parmesan, plus more for serving (optional)
1 teaspoon salt
½ teaspoon black pepper
½ cup fresh basil

1. Preheat the Ninja Foodi cooker to 190ºC. 2. In a small bowl, combine the prawns, 1 tablespoon olive oil, garlic powder, and cayenne. Toss to coat the prawns. 3. Place the prawns into the cook & crisp basket and roast for 5 minutes. Remove the prawns and set aside. 4. Cook the pasta according to package directions. Once done cooking, reserve ½ cup pasta water, then drain. 5. Meanwhile, in a large skillet, heat 120 ml of olive oil over medium heat. Add the garlic and mushrooms and cook down for 5 minutes. 6. Pour the pasta, reserved pasta water, Parmesan, salt, pepper, and basil into the skillet with the vegetable-and-oil mixture, and stir to coat the pasta. 7. Toss in the prawns and remove from heat, then let the mixture sit for 5 minutes before serving with additional Parmesan, if desired.

Mussels with Fennel and Leeks

Prep time: 20 minutes | Cook time: 6 minutes | Serves 4

1 tablespoon extra-virgin olive oil, plus extra for drizzling
1 fennel bulb, 1 tablespoon fronds minced, stalks discarded, bulb halved, cored, and sliced thin
1 leek, ends trimmed, leek halved lengthwise, sliced 1 inch thick, and washed thoroughly
4 garlic cloves, minced
3 sprigs fresh thyme
¼ teaspoon red pepper flakes
120 ml dry white wine
1.4 kg mussels, scrubbed and debearded

1. Using highest sauté function, heat oil in Ninja Foodi cooker until shimmering. Add fennel and leek and cook until softened, about 5 minutes. Stir in garlic, thyme sprigs, and pepper flakes and cook until fragrant, about 30 seconds. Stir in wine, then add mussels. 2. Lock lid in place and close pressure release valve. Select high pressure and set cook time for 0 minutes. Once Ninja Foodi cooker has reached pressure, immediately turn off pot and quick-release pressure. Carefully remove lid, allowing steam to escape away from you. 3. Discard thyme sprigs and any mussels that have not opened. Transfer mussels to individual serving bowls, sprinkle with fennel fronds, and drizzle with extra oil. Serve.

Aromatic Monkfish Stew

Prep time: 5 minutes | Cook time: 6 minutes | Serves 6

Juice of 1 lemon
1 tablespoon fresh basil
1 tablespoon fresh parsley
1 tablespoon olive oil
1 teaspoon garlic, minced
680 g monkfish
1 tablespoon butter
1 bell pepper, chopped
1 onion, sliced
½ teaspoon cayenne pepper
½ teaspoon mixed peppercorns
¼ teaspoon turmeric powder
¼ teaspoon ground cumin
Sea salt and ground black pepper, to taste
480 ml fish stock
120 ml water
60 ml dry white wine
2 bay leaves
1 ripe tomato, crushed

1. Stir together the lemon juice, basil, parsley, olive oil, and garlic in a ceramic dish. Add the monkfish and marinate for 30 minutes. 2. Set your Ninja Foodi cooker to Sauté. Add and melt the butter. Once hot, cook the bell pepper and onion until fragrant. 3. Stir in the remaining ingredients. 4. Lock the lid. Set the cooking time for 6 minutes at High Pressure. 5. When the timer beeps, perform a quick pressure release. Carefully remove the lid. 6. Discard the bay leaves and divide your stew into serving bowls. Serve hot.

Snapper in Spicy Tomato Sauce

Prep time: 5 minutes | Cook time: 5 minutes | Serves 6

2 teaspoons coconut oil, melted	1 (113 g) can fire-roasted diced tomatoes
1 teaspoon celery seeds	1 bell pepper, sliced
½ teaspoon fresh grated ginger	1 jalapeño pepper, minced
½ teaspoon cumin seeds	Sea salt and ground black pepper, to taste
1 brown onion, chopped	¼ teaspoon chili flakes
2 cloves garlic, minced	½ teaspoon turmeric powder
680 g snapper fillets	
180 ml vegetable broth	

1. Set the Ninja Foodi cooker to Sauté. Add and heat the sesame oil until hot. Sauté the celery seeds, fresh ginger, and cumin seeds. 2. Add the onion and continue to sauté until softened and fragrant. 3. Mix in the minced garlic and continue to cook for 30 seconds. Add the remaining ingredients and stir well. 4. Lock the lid. Set the cooking time for 3 minutes at Low Pressure. 5. When the timer beeps, perform a quick pressure release. Carefully remove the lid. 6. Serve warm

Creamy Haddock

Prep time: 10 minutes | Cook time: 8 minutes | Serves 4

455 g haddock fillet	1 teaspoon coconut oil
1 teaspoon cayenne pepper	120 ml heavy cream
1 teaspoon salt	

1. Grease a baking pan with coconut oil. 2. Then put haddock fillet inside and sprinkle it with cayenne pepper, salt, and heavy cream. Put the baking pan in the cook & crisp basket and cook at 190°C for 8 minutes.

Steamed Cod with Garlic and Swiss Chard

Prep time: 5 minutes | Cook time: 12 minutes | Serves 4

1 teaspoon salt	½ white onion, thinly sliced
½ teaspoon dried oregano	135 g Swiss chard, washed, stemmed, and torn into pieces
½ teaspoon dried thyme	60 ml olive oil
½ teaspoon garlic powder	1 lemon, quartered
4 cod fillets	

1. Preheat the Ninja Foodi cooker to 190°C. 2. In a small bowl, whisk together the salt, oregano, thyme, and garlic powder. 3. Tear off four pieces of aluminum foil, with each sheet being large enough to envelop one cod fillet and a quarter of the vegetables. 4. Place a cod fillet in the middle of each sheet of foil, then sprinkle on all sides with the spice mixture. 5. In each foil packet, place a quarter of the onion slices and 30 g Swiss chard, then drizzle 1 tablespoon olive oil and squeeze ¼ lemon over the contents of each foil packet. 6. Fold and seal the sides of the foil packets and then place them into the cook & crisp basket. Steam for 12 minutes. 7. Remove from the basket, and carefully open each packet to avoid a steam burn.

Tandoori Prawns

Prep time: 25 minutes | Cook time: 6 minutes | Serves 4

455 g jumbo raw prawns (21 to 25 count), peeled and deveined	1 teaspoon garam masala
1 tablespoon minced fresh ginger	1 teaspoon smoked paprika
3 cloves garlic, minced	1 teaspoon kosher or coarse sea salt
5 g chopped fresh coriander or parsley, plus more for garnish	½ to 1 teaspoon cayenne pepper
1 teaspoon ground turmeric	2 tablespoons olive oil (for Paleo) or melted ghee
	2 teaspoons fresh lemon juice

1. In a large bowl, combine the prawns, ginger, garlic, coriander, turmeric, garam masala, paprika, salt, and cayenne. Toss well to coat. Add the oil or ghee and toss again. Marinate at room temperature for 15 minutes, or cover and refrigerate for up to 8 hours. 2. Place the prawns in a single layer in the cook & crisp basket. Set the Ninja Foodi cooker to 165°C for 6 minutes. Transfer the prawns to a serving platter. Cover and let the prawns finish cooking in the residual heat, about 5 minutes. 3. Sprinkle the prawns with the lemon juice and toss to coat. Garnish with additional cilantro and serve.

Prawn Caesar Salad

Prep time: 30 minutes | Cook time: 4 to 6 minutes | Serves 4

340 g fresh large prawns, peeled and deveined	¼ teaspoon freshly ground black pepper, plus additional to season the marinade
1 tablespoon plus 1 teaspoon freshly squeezed lemon juice, divided	735 g mayonnaise
4 tablespoons olive oil or avocado oil, divided	2 tablespoons freshly grated Parmesan cheese
2 garlic cloves, minced, divided	1 teaspoon Dijon mustard
¼ teaspoon sea salt, plus additional to season the marinade	1 tinned anchovy, mashed
	340 g romaine lettuce hearts, torn

1. Place the prawns in a large bowl. Add 1 tablespoon of lemon juice, 1 tablespoon of olive oil, and 1 minced garlic clove. Season with salt and pepper. Toss well and refrigerate for 15 minutes. 2. While the prawns marinates, make the dressing: In a blender, combine the mayonnaise, Parmesan cheese, Dijon mustard, the remaining 1 teaspoon of lemon juice, the anchovy, the remaining minced garlic clove, ¼ teaspoon of salt, and ¼ teaspoon of pepper. Process until smooth. With the blender running, slowly stream in the remaining 3 tablespoons of oil. Transfer the mixture to a jar; seal and refrigerate until ready to serve. 3. Remove the prawns from its marinade and place it in the cook & crisp basket in a single layer. Set the Ninja Foodi cooker to 205°C and air crisp for 2 minutes. Flip the prawns and cook for 2 to 4 minutes more, until the flesh turns opaque. 4. Place the romaine in a large bowl and toss with the desired amount of dressing. Top with the prawns and serve immediately.

Sole and Cauliflower Fritters

Prep time: 5 minutes | Cook time: 24 minutes | Serves 2

230 g sole fillets
230 g mashed cauliflower
75 g red onion, chopped
1 bell pepper, finely chopped
1 egg, beaten
2 garlic cloves, minced
2 tablespoons fresh parsley, chopped

1 tablespoon olive oil
1 tablespoon coconut aminos or tamari
½ teaspoon scotch bonnet pepper, minced
½ teaspoon paprika
Salt and white pepper, to taste
Cooking spray

1. Preheat the Ninja Foodi cooker to 200°C. Spray the cook & crisp basket with cooking spray. 2. Place the sole fillets in the basket and air crisp for 10 minutes, flipping them halfway through. 3. When the fillets are done, transfer them to a large bowl. Mash the fillets into flakes. Add the remaining ingredients and stir to combine. 4. Make the fritters: Scoop out 2 tablespoons of the fish mixture and shape into a patty about ½ inch thick with your hands. Repeat with the remaining fish mixture. 5. Arrange the patties in the cook & crisp basket and bake for 14 minutes, flipping the patties halfway through, or until they are golden brown and cooked through. 6. Cool for 5 minutes and serve on a plate.

Chapter 5 Poultry

Chicken and Mixed Greens Salad

Prep time: 5 minutes | Cook time: 20 minutes | Serves 4

Chicken:
2 tablespoons avocado oil
450 g chicken breast, cubed
120 ml filtered water
½ teaspoon ground turmeric
½ teaspoon dried parsley
½ teaspoon dried basil
½ teaspoon rock salt
½ teaspoon freshly ground black pepper
Salad:
1 avocado, mashed
240 ml chopped rocket
240 ml chopped Swiss chard
240 ml chopped kale
120 ml chopped spinach
2 tablespoons pine nuts, toasted

1. Combine all the chicken ingredients in the Ninja Foodi cooker. 2. Secure the lid. Set the cooking time for 20 minutes at High Pressure. 3. Meanwhile, toss all the salad ingredients in a large salad bowl. 4. Once cooking is complete, do a quick pressure release. Carefully open the lid. 5. Remove the chicken to the salad bowl and serve.

Tuscan Chicken Drumsticks

Prep time: 15 minutes | Cook time: 12 minutes | Serves 4

4 chicken drumsticks
240 ml chopped spinach
1 teaspoon minced garlic
1 teaspoon ground paprika
240 ml double cream
1 teaspoon cayenne pepper
30 g sun-dried tomatoes, chopped

1. Put all ingredients in the Ninja Foodi cooker. 2. Close and seal the lid. 3. Cook the meal on High Pressure for 12 minutes. 4. Then allow the natural pressure release for 10 minutes. 5. Serve the chicken with hot sauce from the Ninja Foodi cooker.

Kung Pao Chicken

Prep time: 5 minutes | Cook time: 17 minutes | Serves 5

2 tablespoons coconut oil
450 g boneless, skinless chicken breasts, cubed
240 ml cashews, chopped
6 tablespoons hot sauce
½ teaspoon chili powder
½ teaspoon finely grated ginger
½ teaspoon rock salt
½ teaspoon freshly ground black pepper

1. Set the Ninja Foodi cooker to Sauté and melt the coconut oil. 2. Add the remaining ingredients to the Ninja Foodi cooker and mix well. 3. Secure the lid. Set the cooking time for 17 minutes at High Pressure. 4. Once cooking is complete, do a quick pressure release. Carefully open the lid. 5. Serve warm.

Curried Orange Honey Chicken

Prep time: 10 minutes | Cook time: 16 to 19 minutes | Serves 4

340 g boneless, skinless chicken thighs, cut into 1-inch pieces
1 yellow bell pepper, cut into 1½-inch pieces
1 small red onion, sliced
Olive oil for misting
60 ml chicken stock
2 tablespoons honey
60 ml orange juice
1 tablespoon cornflour
2 to 3 teaspoons curry powder

1. Preheat the Ninja Foodi cooker to 190ºC. 2. Put the chicken thighs, pepper, and red onion in the cook & crisp basket and mist with olive oil. 3. Roast for 12 to 14 minutes or until the chicken is cooked to 75ºC, shaking the basket halfway through cooking time. 4. Remove the chicken and vegetables from the cook & crisp basket and set aside. 5. In a metal bowl, combine the stock, honey, orange juice, cornflour, and curry powder, and mix well. Add the chicken and vegetables, stir, and put the bowl in the basket. 6. Return the basket to the Ninja Foodi cooker and roast for 2 minutes. Remove and stir, then roast for 2 to 3 minutes or until the sauce is thickened and bubbly. 7. Serve warm.

Sesame Chicken Breast

Prep time: 10 minutes | Cook time: 18 minutes | Serves 6

Oil, for spraying
2 (170 g) boneless, skinless chicken breasts, cut into bite-size pieces
60 g cornflour plus 1 tablespoon
60 ml soy sauce
2 tablespoons packed light brown sugar
2 tablespoons pineapple juice
1 tablespoon molasses
½ teaspoon ground ginger
1 tablespoon water
2 teaspoons sesame seeds

1. Line the cook & crisp basket with parchment and spray lightly with oil. 2. Place the chicken and 60 g of cornflour in a zip-top plastic bag, seal, and shake well until evenly coated. 3. Place the chicken in an even layer in the prepared basket and spray liberally with oil. You may need to work in batches, depending on the size of your fryer. 4. Air crisp at 200ºC for 9 minutes, flip, spray with more oil, and cook for another 8 to 9 minutes, or until the internal temperature reaches 75ºC. 5. In a small saucepan, combine the soy sauce, brown sugar, pineapple juice, molasses, and ginger over medium heat and cook, stirring frequently, until the brown sugar has dissolved. 6. In a small bowl, mix together the water and remaining 1 tablespoon of cornflour. Pour it into the soy sauce mixture. 7. Bring the mixture to a boil, stirring frequently, until the sauce thickens. Remove from the heat. 8. Transfer the chicken to a large bowl, add the sauce, and toss until evenly coated. Sprinkle with the sesame seeds and serve.

Chicken Casserole

Prep time: 15 minutes | Cook time: 15 minutes | Serves 4

240 ml broccoli florets
360 ml Alfredo sauce
120 ml chopped fresh spinach
60 ml whole-milk ricotta cheese
½ teaspoon salt
¼ teaspoon pepper
450 g thin-sliced deli chicken
240 ml shredded whole-milk Mozzarella cheese
240 ml water

1. Put the broccoli florets in a large bowl. Add the Alfredo sauce, spinach, ricotta, salt, and pepper to the bowl and stir to mix well. Using a spoon, separate the veggie mix into three sections. 2. Layer the chicken into the bottom of a 1.7-liters glass bowl. Place one section of the veggie mix on top in an even layer and top with a layer of shredded Mozzarella cheese. Repeat until all veggie mix has been used and finish with a layer of Mozzarella cheese. Cover the dish with aluminium foil. 3. Pour the water into the Ninja Foodi cooker and insert the reversible rack. Place the dish on the reversible rack. 4. Secure the lid. Set the cooking time for 15 minutes at High Pressure. 5. Once cooking is complete, do a quick pressure release. Carefully open the lid. 6. If desired, broil in oven for 3 to 5 minutes until golden. Serve warm.

Broccoli Chicken Divan

Prep time: 15 minutes | Cook time: 10 minutes | Serves 4

240 ml chopped broccoli
2 tablespoons cream cheese
120 ml double cream
1 tablespoon curry powder
60 ml chicken broth
120 ml grated Cheddar cheese
170 g chicken fillet, cooked and chopped

1. Mix up broccoli and curry powder and put the mixture in the Ninja Foodi cooker. 2. Add double cream and cream cheese. 3. Then add chicken and mix up the ingredients. 4. Then add chicken broth and double cream. 5. Top the mixture with Cheddar cheese. Close and seal the lid. 6. Cook the meal on High Pressure for 10 minutes. Allow the natural pressure release for 5 minutes, open the lid and cool the meal for 10 minutes.

Mediterranean Stuffed Chicken Breasts

Prep time: 5 minutes | Cook time: 20 to 25 minutes | Serves 4

4 small boneless, skinless chicken breast halves (about 680 g)
Salt and freshly ground black pepper, to taste
115 g goat cheese
6 pitted Kalamata olives, coarsely chopped
Zest of ½ lemon
1 teaspoon minced fresh rosemary or ½ teaspoon ground dried rosemary
50 g almond meal
60 ml balsamic vinegar
6 tablespoons unsalted butter

1. Preheat the Ninja Foodi cooker to 180°C. 2. With a boning knife, cut a wide pocket into the thickest part of each chicken breast half, taking care not to cut all the way through. Season the chicken evenly on both sides with salt and freshly ground black pepper. 3. In a small bowl, mix the cheese, olives, lemon zest, and rosemary. Stuff the pockets with the cheese mixture and secure with toothpicks. 4. Place the almond meal in a shallow bowl and dredge the chicken, shaking off the excess. Coat lightly with olive oil spray. 5. Working in batches if necessary, arrange the chicken breasts in a single layer in the cook & crisp basket. Pausing halfway through the cooking time to flip the chicken, air crisp for 20 to 25 minutes, until a thermometer inserted into the thickest part registers 75°C. 6. While the chicken is baking, prepare the sauce. In a small pan over medium heat, simmer the balsamic vinegar until thick and syrupy, about 5 minutes. Set aside until the chicken is done. When ready to serve, warm the sauce over medium heat and whisk in the butter, 1 tablespoon at a time, until melted and smooth. Season to taste with salt and pepper. 7. Serve the chicken breasts with the sauce drizzled on top.

Apricot-Glazed Chicken Drumsticks

Prep time: 15 minutes | Cook time: 30 minutes | Makes 6 drumsticks

For the Glaze:
160 g apricot preserves
½ teaspoon tamari
¼ teaspoon chili powder
2 teaspoons Dijon mustard
For the Chicken:
6 chicken drumsticks
½ teaspoon seasoning salt
1 teaspoon salt
½ teaspoon ground black pepper
Cooking spray

Make the glaze: 1. Combine the ingredients for the glaze in a saucepan, then heat over low heat for 10 minutes or until thickened. 2. Turn off the heat and sit until ready to use. Make the Chicken: 1. Preheat the Ninja Foodi cooker to 190°C. Spritz the cook & crisp basket with cooking spray. 2. Combine the seasoning salt, salt, and pepper in a small bowl. Stir to mix well. 3. Place the chicken drumsticks in the preheated Ninja Foodi cooker. Spritz with cooking spray and sprinkle with the salt mixture on both sides. 4. Air crisp for 20 minutes or until well browned. Flip the chicken halfway through. 5. Baste the chicken with the glaze and Ninja Foodi cooker for 2 more minutes or until the chicken tenderloin is glossy. 6. Serve immediately.

Chipotle Drumsticks

Prep time: 15 minutes | Cook time: 20 minutes | Serves 4

1 tablespoon tomato paste
½ teaspoon chipotle powder
¼ teaspoon apple cider vinegar
¼ teaspoon garlic powder
8 chicken drumsticks
½ teaspoon salt
⅛ teaspoon ground black pepper

1. In a small bowl, combine tomato paste, chipotle powder, vinegar, and garlic powder. 2. Sprinkle drumsticks with salt and pepper, then place into a large bowl and pour in tomato paste mixture. Toss or stir to evenly coat all drumsticks in mixture. 3. Place drumsticks into ungreased cook & crisp basket. Adjust the temperature to 200°C and air crisp for 25 minutes, turning drumsticks halfway through cooking. Drumsticks will be dark red with an internal temperature of at least 75°C when done. Serve warm.

Bruschetta Chicken

Prep time: 10 minutes | Cook time: 20 minutes | Serves 4

Bruschetta Stuffing:
1 tomato, diced
3 tablespoons balsamic vinegar
1 teaspoon Italian seasoning
2 tablespoons chopped fresh basil
3 garlic cloves, minced
2 tablespoons extra-virgin olive oil
Chicken:
4 (115 g) boneless, skinless chicken breasts, cut 4 slits each
1 teaspoon Italian seasoning
Chicken seasoning or rub, to taste
Cooking spray

1. Preheat the Ninja Foodi cooker to 190°. Spritz the cook & crisp basket with cooking spray. 2. Combine the ingredients for the bruschetta stuffing in a bowl. Stir to mix well. Set aside. 3. Rub the chicken breasts with Italian seasoning and chicken seasoning on a clean work surface. 4. Arrange the chicken breasts, slits side up, in a single layer in the cook & crisp basket and spritz with cooking spray. You may need to work in batches to avoid overcrowding. 5. Air crisp for 7 minutes, then open the Ninja Foodi cooker and fill the slits in the chicken with the bruschetta stuffing. Cook for another 3 minutes or until the chicken is well browned. 6. Serve immediately.

Ann's Chicken Cacciatore

Prep time: 25 minutes | Cook time: 3 to 9 minutes | Serves 8

1 large onion, thinly sliced
1.4 kg chicken, cut up, skin removed, trimmed of fat
2 (170 g) cans tomato paste
110 g can sliced mushrooms, drained
1 teaspoon salt
60 ml dry white wine
¼ teaspoons pepper
1–2 garlic cloves, minced
1–2 teaspoons dried oregano
½ teaspoon dried basil
½ teaspoon celery seed, optional
1 bay leaf

1. In the inner pot of the Ninja Foodi cooker, place the onion and chicken. 2. Combine remaining ingredients and pour over the chicken. 3. Secure the lid and make sure vent is at sealing. Cook on Slow Cook mode, low 7–9 hours, or high 3–4 hours.

Sesame Chicken with Broccoli

Prep time: 15 minutes | Cook time: 12 minutes | Serves 2
½ teaspoon five spices
½ teaspoon sesame seeds
120 ml chopped broccoli
170 g chicken fillet, sliced
120 ml chicken broth
1 teaspoon coconut aminos
1 tablespoon avocado oil

1. In the mixing bowl, mix up avocado oil, coconut aminos, and sesame seeds. 2. Add five spices. 3. After this, mix up sliced chicken fillet and coconut aminos mixture. 4. Put the chicken in the Ninja Foodi cooker. Add chicken broth and broccoli. 5. Close and seal the lid. 6. Cook the meal on High Pressure for 12 minutes. Make a quick pressure release.

Chicken Enchiladas

Prep time: 10 minutes | Cook time: 8 minutes | Serves 4

Oil, for spraying
420 g shredded cooked chicken
1 package taco seasoning
8 flour tortillas, at room temperature
60 g canned black beans, rinsed and drained
1 (115 g) can diced green chilies, drained
1 (280 g) can red or green enchilada sauce
235 g shredded Cheddar cheese

1. Line the cook & crisp basket with parchment and spray lightly with oil. (Do not skip the step of lining the basket; the parchment will keep the sauce and cheese from dripping through the holes.) 2. In a small bowl, mix together the chicken and taco seasoning. 3. Divide the mixture among the tortillas. Top with the black beans and green chilis. Carefully roll up each tortilla. 4. Place the enchiladas, seam-side down, in the prepared basket. You may need to work in batches, depending on the size of your Ninja Foodi cooker. 5. Spoon the enchilada sauce over the enchiladas. Use just enough sauce to keep them from drying out. You can add more sauce when serving. Sprinkle the cheese on top. 6. Air crisp at 180°C for 5 to 8 minutes, or until heated through and the cheese is melted. 7. Place 2 enchiladas on each plate and top with more enchilada sauce, if desired.

Classic Chicken Kebab

Prep time: 35 minutes | Cook time: 25 minutes | Serves 4

60 ml olive oil
1 teaspoon garlic powder
1 teaspoon onion powder
1 teaspoon ground cumin
½ teaspoon dried oregano
½ teaspoon dried basil
60 ml lemon juice
1 tablespoon apple cider vinegar
Olive oil cooking spray
450 g boneless skinless chicken thighs, cut into 1-inch pieces
1 red bell pepper, cut into 1-inch pieces
1 red onion, cut into 1-inch pieces
1 courgette, cut into 1-inch pieces
12 cherry tomatoes

1. In a large bowl, mix together the olive oil, garlic powder, onion powder, cumin, oregano, basil, lemon juice, and apple cider vinegar. 2. Spray six skewers with olive oil cooking spray. 3. On each skewer, slide on a piece of chicken, then a piece of bell pepper, onion, courgette, and finally a tomato and then repeat. Each skewer should have at least two pieces of each item. 4. Once all of the skewers are prepared, place them in a 9-by-13-inch baking dish and pour the olive oil marinade over the top of the skewers. Turn each skewer so that all sides of the chicken and vegetables are coated. 5. Cover the dish with plastic wrap and place it in the refrigerator for 30 minutes. 6. After 30 minutes, Preheat the Ninja Foodi cooker to 190°C. (If using a grill attachment, make sure it is inside the Ninja Foodi cooker during preheating.) 7. Remove the skewers from the marinade and lay them in a single layer in the cook & crisp basket. 8. Cook for 10 minutes. Rotate the kebabs, then cook them for 15 minutes more. 9. Remove the skewers from the Ninja Foodi cooker and let them rest for 5 minutes before serving.

Chicken and Ham Meatballs with Dijon Sauce

Prep time: 10 minutes | Cook time: 15 minutes | Serves 4

Meatballs:
230 g ham, diced
230 g chicken mince
110 g grated Swiss cheese
1 large egg, beaten
3 cloves garlic, minced
15 g chopped onions
1½ teaspoons sea salt
1 teaspoon ground black pepper
Cooking spray
Dijon Sauce:
3 tablespoons Dijon mustard
2 tablespoons lemon juice
60 ml chicken broth, warmed
¾ teaspoon sea salt
¼ teaspoon ground black pepper
Chopped fresh thyme leaves, for garnish

1. Preheat the Ninja Foodi cooker to 200°C. Spritz the cook & crisp basket with cooking spray. 2. Combine the ingredients for the meatballs in a large bowl. Stir to mix well, then shape the mixture in twelve 1½-inch meatballs. 3. Arrange the meatballs in a single layer in the cook & crisp basket. Air crisp for 15 minutes or until lightly browned. Flip the balls halfway through. You may need to work in batches to avoid overcrowding. 4. Meanwhile, combine the ingredients, except for the thyme leaves, for the sauce in a small bowl. Stir to mix well. 5. Transfer the cooked meatballs on a large plate, then baste the sauce over. Garnish with thyme leaves and serve.

Smoky Whole Chicken

Prep time: 20 minutes | Cook time: 21 minutes | Serves 6

2 tablespoons extra-virgin olive oil
1 tablespoon rock salt
1½ teaspoons smoked paprika
1 teaspoon freshly ground black pepper
½ teaspoon herbes de Provence
¼ teaspoon cayenne pepper
1 (1.6 kg) whole chicken, rinsed and patted dry, giblets removed
1 large lemon, halved
6 garlic cloves, peeled and crushed with the flat side of a knife
1 large onion, cut into 8 wedges, divided
240 ml Chicken Bone Broth, store-bought chicken broth, or water
2 large carrots, each cut into 4 pieces
2 celery stalks, each cut into 4 pieces

1. In a small bowl, combine the olive oil, salt, paprika, pepper, herbes de Provence, and cayenne. 2. Place the chicken on a cutting board and rub the olive oil mixture under the skin and all over the outside. Stuff the cavity with the lemon halves, garlic cloves, and 3 to 4 wedges of onion. 3. Pour the broth into the electric pressure cooker. Add the remaining onion wedges, carrots, and celery. Insert a wire rack or reversible rack on top of the vegetables. 4. Place the chicken, breast-side up, on the rack. 5. Close and lock the lid of the pressure cooker. Set the valve to sealing. 6. Cook on high pressure for 21 minutes. 7. When the cooking is complete, hit Start/Stop and allow the pressure to release naturally for 15 minutes, then quick release any remaining pressure. 8. Once the pin drops, unlock and remove the lid. 9. Carefully remove the chicken to a clean cutting board. Remove the skin and cut the chicken into pieces or shred/chop the meat, and serve.

Chicken Tagine

Prep time: 15 minutes | Cook time: 11 minutes | Serves 4

2 (425 g) cans chickpeas, rinsed, divided
1 tablespoon extra-virgin olive oil
5 garlic cloves, minced
1½ teaspoons paprika
½ teaspoon ground turmeric
½ teaspoon ground cumin
¼ teaspoon ground ginger
¼ teaspoon cayenne pepper
1 fennel bulb, 1 tablespoon fronds minced, stalks discarded, bulb halved and cut lengthwise into ½-inch-thick wedges
240 ml chicken broth
3 (2-inch) strips lemon zest, plus lemon wedges for serving
4 (142 to 198 g) bone-in chicken thighs, skin removed, trimmed
½ teaspoon table salt
120 ml pitted large brine-cured green or black olives, halved
80 ml raisins
2 tablespoons chopped fresh parsley

1. Using potato masher, mash 120 ml chickpeas in bowl to paste. Using highest sauté function, cook oil, garlic, paprika, turmeric, cumin, ginger, and cayenne in Ninja Foodi cooker until fragrant, about 1 minute. Turn off Ninja Foodi cooker, then stir in remaining whole chickpeas, mashed chickpeas, fennel wedges, broth, and zest. 2. Sprinkle chicken with salt. Nestle chicken skinned side up into pot and spoon some of cooking liquid over top. Lock lid in place and close pressure release valve. Select high pressure and cook for 10 minutes. 3. Turn off Ninja Foodi cooker and quick-release pressure. Carefully remove lid, allowing steam to escape away from you. Discard lemon zest. Stir in olives, raisins, parsley, and fennel fronds. Season with salt and pepper to taste. Serve with lemon wedges.

Chicken and Vegetable Fajitas

Prep time: 15 minutes | Cook time: 23 minutes | Serves 6

Chicken:
450 g boneless, skinless chicken thighs, cut crosswise into thirds
1 tablespoon vegetable oil
4½ teaspoons taco seasoning
Vegetables:
50 g sliced onion
150 g sliced bell pepper
1 or 2 jalapeños, quartered lengthwise
1 tablespoon vegetable oil
½ teaspoon kosher salt
½ teaspoon ground cumin
For Serving:
Tortillas
Sour cream
Shredded cheese
Guacamole
Salsa

1. For the chicken: In a medium bowl, toss together the chicken, vegetable oil, and taco seasoning to coat. 2. For the vegetables: In a separate bowl, toss together the onion, bell pepper, jalapeño(s), vegetable oil, salt, and cumin to coat. 3. Place the chicken in the cook & crisp basket. Set the Ninja Foodi cooker to (190°C for 10 minutes. Add the vegetables to the basket, toss everything together to blend the seasonings, and Set the Ninja Foodi cooker for 13 minutes more. Use a meat thermometer to ensure the chicken has reached an internal temperature of 75°C. 4. Transfer the chicken and vegetables to a serving platter. Serve with tortillas and the desired fajita fixings.

Ham Chicken with Cheese

Prep time: 15 minutes | Cook time: 25 minutes | Serves 4

55 g unsalted butter, softened
115 g cream cheese, softened
1½ teaspoons Dijon mustard
2 tablespoons white wine vinegar
60 ml water
280 g shredded cooked chicken
115 g ham, chopped
115 g sliced Swiss or Provolone cheese

1. Preheat the Ninja Foodi cooker to 190ºC. Lightly coat a casserole dish that will fit in the Ninja Foodi cooker, such as an 8-inch round pan, with olive oil and set aside. 2. In a large bowl and using an electric mixer, combine the butter, cream cheese, Dijon mustard, and vinegar. With the motor running at low speed, slowly add the water and beat until smooth. Set aside. 3. Arrange an even layer of chicken in the bottom of the prepared pan, followed by the ham. Spread the butter and cream cheese mixture on top of the ham, followed by the cheese slices on the top layer. Air crisp for 20 to 25 minutes until warmed through and the cheese has browned.

Barbecue Shredded Chicken

Prep time: 5 minutes | Cook time: 25 minutes | Serves 4

1 (2.2 kg) whole chicken
3 teaspoons salt
1 teaspoon pepper
1 teaspoon dried parsley
1 teaspoon garlic powder
½ medium onion, cut into 3 to 4 large pieces
240 ml water
120 ml sugar-free barbecue sauce, divided

1. Scatter the chicken with salt, pepper, parsley, and garlic powder. Put the onion pieces inside the chicken cavity. 2. Pour the water into the Ninja Foodi cooker and insert the reversible rack. Place seasoned chicken on the reversible rack. Brush with half of the barbecue sauce. 3. Lock the lid. Set the cooking time for 25 minutes at High Pressure. 4. When the timer beeps, perform a natural pressure release for 10 minutes, then release any remaining pressure. Carefully remove the lid. 5. Using a clean brush, add the remaining half of the sauce to chicken. For crispy skin or thicker sauce, you can broil in the oven for 5 minutes until lightly browned. 6. Slice or shred the chicken and serve warm.

Mexican Chicken with Red Salsa

Prep time: 10 minutes | Cook time: 20 minutes | Serves 8

900 g boneless, skinless chicken thighs, cut into bite-size pieces
1½ tablespoons ground cumin
1½ tablespoons chili powder
1 tablespoon salt
2 tablespoons vegetable oil
1 (411 g) can diced tomatoes, undrained
1 (142 g) can sugar-free tomato paste
1 small onion, chopped
3 garlic cloves, minced
60 g pickled jalapeños from a can, with juice
120 ml sour cream

1. Preheat the Ninja Foodi cooker by selecting Sauté and adjusting to high heat. 2. In a medium bowl, coat the chicken with the cumin, chili powder, and salt. 3. Put the oil in the inner cooking pot. When it is shimmering, add the coated chicken pieces. (This step lets the spices bloom a bit to get their full flavor.) Cook the chicken for 4 to 5 minutes. 4. Add the tomatoes, tomato paste, onion, garlic, and jalapeños. 5. Lock the lid into place. Adjust the pressure to High. Cook for 15 minutes. When the cooking is complete, let the pressure release naturally for 10 minutes, then quick-release any remaining pressure. Unlock and remove the lid. 6. Use two forks to shred the chicken. Serve topped with the sour cream. This dish is good with mashed cauliflower, steamed vegetables, or a salad.

Chicken Wings with Piri Piri Sauce

Prep time: 30 minutes | Cook time: 30 minutes | Serves 6

12 chicken wings
45 g butter, melted
1 teaspoon onion powder
½ teaspoon cumin powder
1 teaspoon garlic paste
Sauce:
60 g piri piri peppers, stemmed and chopped
1 tablespoon pimiento, seeded and minced
1 garlic clove, chopped
2 tablespoons fresh lemon juice
⅓ teaspoon sea salt
½ teaspoon tarragon

1. Steam the chicken wings using a steamer basket that is placed over a saucepan with boiling water; reduce the heat. 2. Now, steam the wings for 10 minutes over a moderate heat. Toss the wings with butter, onion powder, cumin powder, and garlic paste. 3. Let the chicken wings cool to room temperature. Then, refrigerate them for 45 to 50 minutes. 4. Roast in the preheated Ninja Foodi cooker at 170ºC for 25 to 30 minutes; make sure to flip them halfway through. 5. While the chicken wings are cooking, prepare the sauce by mixing all of the sauce ingredients in a food processor. Toss the wings with prepared Piri Piri Sauce and serve.

Mexican Turkey Tenderloin

Prep time: 5 minutes | Cook time: 8 minutes | Serves 6

240 ml Salsa or bottled salsa
1 teaspoon chili powder
½ teaspoon ground cumin
¼ teaspoon dried oregano
680 g unseasoned turkey tenderloin or boneless turkey breast, cut into 6 pieces
Freshly ground black pepper
120 ml shredded Monterey Jack cheese or Mexican cheese blend

1. In a small bowl or measuring cup, combine the salsa, chili powder, cumin, and oregano. Pour half of the mixture into the electric pressure cooker. 2. Nestle the turkey into the sauce. Grind some pepper onto each piece of turkey. Pour the remaining salsa mixture on top. 3. Close and lock the lid of the pressure cooker. Set the valve to sealing. 4. Cook on high pressure for 8 minutes. 5. When the cooking is complete, hit Start/Stop. Allow the pressure to release naturally for 10 minutes, then quick release any remaining pressure. 6. Once the pin drops, unlock and remove the lid. 7. Sprinkle the cheese on top, and put the lid back on for a few minutes to let the cheese melt. 8. Serve immediately.

Barbecued Chicken with Creamy Coleslaw

Prep time: 10 minutes | Cook time: 20 minutes | Serves 2

270 g shredded coleslaw mix
Salt and pepper
2 (340 g) bone-in split chicken breasts, trimmed
1 teaspoon vegetable oil
2 tablespoons barbecue sauce, plus extra for serving
2 tablespoons mayonnaise
2 tablespoons sour cream
1 teaspoon distilled white vinegar, plus extra for seasoning
¼ teaspoon sugar

1. Preheat the Ninja Foodi cooker to 180°C. 2. Toss coleslaw mix and ¼ teaspoon salt in a colander set over bowl. Let sit until wilted slightly, about 30 minutes. Rinse, drain, and dry well with a dish towel. 3. Meanwhile, pat chicken dry with paper towels, rub with oil, and season with salt and pepper. Arrange breasts skin-side down in cook & crisp basket, spaced evenly apart, alternating ends. Bake for 10 minutes. Flip breasts and brush skin side with barbecue sauce. Return basket to Ninja Foodi cooker and bake until well browned and chicken registers 70°C, 10 to 15 minutes. 4. Transfer chicken to serving platter, tent loosely with aluminum foil, and let rest for 5 minutes. While chicken rests, whisk mayonnaise, sour cream, vinegar, sugar, and pinch pepper together in a large bowl. Stir in coleslaw mix and season with salt, pepper, and additional vinegar to taste. Serve chicken with coleslaw, passing extra barbecue sauce separately.

Lemon Garlic Chicken

Prep time: 20 minutes | Cook time: 30 minutes | Serves 6

900 g skinless chicken thighs
1 tablespoon avocado oil
1 teaspoon minced garlic
½ teaspoon ground coriander
1 teaspoon lemon zest
1 teaspoon lemon juice
80 ml chicken broth
240 ml water

1. Pour water and insert the steamer rack in the Ninja Foodi cooker. Pour water and chicken broth in the Ninja Foodi cooker bowl. 2. Put the chicken thighs in the bowl and sprinkle them with avocado oil, minced garlic, ground coriander, lemon zest, and lemon juice. 3. Then shake the chicken thighs gently and transfer them on the steamer rack. 4. Close and seal the lid. 5. Cook the chicken for 15 minutes on High Pressure. Then make a quick pressure release and transfer the chicken thighs on the plate.

Chicken Thighs with Coriander

Prep time: 15 minutes | Cook time: 25 minutes | Serves 4

1 tablespoon olive oil
Juice of ½ lime
1 tablespoon coconut aminos
1½ teaspoons Montreal chicken seasoning
8 bone-in chicken thighs, skin on
2 tablespoons chopped fresh coriander

1. In a gallon-size resealable bag, combine the olive oil, lime juice, coconut aminos, and chicken seasoning. Add the chicken thighs, seal the bag, and massage the bag to ensure the chicken is thoroughly coated. Refrigerate for at least 2 hours, preferably overnight. 2. Preheat the Ninja Foodi cooker to 200°C. 3. Remove the chicken from the marinade (discard the marinade) and arrange in a single layer in the cook & crisp basket. Pausing halfway through the cooking time to flip the chicken, air crisp for 20 to 25 minutes, until a thermometer inserted into the thickest part registers 75°C. 4. Transfer the chicken to a serving platter and top with the coriander before serving.

Chili Lime Turkey Burgers

Prep time: 10 minutes | Cook time: 3 minutes | Serves 4

Burgers:
900 g ground turkey
45 g diced red onion
2 cloves garlic, minced
1½ teaspoons minced coriander
1½ teaspoons salt
1 teaspoon Mexican chili powder
Juice and zest of 1 lime
120 ml water
Dipping Sauce:
120 ml sour cream
4 teaspoons sriracha
1 tablespoon chopped coriander, plus more for garnish
1 teaspoon lime juice

1. Make the burgers: In a large bowl, add the turkey, onion, garlic, coriander, salt, chili powder, and lime juice and zest. Use a wooden spoon to mix until the ingredients are well distributed. 2. Divide the meat into four 227-g balls. Use a kitchen scale to measure for accuracy. Pat the meat into thick patties, about 1 inch thick. 3. Add the water and reversible rack to the Ninja Foodi cooker. Place the turkey patties on top of the reversible rack, overlapping if necessary. 4. Close the lid and seal the vent. Cook on High Pressure for 3 minutes. Quick release the steam. 5. Remove the patties from the pot. 6. Make the dipping sauce: In a small bowl, whisk together the sour cream, sriracha, coriander, and lime juice. 7. Top each patty with 2 tablespoons of the sauce and garnish with fresh coriander.

One-Dish Chicken and Rice

Prep time: 10 minutes | Cook time: 40 minutes | Serves 4

190 g long-grain white rice, rinsed and drained
120 g cut frozen green beans (do not thaw)
1 tablespoon minced fresh ginger
3 cloves garlic, minced
1 tablespoon toasted sesame oil
1 teaspoon kosher salt
1 teaspoon black pepper
450 g chicken wings, preferably drumettes

1. In a baking pan, combine the rice, green beans, ginger, garlic, sesame oil, salt, and pepper. Stir to combine. Place the chicken wings on top of the rice mixture. 2. Cover the pan with foil. Make a long slash in the foil to allow the pan to vent steam. Place the pan in the cook & crisp basket. Set the Ninja Foodi cooker to (190°C for 30 minutes. 3. Remove the foil. Set the Ninja Foodi cooker to 200°C for 10 minutes, or until the wings have browned and rendered fat into the rice and vegetables, turning the wings halfway through the cooking time.

Crispy Duck with Cherry Sauce

Prep time: 10 minutes | Cook time: 33 minutes | Serves 2 to 4

1 whole duck (2.3 kg), split in half, back and rib bones removed
1 teaspoon olive oil
Salt and freshly ground black pepper, to taste
Cherry Sauce:
1 tablespoon butter
1 shallot, minced
120 ml sherry
240 g cherry preserves
240 ml chicken stock
1 teaspoon white wine vinegar
1 teaspoon fresh thyme leaves
Salt and freshly ground black pepper, to taste

1. Preheat the Ninja Foodi cooker to 200ºC. 2. Trim some of the fat from the duck. Rub olive oil on the duck and season with salt and pepper. Place the duck halves in the cook & crisp basket, breast side up and facing the centre of the basket. 3. Air crisp the duck for 20 minutes. Turn the duck over and air crisp for another 6 minutes. 4. While duck is air frying, make the cherry sauce. Melt the butter in a large sauté pan. Add the shallot and sauté until it is just starting to brown, about 2 to 3 minutes. Add the sherry and deglaze the pan by scraping up any brown bits from the bottom of the pan. Simmer the liquid for a few minutes, until it has reduced by half. Add the cherry preserves, chicken stock and white wine vinegar. Whisk well to combine all the ingredients. Simmer the sauce until it thickens and coats the back of a spoon, about 5 to 7 minutes. Season with salt and pepper and stir in the fresh thyme leaves. 5. When the Ninja Foodi cooker timer goes off, spoon some cherry sauce over the duck and continue to air crisp at 200ºC for 4 more minutes. Then, turn the duck halves back over so that the breast side is facing up. Spoon more cherry sauce over the top of the duck, covering the skin completely. Air crisp for 3 more minutes and then remove the duck to a plate to rest for a few minutes. 6. Serve the duck in halves, or cut each piece in half again for a smaller serving. Spoon any additional sauce over the duck or serve it on the side.

Coconut Chicken Meatballs

Prep time: 10 minutes | Cook time: 14 minutes | Serves 4

450 g chicken mince
2 spring onions, finely chopped
20 g chopped fresh corinader leaves
20 g unsweetened shredded coconut
1 tablespoon hoisin sauce
1 tablespoon soy sauce
2 teaspoons Sriracha or other hot sauce
1 teaspoon toasted sesame oil
½ teaspoon kosher salt
1 teaspoon black pepper

1. In a large bowl, gently mix the chicken, spring onions, coriander, coconut, hoisin, soy sauce, Sriracha, sesame oil, salt, and pepper until thoroughly combined (the mixture will be wet and sticky). 2. Place a sheet of parchment paper in the cook & crisp basket. Using a small scoop or teaspoon, drop rounds of the mixture in a single layer onto the parchment paper. 3. Set the Ninja Foodi cooker to 180ºC for 10 minutes, turning the meatballs halfway through the cooking time. Raise the Ninja Foodi cooker temperature to 200ºC and cook for 4 minutes more to brown the outsides of the meatballs. Use a meat thermometer to ensure the meatballs have reached an internal temperature of 75ºC. 4. Transfer the meatballs to a serving platter. Repeat with any remaining chicken mixture.

Thai Coconut Chicken

Prep time: 10 minutes | Cook time: 15 minutes | Serves 4

1 tablespoon coconut oil
450 g chicken, cubed
2 cloves garlic, minced
1 shallot, peeled and chopped
1 teaspoon Thai chili, minced
1 teaspoon fresh ginger root, julienned
⅓ teaspoon cumin powder
1 tomato, peeled and chopped
240 ml vegetable broth
80 ml unsweetened coconut milk
2 tablespoons coconut aminos
1 teaspoon Thai curry paste
Salt and freshly ground black pepper, to taste

1. Set your Ninja Foodi cooker to Sauté and heat the coconut oil. 2. Brown the chicken cubes for 2 to 3 minutes, stirring frequently. Reserve the chicken in a bowl. 3. Add the garlic and shallot and sauté for 2 minutes until tender. Add a splash of vegetable broth to the pot, if needed. 4. Stir in the Thai chili, ginger, and cumin powder and cook for another 1 minute or until fragrant. 5. Add the cooked chicken, tomato, vegetable broth, milk, coconut aminos, and curry paste to the Ninja Foodi cooker and stir well. 6. Lock the lid. Set the cooking time for 10 minutes at High Pressure. 7. When the timer beeps, perform a quick pressure release. Carefully remove the lid. Season with salt and pepper to taste and serve.

Porchetta-Style Chicken Breasts

Prep time: 10 minutes | Cook time: 15 minutes | Serves 4

25 g fresh parsley leaves
10 g roughly chopped fresh chives
4 cloves garlic, peeled
2 tablespoons lemon juice
3 teaspoons fine sea salt
1 teaspoon dried rubbed sage
1 teaspoon fresh rosemary leaves
1 teaspoon ground fennel
½ teaspoon red pepper flakes
4 (115 g) boneless, skinless chicken breasts, pounded to ¼ inch thick
8 slices bacon
Sprigs of fresh rosemary, for garnish (optional)

1. Spray the cook & crisp basket with avocado oil. Preheat the Ninja Foodi cooker to 170ºC. 2. Place the parsley, chives, garlic, lemon juice, salt, sage, rosemary, fennel, and red pepper flakes in a food processor and purée until a smooth paste forms. 3. Place the chicken breasts on a cutting board and rub the paste all over the tops. With a short end facing you, roll each breast up like a jelly roll to make a log and secure it with toothpicks. 4. Wrap 2 slices of bacon around each chicken breast log to cover the entire breast. Secure the bacon with toothpicks. 5. Place the chicken breast logs in the cook & crisp basket and air crisp for 5 minutes, flip the logs over, and cook for another 5 minutes. Increase the heat to 200ºC and cook until the bacon is crisp, about 5 minutes more. 6. Remove the toothpicks and garnish with fresh rosemary sprigs, if desired, before serving. Store leftovers in an airtight container in the refrigerator for up to 4 days or in the freezer for up to a month. Reheat in a preheated 180ºC Ninja Foodi cooker for 5 minutes, then increase the heat to 200ºC and cook for 2 minutes to crisp the bacon.

Chicken Reuben Bake

Prep time: 10 minutes | Cook time: 6 to 8 hours | Serves 6

- 4 boneless, skinless chicken-breast halves
- 60 ml water
- 1 bag (450 g) sauerkraut, drained and rinsed
- 4–5 (30 g each) slices Swiss cheese
- 180 ml fat-free Thousand Island salad dressing
- 2 tablespoons chopped fresh parsley

1. Place chicken and water in inner pot of the Ninja Foodi cooker along with 60 ml water. Layer sauerkraut over chicken. Add cheese. Top with salad dressing. Sprinkle with parsley. 2. Secure the lid and cook on the Slow Cook setting on low 6–8 hours.

Hoisin Turkey Burgers

Prep time: 30 minutes | Cook time: 20 minutes | Serves 4

- Olive oil
- 450 g lean turkey mince
- 30 g whole-wheat bread crumbs
- 60 ml hoisin sauce
- 2 tablespoons soy sauce
- 4 whole-wheat buns

1. Spray the cook & crisp basket lightly with olive oil. 2. In a large bowl, mix together the turkey, bread crumbs, hoisin sauce, and soy sauce. 3. Form the mixture into 4 equal patties. Cover with plastic wrap and refrigerate the patties for 30 minutes. 4. Place the patties in the cook & crisp basket in a single layer. Spray the patties lightly with olive oil. 5. Air crisp at 190ºC for 10 minutes. Flip the patties over, lightly spray with olive oil, and cook until golden brown, an additional 5 to 10 minutes. 6. Place the patties on buns and top with your choice of low-calorie burger toppings like sliced tomatoes, onions, and cabbage slaw.

Thai Chicken with Cucumber and Chili Salad

Prep time: 25 minutes | Cook time: 25 minutes | Serves 6

- 2 (570 g) small chickens, giblets discarded
- 1 tablespoon fish sauce
- 6 tablespoons chopped fresh coriander
- 2 teaspoons lime zest
- 1 teaspoon ground coriander
- 2 garlic cloves, minced
- 2 tablespoons packed light brown sugar
- 2 teaspoons vegetable oil
- Salt and ground black pepper, to taste
- 1 English cucumber, halved lengthwise and sliced thin
- 1 Thai chili, stemmed, deseeded, and minced
- 2 tablespoons chopped dry-roasted peanuts
- 1 small shallot, sliced thinly
- 1 tablespoon lime juice
- Lime wedges, for serving
- Cooking spray

1. Arrange a chicken on a clean work surface, remove the backbone with kitchen shears, then pound the chicken breast to flat. Cut the breast in half. Repeat with the remaining chicken. 2. Loose the breast and thigh skin with your fingers, then pat the chickens dry and pierce about 10 holes into the fat deposits of the chickens. Tuck the wings under the chickens. 3. Combine 2 teaspoons of fish sauce, coriander, lime zest, coriander, garlic, 4 teaspoons of sugar, 1 teaspoon of vegetable oil, ½ teaspoon of salt, and ⅛ teaspoon of ground black pepper in a small bowl. Stir to mix well. 4. Rub the fish sauce mixture under the breast and thigh skin of the game chickens, then let sit for 10 minutes to marinate. 5. Preheat the Ninja Foodi cooker to 200ºC. Spritz the cook & crisp basket with cooking spray. 6. Arrange the marinated chickens in the preheated Ninja Foodi cooker, skin side down. 7. Air crisp for 15 minutes, then gently turn the game hens over and air crisp for 10 more minutes or until the skin is golden brown and the internal temperature of the chickens reads at least 75ºC. 8. Meanwhile, combine all the remaining ingredients, except for the lime wedges, in a large bowl and sprinkle with salt and black pepper. Toss to mix well. 9. Transfer the fried chickens on a large plate, then sit the salad aside and squeeze the lime wedges over before serving.

Garlic Dill Wings

Prep time: 5 minutes | Cook time: 25 minutes | Serves 4

- 900 g bone-in chicken wings, separated at joints
- ½ teaspoon salt
- ½ teaspoon ground black pepper
- ½ teaspoon onion powder
- ½ teaspoon garlic powder
- 1 teaspoon dried dill

1. In a large bowl, toss wings with salt, pepper, onion powder, garlic powder, and dill until evenly coated. Place wings into ungreased cook & crisp basket in a single layer, working in batches if needed. 2. Adjust the temperature to 200ºC and air crisp for 25 minutes, shaking the basket every 7 minutes during cooking. Wings should have an internal temperature of at least 75ºC and be golden brown when done. Serve warm.

Gold Livers

Prep time: 10 minutes | Cook time: 20 minutes | Serves 4

- 2 eggs
- 2 tablespoons water
- 90 g flour
- 240 g panko breadcrumbs
- 1 teaspoon salt
- ½ teaspoon ground black pepper
- 570 g chicken livers
- Cooking spray

1. Preheat the Ninja Foodi cooker to 200ºC. Spritz the cook & crisp basket with cooking spray. 2. Whisk the eggs with water in a large bowl. Pour the flour in a separate bowl. Pour the panko on a shallow dish and sprinkle with salt and pepper. 3. Dredge the chicken livers in the flour. Shake the excess off, then dunk the livers in the whisked eggs, and then roll the livers over the panko to coat well. 4. Arrange the livers in the preheated Ninja Foodi cooker and spritz with cooking spray. Work in batches to avoid overcrowding. 5. Air crisp for 10 minutes or until the livers are golden and crispy. Flip the livers halfway through. Repeat with remaining livers. 6. Serve immediately.

Crack Chicken Breasts

Prep time: 5 minutes | Cook time: 15 minutes | Serves 2

230 g boneless, skinless chicken breasts
60 g cream cheese, softened
120 ml grass-fed bone broth
60 ml tablespoons keto-friendly ranch dressing
120 ml shredded full-fat Cheddar cheese
3 slices bacon, cooked and chopped into small pieces

1. Combine all the ingredients except the Cheddar cheese and bacon in the Ninja Foodi cooker. 2. Secure the lid. Set the cooking time for 15 minutes at High Pressure. 3. Once cooking is complete, do a quick pressure release. Carefully open the lid. 4. Add the Cheddar cheese and bacon and stir well, then serve.

African Chicken Peanut Stew

Prep time: 10 minutes | Cook time: 10 minutes | Serves 6

240 ml chopped onion
2 tablespoons minced garlic
1 tablespoon minced fresh ginger
1 teaspoon salt
½ teaspoon ground cumin
½ teaspoon ground coriander
½ teaspoon freshly ground black pepper
½ teaspoon ground cinnamon
⅛ teaspoon ground cloves
1 tablespoon sugar-free tomato paste
450 g boneless, skinless chicken breasts or thighs, cut into large chunks
700 ml- 1 L chopped Swiss chard
240 ml cubed raw pumpkin
120 ml water
240 ml chunky peanut butter

1. In the inner cooking pot of the Ninja Foodi cooker, stir together the onion, garlic, ginger, salt, cumin, coriander, pepper, cinnamon, cloves, and tomato paste. Add the chicken, chard, pumpkin, and water. 2. Lock the lid into place. Adjust the pressure to High. Cook for 10 minutes. When the cooking is complete, let the pressure release naturally. Unlock the lid. 3. Mix in the peanut butter a little at a time. Taste with each addition, as your reward for cooking. The final sauce should be thick enough to coat the back of a spoon in a thin layer. 4. Serve over mashed cauliflower, cooked courgette noodles, steamed vegetables, or with a side salad.

Brazilian Tempero Baiano Chicken Drumsticks

Prep time: 30 minutes | Cook time: 20 minutes | Serves 4

1 teaspoon cumin seeds
1 teaspoon dried oregano
1 teaspoon dried parsley
1 teaspoon ground turmeric
½ teaspoon coriander seeds
1 teaspoon kosher salt
½ teaspoon black peppercorns
½ teaspoon cayenne pepper
60 ml fresh lime juice
2 tablespoons olive oil
680 g chicken drumsticks

1. In a clean coffee grinder or spice mill, combine the cumin, oregano, parsley, turmeric, coriander seeds, salt, peppercorns, and cayenne. Process until finely ground. 2. In a small bowl, combine the ground spices with the lime juice and oil. Place the chicken in a resealable plastic bag. Add the marinade, seal, and massage until the chicken is well coated. Marinate at room temperature for 30 minutes or in the refrigerator for up to 24 hours. 3. When you are ready to cook, place the drumsticks skin side up in the cook & crisp basket. Set the Ninja Foodi cooker to 200ºC for 20 to 25 minutes, turning the legs halfway through the cooking time. Use a meat thermometer to ensure that the chicken has reached an internal temperature of 75ºC. 4. Serve with plenty of napkins.

Harissa-Rubbed Chicken

Prep time: 30 minutes | Cook time: 21 minutes | Serves 4

Harissa:
120 ml olive oil
6 cloves garlic, minced
2 tablespoons smoked paprika
1 tablespoon ground coriander
1 tablespoon ground cumin
1 teaspoon ground caraway
1 teaspoon kosher salt
½ to 1 teaspoon cayenne pepper
Chickens:
120 g yogurt
2 small chickens, any giblets removed, split in half lengthwise

1. For the harissa: In a medium microwave-safe bowl, combine the oil, garlic, paprika, coriander, cumin, caraway, salt, and cayenne. Microwave on high for 1 minute, stirring halfway through the cooking time. (You can also heat this on the stovetop until the oil is hot and bubbling. Or, if you must use your Ninja Foodi cooker for everything, cook it in the Ninja Foodi cooker at 180ºC for 5 to 6 minutes, or until the paste is heated through.) 2. For the chicken: In a small bowl, combine 1 to 2 tablespoons harissa and the yogurt. Whisk until well combined. Place the chicken halves in a resealable plastic bag and pour the marinade over. Seal the bag and massage until all of the pieces are thoroughly coated. Marinate at room temperature for 30 minutes or in the refrigerator for up to 24 hours. 3. Arrange the hen halves in a single layer in the cook & crisp basket. (If you have a smaller Ninja Foodi cooker, you may have to cook this in two batches.) Set the Ninja Foodi cooker to 200ºC for 20 minutes. Use a meat thermometer to ensure the chickens have reached an internal temperature of 75ºC.

Fajita Chicken Strips

Prep time: 10 minutes | Cook time: 15 minutes | Serves 4

450 g boneless, skinless chicken tenderloins, cut into strips
3 bell peppers, any color, cut into chunks
1 onion, cut into chunks
1 tablespoon olive oil
1 tablespoon fajita seasoning mix
Cooking spray

1. Preheat the Ninja Foodi cooker to 190ºC. 2. In a large bowl, mix together the chicken, bell peppers, onion, olive oil, and fajita seasoning mix until completely coated. 3. Spray the cook & crisp basket lightly with cooking spray. 4. Place the chicken and vegetables in the cook & crisp basket and lightly spray with cooking spray. 5. Air crisp for 7 minutes. Shake the basket and air crisp for an additional 5 to 8 minutes, until the chicken is cooked through and the veggies are starting to char. 6. Serve warm.

BLT Chicken Salad

Prep time: 15 minutes | Cook time: 17 minutes | Serves 4

4 slices bacon
2 (170 g) chicken breasts
1 teaspoon salt
½ teaspoon garlic powder
¼ teaspoon dried parsley
¼ teaspoon pepper
¼ teaspoon dried thyme
240 ml water
480 ml chopped romaine lettuce
Sauce:
80 ml mayonnaise
30 g chopped pecans
120 ml diced plum tomatoes
½ avocado, diced
1 tablespoon lemon juice

1. Press the Sauté button to heat your Ninja Foodi cooker. 2. Add the bacon and cook for about 7 minutes, flipping occasionally, until crisp. Remove and place on a paper towel to drain. When cool enough to handle, crumble the bacon and set aside. 3. Sprinkle the chicken with salt, garlic powder, parsley, pepper, and thyme. 4. Pour the water into the Ninja Foodi cooker. Use a wooden spoon to ensure nothing is stuck to the bottom of the pot. Add the reversible rack to the pot and place the chicken on top of the reversible rack. 5. Secure the lid. Set the cooking time for 10 minutes at High Pressure. 6. Meanwhile, whisk together all the ingredients for the sauce in a large salad bowl. 7. Once cooking is complete, do a quick pressure release. Carefully open the lid. 8. Remove the chicken and let sit for 10 minutes. Cut the chicken into cubes and transfer to the salad bowl, along with the cooked bacon. Gently stir until the chicken is thoroughly coated. Mix in the lettuce right before serving.

Buffalo Crispy Chicken Strips

Prep time: 15 minutes | Cook time: 13 to 17 minutes per batch | Serves 4

90 g all-purpose flour
2 eggs
2 tablespoons water
120 g seasoned panko bread crumbs
2 teaspoons granulated garlic
1 teaspoon salt
1 teaspoon freshly ground black pepper
16 chicken breast strips, or 3 large boneless, skinless chicken breasts, cut into 1-inch strips
Olive oil spray
60 ml Buffalo sauce, plus more as needed

1. Put the flour in a small bowl. 2. In another small bowl, whisk the eggs and the water. 3. In a third bowl, stir together the panko, granulated garlic, salt, and pepper. 4. Dip each chicken strip in the flour, in the egg, and in the panko mixture to coat. Press the crumbs onto the chicken with your fingers. 5. Insert the crisper plate into the basket and the basket into the unit. Preheat the unit by selecting AIR FRY, setting the temperature to 190ºC, and setting the time to 3 minutes. Select START/STOP to begin. 6. Once the unit is preheated, place a parchment paper liner into the basket. Working in batches if needed, place the chicken strips into the basket. Do not stack unless using a wire rack for the second layer. Spray the top of the chicken with olive oil. 7. Select AIR FRY, set the temperature to 190ºC, and set the time to 17 minutes. Select START/STOP to begin. 8. After 10 or 12 minutes, remove the basket, flip the chicken, and spray again with olive oil. Reinsert the basket to resume cooking. 9. When the cooking is complete, the chicken should be golden brown and crispy and a food thermometer inserted into the chicken should register 75ºC. 10. Repeat steps 6, 7, and 8 with any remaining chicken. 11. Transfer the chicken to a large bowl. Drizzle the Buffalo sauce over the top of the cooked chicken, toss to coat, and serve.

Fried Chicken Breasts

Prep time: 30 minutes | Cook time: 12 to 14 minutes | Serves 4

450 g boneless, skinless chicken breasts
180 ml dill pickle juice
70 g finely ground blanched almond flour
70 g finely grated Parmesan cheese
½ teaspoon sea salt
½ teaspoon freshly ground black pepper
2 large eggs
Avocado oil spray

1. Place the chicken breasts in a zip-top bag or between two pieces of plastic wrap. Using a meat mallet or heavy skillet, pound the chicken to a uniform ½-inch thickness. 2. Place the chicken in a large bowl with the pickle juice. Cover and allow to brine in the refrigerator for up to 2 hours. 3. In a shallow dish, combine the almond flour, Parmesan cheese, salt, and pepper. In a separate, shallow bowl, beat the eggs. 4. Drain the chicken and pat it dry with paper towels. Dip in the eggs and then in the flour mixture, making sure to press the coating into the chicken. Spray both sides of the coated breasts with oil. 5. Spray the cook & crisp basket with oil and put the chicken inside. Set the temperature to 200ºC and air crisp for 6 to 7 minutes. 6. Carefully flip the breasts with a spatula. Spray the breasts again with oil and continue cooking for 6 to 7 minutes more, until golden and crispy.

Bruschetta and Cheese Stuffed Chicken

Prep time: 10 minutes | Cook time: 10 minutes | Serves 4

170 g diced plum tomatoes
2 tablespoons avocado oil
1 tablespoon thinly sliced fresh basil, plus more for garnish
1½ teaspoons balsamic vinegar
Pinch of salt
Pinch of black pepper
4 boneless, skinless chicken breasts (about 900 g)
340 g goat cheese, divided
2 teaspoons Italian seasoning, divided
240 ml water

1. Prepare the bruschetta by mixing the tomatoes, avocado oil, basil, vinegar, salt, and pepper in a small bowl. Let it marinate until the chicken is done. 2. Pat the chicken dry with a paper towel. Butterfly the breast open but do not cut all the way through. Stuff each breast with 85 g of the goat cheese. Use toothpicks to close the edges. 3. Sprinkle ½ teaspoon of the Italian seasoning on top of each breast. 4. Pour the water into the pot. Place the reversible rack inside. Lay a piece of aluminium foil on top of the reversible rack and place the chicken breasts on top. It is okay if they overlap. 5. Close the lid and seal the vent. Cook on High Pressure for 10 minutes. Quick release the steam. 6. Remove the toothpicks and top each breast with one-fourth of the bruschetta.

Gochujang Chicken Wings

Prep time: 15 minutes | Cook time: 25 minutes | Serves 4

Wings:
900 g chicken wings
1 teaspoon kosher salt
1 teaspoon black pepper or gochugaru (Korean red pepper)
Sauce:
2 tablespoons gochujang (Korean chili paste)
1 tablespoon mayonnaise
1 tablespoon toasted sesame oil
1 tablespoon minced fresh ginger
1 tablespoon minced garlic
1 teaspoon sugar
1 teaspoon agave nectar or honey
For Serving
1 teaspoon sesame seeds
25 g chopped spring onions

1. For the wings: Season the wings with the salt and pepper and place in the cook & crisp basket. Set the Ninja Foodi cooker to 200ºC for 20 minutes, turning the wings halfway through the cooking time. 2. Meanwhile, for the sauce: In a small bowl, combine the gochujang, mayonnaise, sesame oil, ginger, garlic, sugar, and agave; set aside. 3. As you near the 20-minute mark, use a meat thermometer to check the meat. When the wings reach 70ºC, transfer them to a large bowl. Pour about half the sauce on the wings; toss to coat (serve the remaining sauce as a dip). 4. Return the wings to the cook & crisp basket and cook for 5 minutes, until the sauce has glazed. 5. Transfer the wings to a serving platter. Sprinkle with the sesame seeds and spring onions. Serve with the reserved sauce on the side for dipping.

Simple Chicken Masala

Prep time: 10 minutes | Cook time: 17 minutes | Serves 3

340 g chicken fillet
1 tablespoon masala spices
1 tablespoon avocado oil
3 tablespoons organic almond milk

1. Heat up avocado oil in the Ninja Foodi cooker on Sauté mode for 2 minutes. 2. Meanwhile, chop the chicken fillet roughly and mix it up with masala spices. 3. Add almond milk and transfer the chicken in the Ninja Foodi cooker. 4. Cook the chicken bites on Sauté mode for 15 minutes. Stir the meal occasionally.

Chicken and Broccoli Casserole

Prep time: 5 minutes | Cook time: 20 to 25 minutes | Serves 4

230 g broccoli, chopped into florets
280 g shredded cooked chicken
115 g cream cheese
80 g heavy cream
1½ teaspoons Dijon mustard
½ teaspoon garlic powder
Salt and freshly ground black pepper, to taste
2 tablespoons chopped fresh basil
230 g shredded Cheddar cheese

1. Preheat the Ninja Foodi cooker to 200ºC. Lightly coat a casserole dish that will fit in Ninja Foodi cooker, with olive oil and set aside. 2. Place the broccoli in a large glass bowl with 1 tablespoon of water and cover with a microwavable plate. Microwave on high for 2 to 3 minutes until the broccoli is bright green but not mushy. Drain if necessary and add to another large bowl along with the shredded chicken. 3. In the same glass bowl used to microwave the broccoli, combine the cream cheese and cream. Microwave for 30 seconds to 1 minute on high and stir until smooth. Add the mustard and garlic powder and season to taste with salt and freshly ground black pepper. Whisk until the sauce is smooth. 4. Pour the warm sauce over the broccoli and chicken mixture and then add the basil. Using a silicone spatula, gently fold the mixture until thoroughly combined. 5. Transfer the chicken mixture to the prepared casserole dish and top with the cheese. Air crisp for 20 to 25 minutes until warmed through and the cheese has browned.

Ninja Foodi cooker Crack Chicken

Prep time: 15 minutes | Cook time: 20 minutes | Serves 4

240 ml chicken broth
1 teaspoon dried dill
1 teaspoon dried oregano
½ teaspoon onion powder
450 g skinless, boneless chicken breast
½ teaspoon salt
2 tablespoons mascarpone cheese
60 g Cheddar cheese, shredded

1. Pour the chicken broth in the Ninja Foodi cooker. 2. Add dried ill, oregano, onion powder, chicken breast, and salt. 3. Close and seal the lid. 4. Cook the chicken breast on High Pressure for 15 minutes. 5. Then make a quick pressure release and transfer the cooked chicken in the bowl. 6. Blend the chicken broth mixture with the help of the immersion blender. 7. Add mascarpone cheese and Cheddar cheese. Sauté the liquid for 2 minutes on Sauté mode. 8. Meanwhile, shred the chicken. 9. Add it in the mascarpone mixture and mix it up. Sauté the meal for 3 minutes more.

Spanish Chicken and Mini Sweet Pepper Baguette

Prep time: 10 minutes | Cook time: 20 minutes | Serves 2

570 g assorted small chicken parts, breasts cut into halves
¼ teaspoon salt
¼ teaspoon ground black pepper
2 teaspoons olive oil
230 g mini sweet peppers
60 g light mayonnaise
¼ teaspoon smoked paprika
½ clove garlic, crushed
Baguette, for serving
Cooking spray

1. Preheat the Ninja Foodi cooker to 190ºC. Spritz the cook & crisp basket with cooking spray. 2. Toss the chicken with salt, ground black pepper, and olive oil in a large bowl. 3. Arrange the sweet peppers and chicken in the preheated Ninja Foodi cooker and air crisp for 10 minutes, then transfer the peppers on a plate. 4. Flip the chicken and air crisp for 10 more minutes or until well browned. 5. Meanwhile, combine the mayo, paprika, and garlic in a small bowl. Stir to mix well. 6. Assemble the baguette with chicken and sweet pepper, then spread with mayo mixture and serve.

Easy Cajun Chicken Drumsticks

Prep time: 5 minutes | Cook time: 40 minutes | Serves 5

1 tablespoon olive oil
10 chicken drumsticks
1½ tablespoons Cajun seasoning
Salt and ground black pepper, to taste

1. Preheat the Ninja Foodi cooker to 200°C. Grease the cook & crisp basket with olive oil. 2. On a clean work surface, rub the chicken drumsticks with Cajun seasoning, salt, and ground black pepper. 3. Arrange the seasoned chicken drumsticks in a single layer in the Ninja Foodi cooker. You need to work in batches to avoid overcrowding. 4. Air crisp for 18 minutes or until lightly browned. Flip the drumsticks halfway through. 5. Remove the chicken drumsticks from the Ninja Foodi cooker. Serve immediately.

African Merguez Meatballs

Prep time: 30 minutes | Cook time: 10 minutes | Serves 4

450 g chicken mince
2 garlic cloves, finely minced
1 tablespoon sweet Hungarian paprika
1 teaspoon kosher salt
1 teaspoon sugar
1 teaspoon ground cumin
½ teaspoon black pepper
½ teaspoon ground fennel
½ teaspoon ground coriander
½ teaspoon cayenne pepper
¼ teaspoon ground allspice

1. In a large bowl, gently mix the chicken, garlic, paprika, salt, sugar, cumin, black pepper, fennel, coriander, cayenne, and allspice until all the ingredients are incorporated. Let stand for 30 minutes at room temperature, or cover and refrigerate for up to 24 hours. 2. Form the mixture into 16 meatballs. Arrange them in a single layer in the cook & crisp basket. Set the Ninja Foodi cooker to 200°C for 10 minutes, turning the meatballs halfway through the cooking time. Use a meat thermometer to ensure the meatballs have reached an internal temperature of 75°C.

Garlic Parmesan Drumsticks

Prep time: 5 minutes | Cook time: 25 minutes | Serves 4

8 (115 g) chicken drumsticks
½ teaspoon salt
⅛ teaspoon ground black pepper
½ teaspoon garlic powder
2 tablespoons salted butter, melted
45 g grated Parmesan cheese
1 tablespoon dried parsley

1. Sprinkle drumsticks with salt, pepper, and garlic powder. Place drumsticks into ungreased cook & crisp basket. 2. Adjust the temperature to 200°C and air crisp for 25 minutes, turning drumsticks halfway through cooking. Drumsticks will be golden and have an internal temperature of at least 75°C when done. 3. Transfer drumsticks to a large serving dish. Pour butter over drumsticks, and sprinkle with Parmesan and parsley. Serve warm.

Chicken Piccata

Prep time: 5 minutes | Cook time: 25 minutes | Serves 4

4 (170 g) boneless, skinless chicken breasts
½ teaspoon salt
½ teaspoon garlic powder
¼ teaspoon pepper
2 tablespoons coconut oil
240 ml water
2 cloves garlic, minced
4 tablespoons butter
Juice of 1 lemon
¼ teaspoon xanthan gum

1. Sprinkle the chicken with salt, garlic powder, and pepper. 2. Set your Ninja Foodi cooker to Sauté and melt the coconut oil. 3. Add the chicken and sear each side for about 5 to 7 minutes until golden brown. 4. Remove the chicken and set aside on a plate. 5. Pour the water into the Ninja Foodi cooker. Using a wooden spoon, scrape the bottom if necessary to remove any stuck-on seasoning or meat. Insert the reversible rack and place the chicken on the reversible rack. 6. Secure the lid. Set the cooking time for 10 minutes at High Pressure. 7. Once cooking is complete, do a natural pressure release for 10 minutes, then release any remaining pressure. Carefully open the lid. 8. Remove the chicken and set aside. Strain the broth from the Ninja Foodi cooker into a large bowl and return to the pot. 9. Set your Ninja Foodi cooker to Sauté again and add the remaining ingredients. Cook for at least 5 minutes, stirring frequently, or until the sauce is cooked to your desired thickness. 10. Pour the sauce over the chicken and serve warm.

Buttermilk Breaded Chicken

Prep time: 7 minutes | Cook time: 20 to 25 minutes | Serves 4

125 g all-purpose flour
2 teaspoons paprika
Pinch salt
Freshly ground black pepper, to taste
80 ml buttermilk
2 eggs
2 tablespoons extra-virgin olive oil
185 g bread crumbs
6 chicken pieces, drumsticks, breasts, and thighs, patted dry
Cooking oil spray

1. In a shallow bowl, stir together the flour, paprika, salt, and pepper. 2. In another bowl, beat the buttermilk and eggs until smooth. 3. In a third bowl, stir together the olive oil and bread crumbs until mixed. 4. Dredge the chicken in the flour, dip in the eggs to coat, and finally press into the bread crumbs, patting the crumbs firmly onto the chicken skin. 5. Insert the crisper plate into the basket and the basket into the unit. Preheat the unit by selecting AIR FRY, setting the temperature to 190°C, and setting the time to 3 minutes. Select START/STOP to begin. 6. Once the unit is preheated, spray the crisper plate with cooking oil. Place the chicken into the basket. 7. Select AIR FRY, set the temperature to 190°C, and set the time to 25 minutes. Select START/STOP to begin. 8. After 10 minutes, flip the chicken. Resume cooking. After 10 minutes more, check the chicken. If a food thermometer inserted into the chicken registers 75°C and the chicken is brown and crisp, it is done. Otherwise, resume cooking for up to 5 minutes longer. 9. When the cooking is complete, let cool for 5 minutes, then serve.

Chicken Enchilada Bowl

Prep time: 10 minutes | Cook time: 35 minutes | Serves 4

2 (170 g) boneless, skinless chicken breasts
2 teaspoons chili powder
½ teaspoon garlic powder
½ teaspoon salt
¼ teaspoon pepper
2 tablespoons coconut oil
180 ml red enchilada sauce
60 ml chicken broth
1 (110 g) can green chilies
60 ml diced onion
480 ml cooked cauliflower rice
1 avocado, diced
120 ml sour cream
240 ml shredded Cheddar cheese

1. Sprinkle the chili powder, garlic powder, salt, and pepper on chicken breasts. 2. Set your Ninja Foodi cooker to Sauté and melt the coconut oil. Add the chicken breasts and sear each side for about 5 minutes until golden brown. 3. Pour the enchilada sauce and broth over the chicken. Using a wooden spoon or rubber spatula, scrape the bottom of pot to make sure nothing is sticking. Stir in the chilies and onion. 4. Secure the lid. Set the cooking time for 25 minutes at High Pressure. 5. Once cooking is complete, do a quick pressure release. Carefully open the lid. 6. Remove the chicken and shred with two forks. Serve the chicken over the cauliflower rice and place the avocado, sour cream, and Cheddar cheese on top.

Barbecue Chicken and Coleslaw Tostadas

Prep time: 15 minutes | Cook time: 40 minutes | Makes 4 tostadas

Coleslaw:
60 g sour cream
25 g small green cabbage, finely chopped
½ tablespoon white vinegar
½ teaspoon garlic powder
½ teaspoon salt
¼ teaspoon ground black pepper

Tostadas:
280 g pulled rotisserie chicken
120 ml barbecue sauce
4 corn tortillas
110 g shredded Mozzarella cheese
Cooking spray

Make the Coleslaw: 1. Combine the ingredients for the coleslaw in a large bowl. Toss to mix well. 2. Refrigerate until ready to serve. Make the Tostadas: 1. Preheat the Ninja Foodi cooker to 190°C. Spritz the cook & crisp basket with cooking spray. 2. Toss the chicken with barbecue sauce in a separate large bowl to combine well. Set aside. 3. Place one tortilla in the preheated Ninja Foodi cooker and spritz with cooking spray. Work in batches to avoid overcrowding. 4. Air crisp the tortilla for 5 minutes or until lightly browned, then spread a quarter of the barbecue chicken and cheese over. 5. Air crisp for another 5 minutes or until the cheese melts. Repeat with remaining tortillas, chicken, and cheese. 6. Serve the tostadas with coleslaw on top.

Chicken Tacos with Fried Cheese Shells

Prep time: 5 minutes | Cook time: 25 minutes | Serves 6

Chicken:
4 (170 g) boneless, skinless chicken breasts
240 ml chicken broth
1 teaspoon salt
¼ teaspoon pepper
1 tablespoon chili powder
2 teaspoons garlic powder
2 teaspoons cumin
Cheese Shells:
360 ml shredded whole-milk Mozzarella cheese

1. Combine all ingredients for the chicken in the Ninja Foodi cooker. 2. Secure the lid. Set the cooking time for 20 minutes at High Pressure. 3. Once cooking is complete, do a quick pressure release. Carefully open the lid. 4. Shred the chicken and serve in bowls or cheese shells. 5. Make the cheese shells: Heat a nonstick skillet over medium heat. 6. Sprinkle 60 ml of Mozzarella cheese in the skillet and fry until golden. Flip and turn off the heat. Allow the cheese to get brown. Fill with chicken and fold. The cheese will harden as it cools. Repeat with the remaining cheese and filling. 7. Serve warm.

Parmesan Carbonara Chicken

Prep time: 15 minutes | Cook time: 25 minutes | Serves 5

450 g chicken, skinless, boneless, chopped
240 ml double cream
240 ml chopped spinach
60 g Parmesan, grated
1 teaspoon ground black pepper
1 tablespoon coconut oil
60 g bacon, chopped

1. Put the coconut oil and chopped chicken in the Ninja Foodi cooker. 2. Sauté the chicken for 10 minutes. Stir it from time to time. 3. Then add ground black pepper, and spinach. Stir the mixture well and sauté for 5 minutes more. 4. Then add double cream and Parmesan. Close and seal the lid. 5. Cook the meal on High Pressure for 10 minutes. Allow the natural pressure release for 10 minutes.

Chapter 6 Snacks and Appetisers

Blackberry Baked Brie

Prep time: 5 minutes | Cook time: 15 minutes | Serves 5

230 g round Brie
240 ml water
60 ml sugar-free blackberry preserves
2 teaspoons chopped fresh mint

1. Slice a grid pattern into the top of the rind of the Brie with a knife. 2. In a 7-inch round baking dish, place the Brie, then cover the baking dish securely with foil. 3. Insert the reversible rack into the inner pot of the Ninja Foodi cooker; pour in the water. 4. Make a foil sling and arrange it on top of the reversible rack. Place the baking dish on top of the reversible rack and foil sling. 5. Secure the lid to the locked position and turn the vent to sealing. 6. Set the Ninja Foodi cooker for 15 minutes on high pressure. 7. When cooking time is up, turn off the Ninja Foodi cooker and do a quick release of the pressure. 8. When the valve has dropped, remove the lid, then remove the baking dish. 9. Remove the top rind of the Brie and top with the preserves. Sprinkle with the fresh mint.

Garlic-Roasted Tomatoes and Olives

Prep time: 5 minutes | Cook time: 20 minutes | Serves 6

475 ml cherry tomatoes
4 garlic cloves, roughly chopped
½ red onion, roughly chopped
240 ml black olives
240 ml green olives
1 tablespoon fresh basil, minced
1 tablespoon fresh oregano, minced
2 tablespoons olive oil
¼ to ½ teaspoon salt

1. Preheat the Ninja Foodi cooker to 190°C. 2. In a large bowl, combine all of the ingredients and toss together so that the tomatoes and olives are coated well with the olive oil and herbs. 3. Pour the mixture into the cook & crisp basket, and roast for 10 minutes. Stir the mixture well, then continue roasting for an additional 10 minutes. 4. Remove from the Ninja Foodi cooker, transfer to a serving bowl, and enjoy.

Tangy Fried Pickle Spears

Prep time: 5 minutes | Cook time: 15 minutes | Serves 6

2 jars sweet and sour pickle spears, patted dry
2 medium-sized eggs
80 ml milk
1 teaspoon garlic powder
1 teaspoon sea salt
½ teaspoon shallot powder
⅓ teaspoon chilli powder
80 ml plain flour
Cooking spray

1. Preheat the Ninja Foodi cooker to 195°C. Spritz the cook & crisp basket with cooking spray. 2. In a bowl, beat together the eggs with milk. In another bowl, combine garlic powder, sea salt, shallot powder, chilli powder and plain flour until well blended. 3. One by one, roll the pickle spears in the powder mixture, then dredge them in the egg mixture. Dip them in the powder mixture a second time for additional coating. 4. Arrange the coated pickles in the prepared basket. Air crisp for 15 minutes until golden and crispy, shaking the basket halfway through to ensure even cooking. 5. Transfer to a plate and let cool for 5 minutes before serving.

Browned Ricotta with Capers and Lemon

Prep time: 10 minutes | Cook time: 8 to 10 minutes | Serves 4 to 6

355 ml whole milk ricotta cheese
2 tablespoons extra-virgin olive oil
2 tablespoons capers, rinsed
Zest of 1 lemon, plus more for garnish
1 teaspoon finely chopped fresh rosemary
Pinch crushed red pepper flakes
Salt and freshly ground black pepper, to taste
1 tablespoon grated Parmesan cheese

1. Preheat the Ninja Foodi cooker to 190°C. 2. In a mixing bowl, stir together the ricotta cheese, olive oil, capers, lemon zest, rosemary, red pepper flakes, salt, and pepper until well combined. 3. Spread the mixture evenly in a baking dish and place it in the cook & crisp basket. 4. Air crisp for 8 to 10 minutes until the top is nicely browned. 5. Remove from the basket and top with a sprinkle of grated Parmesan cheese. 6. Garnish with the lemon zest and serve warm.

Stuffed Figs with Goat Cheese and Honey

Prep time: 5 minutes | Cook time: 10 minutes | Serves 4

8 fresh figs
57 g goat cheese
¼ teaspoon ground cinnamon
1 tablespoon honey, plus more for serving
1 tablespoon olive oil

1. Preheat the Ninja Foodi cooker to 180°C. Line an 8-by-8-inch baking dish with parchment paper that comes up the side so you can lift it out after cooking. 2. In a large bowl, mix together all of the ingredients until well combined. 3. Press the oat mixture into the pan in an even layer. 4. Place the pan into the cook & crisp basket and bake for 15 minutes. 5. Remove the pan from the Ninja Foodi cooker and lift the granola cake out of the pan using the edges of the parchment paper. 6. Allow to cool for 5 minutes before slicing into 6 equal bars. 7. Serve immediately or wrap in plastic wrap and store at room temperature for up to 1 week.

Parmesan Artichoke

Prep time: 1 minute | Cook time: 30 minutes | Serves 2

1 large artichoke
240 ml water
60 ml grated Parmesan cheese
¼ teaspoon salt
¼ teaspoon red pepper flakes

1. Trim artichoke. Remove stem, outer leaves and top. Gently spread leaves. 2. Add water to Ninja Foodi cooker and place steam rack on bottom. Place artichoke on steam rack and sprinkle with Parmesan, salt, and red pepper flakes. Click lid closed. Press the Steam button and adjust time for 30 minutes. 3. When timer beeps, allow a 15-minute natural release and then quick-release the remaining pressure. Enjoy warm topped with additional Parmesan.

Fast Spring Kale Appetizer

Prep time: 5 minutes | Cook time: 2 minutes | Serves 6

3 teaspoons butter
240 ml chopped spring onions
450 g kale, torn into pieces
240 ml water
½ teaspoon cayenne pepper
Himalayan salt and ground black pepper, to taste
120 ml shredded Colby cheese, for serving

1. Set your Ninja Foodi cooker to Sauté and melt the butter. 2. Add the spring onions and sauté for 1 minute until wilted. 3. Add the remaining ingredients except the cheese to the Ninja Foodi cooker and mix well. 4. Lock the lid. Set the cooking time for 1 minute at High Pressure. 5. When the timer beeps, perform a quick pressure release. Carefully remove the lid. 6. Transfer the kale mixture to a bowl and serve topped with the cheese.

Cheese Drops

Prep time: 15 minutes | Cook time: 10 minutes per batch | Serves 8

177 ml plain flour
½ teaspoon rock salt
¼ teaspoon cayenne pepper
¼ teaspoon smoked paprika
¼ teaspoon black pepper
Dash garlic powder (optional)
60 ml butter, softened
240 ml shredded extra mature Cheddar cheese, at room temperature
Olive oil spray

1. In a small bowl, combine the flour, salt, cayenne, paprika, pepper, and garlic powder, if using. 2. Using a food processor, cream the butter and cheese until smooth. Gently add the seasoned flour and process until the dough is well combined, smooth, and no longer sticky. (Or make the dough in a stand mixer fitted with the paddle attachment: Cream the butter and cheese on medium speed until smooth, then add the seasoned flour and beat at low speed until smooth.) 3. Divide the dough into 32 equal-size pieces. On a lightly floured surface, roll each piece into a small ball. 4. Spray the cook & crisp basket with oil spray. Arrange 16 cheese drops in the basket. Set the Ninja Foodi cooker to 165ºC for 10 minutes, or until drops are just starting to brown. Transfer to a wire rack. Repeat with remaining dough, checking for doneness at 8 minutes. 5. Cool the cheese drops completely on the wire rack. Store in an airtight container until ready to serve, or up to 1 or 2 days.

Artichoke and Olive Pitta Flatbread

Prep time: 5 minutes | Cook time: 10 minutes | Serves 4

2 wholewheat pittas
2 tablespoons olive oil, divided
2 garlic cloves, minced
¼ teaspoon salt
120 ml canned artichoke hearts, sliced
60 ml Kalamata olives
60 ml shredded Parmesan
60 ml crumbled feta
Chopped fresh parsley, for garnish (optional)

1. Preheat the Ninja Foodi cooker to 190ºC. 2. Brush each pitta with 1 tablespoon olive oil, then sprinkle the minced garlic and salt over the top. 3. Distribute the artichoke hearts, olives, and cheeses evenly between the two pittas, and place both into the Ninja Foodi cooker to bake for 10 minutes. 4. Remove the pittas and cut them into 4 pieces each before serving. Sprinkle parsley over the top, if desired.

Mayo Chicken Celery

Prep time: 15 minutes | Cook time: 15 minutes | Serves 4

400 g chicken breast, skinless, boneless
240 ml water
4 celery stalks
1 teaspoon salt
½ teaspoon onion powder
1 teaspoon mayonnaise

1. Combine all the ingredients except the mayo in the Ninja Foodi cooker. 2. Secure the lid. Set the cooking time for 15 minutes at High Pressure. 3. Once cooking is complete, do a natural pressure release for 6 minutes, then release any remaining pressure. Carefully open the lid. 4. Remove the chicken and shred with two forks, then return to the Ninja Foodi cooker. 5. Add the mayo and stir well. Serve immediately.

Taco Beef Bites

Prep time: 10 minutes | Cook time: 15 minutes | Serves 6

280 g ground beef
3 eggs, beaten
80 ml shredded Mozzarella
cheese
1 teaspoon taco seasoning
1 teaspoon sesame oil

1. In the mixing bowl mix up ground beef, eggs, Mozzarella, and taco seasoning. 2. Then make the small meat bites from the mixture. 3. Heat up sesame oil in the Ninja Foodi cooker. 4. Put the meat bites in the hot oil and cook them for 5 minutes from each side on Sauté mode.

Parmesan Chicken Balls with Chives

Prep time: 10 minutes | Cook time: 15 minutes | Serves 4

1 teaspoon coconut oil, softened	1 tablespoon chopped chives
240 ml ground chicken	1 teaspoon cayenne pepper
60 ml chicken broth	85 g Parmesan cheese, grated

1. Set your Ninja Foodi cooker to Sauté and heat the coconut oil. 2. Add the remaining ingredients except the cheese to the Ninja Foodi cooker and stir to mix well. 3. Secure the lid. Set the cooking time for 15 minutes at High Pressure. 4. Once cooking is complete, do a quick pressure release. Carefully open the lid. 5. Add the grated cheese and stir until combined. Form the balls from the cooked chicken mixture and allow to cool for 10 minutes, then serve.

Garlic Herb Butter

Prep time: 10 minutes | Cook time: 8 minutes | Serves 4

80 ml butter	½ teaspoon minced garlic
1 teaspoon dried parsley	¼ teaspoon dried thyme
1 tablespoon dried dill	

1. Preheat the Ninja Foodi cooker on Sauté mode. 2. Then add butter and melt it. 3. Add dried parsley, dill, minced garlic, and thyme. Stir the butter mixture well. 4. Transfer it in the butter mold and refrigerate until it is solid.

Chicken and Cabbage Salad

Prep time: 15 minutes | Cook time: 10 minutes | Serves 4

340 g chicken fillet, chopped	cabbage
1 teaspoon Cajun seasoning	1 tablespoon avocado oil
1 tablespoon coconut oil	1 teaspoon sesame seeds
240 ml chopped Chinese	

1. Sprinkle the chopped chicken with the Cajun seasoning. 2. Set your Ninja Foodi cooker to Sauté and heat the coconut oil. Add the chicken and cook for 10 minutes, stirring occasionally. 3. When the chicken is cooked, transfer to a salad bowl. Add the cabbage, avocado oil, and sesame seeds and gently toss to combine. Serve immediately.

Garlic-Parmesan Croutons

Prep time: 3 minutes | Cook time: 12 minutes | Serves 4

Oil, for spraying	3 tablespoons olive oil
1 L cubed French bread	1 tablespoon granulated garlic
1 tablespoon grated Parmesan cheese	½ teaspoon unsalted salt

1. Line the cook & crisp basket with parchment and spray lightly with oil. 2. In a large bowl, mix together the bread, Parmesan cheese, olive oil, garlic, and salt, tossing with your hands to evenly distribute the seasonings. Transfer the coated bread cubes to the prepared basket. 3. Air crisp at 175°C for 10 to 12 minutes, stirring once after 5 minutes, or until crisp and golden brown.

Crispy Chilli Chickpeas

Prep time: 5 minutes | Cook time: 15 minutes | Serves 4

1 (425 g) can cooked chickpeas, drained and rinsed	⅛ teaspoon chilli powder
1 tablespoon olive oil	⅛ teaspoon garlic powder
¼ teaspoon salt	⅛ teaspoon paprika

1. Preheat the Ninja Foodi cooker to 190°C. 2. In a medium bowl, toss all of the ingredients together until the chickpeas are well coated. 3. Pour the chickpeas into the Ninja Foodi cooker and spread them out in a single layer. 4. Roast for 15 minutes, stirring once halfway through the cook time.

Rosemary-Garlic Shoestring Fries

Prep time: 5 minutes | Cook time: 18 minutes | Serves 2

1 large russet or Maris Piper potato (about 340 g), scrubbed clean, and julienned	rosemary
1 tablespoon vegetable oil	Rock salt and freshly ground black pepper, to taste
Leaves from 1 sprig fresh	1 garlic clove, thinly sliced
	Flaky sea salt, for serving

1. Preheat the Ninja Foodi cooker to 205°C. 2. Place the julienned potatoes in a large colander and rinse under cold running water until the water runs clear. Spread the potatoes out on a double-thick layer of paper towels and pat dry. 3. In a large bowl, combine the potatoes, oil, and rosemary. Season with rock salt and pepper and toss to coat evenly. Place the potatoes in the Ninja Foodi cooker and air crisp for 18 minutes, shaking the basket every 5 minutes and adding the garlic in the last 5 minutes of cooking, or until the fries are golden brown and crisp. 4. Transfer the fries to a plate and sprinkle with flaky sea salt while they're hot. Serve immediately.

Parmesan Courgette Fries

Prep time: 15 minutes | Cook time: 5 minutes | Serves 4

1 courgette	½ teaspoon Italian seasoning
30 g Parmesan, grated	1 tablespoon coconut oil
1 tablespoon almond flour	

1. Trim the courgette and cut it into the French fries. 2. Then sprinkle them with grated Parmesan, almond flour, and Italian seasoning. 3. Put coconut oil in the Ninja Foodi cooker and melt it on Sauté mode. 4. Put the courgette in the hot oil in one layer and cook for 2 minutes from each side or until they are golden brown. 5. Dry the courgette fries with paper towels.

Cheesy Hash Brown Bruschetta

Prep time: 5 minutes | Cook time: 6 to 8 minutes | Serves 4

4 frozen hash brown patties
1 tablespoon olive oil
80 ml chopped cherry tomatoes
3 tablespoons diced fresh Mozzarella
2 tablespoons grated Parmesan cheese
1 tablespoon balsamic vinegar
1 tablespoon minced fresh basil

4 frozen hash brown patties 1 tablespoon olive oil 80 ml chopped cherry tomatoes 3 tablespoons diced fresh Mozzarella 2 tablespoons grated Parmesan cheese 1 tablespoon balsamic vinegar 1 tablespoon minced fresh basil

Polenta Fries with Chilli-Lime Mayo

Prep time: 10 minutes | Cook time: 28 minutes | Serves 4

Polenta Fries:
2 teaspoons vegetable or olive oil
¼ teaspoon paprika
450 g prepared polenta, cut into 3-inch × ½-inch strips
Chilli-Lime Mayo:
120 ml mayonnaise
1 teaspoon chilli powder
1 teaspoon chopped fresh coriander
¼ teaspoon ground cumin
Juice of ½ lime
Salt and freshly ground black pepper, to taste

1. Preheat the Ninja Foodi cooker to 205°C. 2. Mix the oil and paprika in a bowl. Add the polenta strips and toss until evenly coated. 3. Transfer the polenta strips to the air crisp basket and air crisp for 28 minutes until the fries are golden brown, shaking the basket once during cooking. Season as desired with salt and pepper. 4. Meanwhile, whisk together all the ingredients for the chilli-lime mayo in a small bowl. 5. Remove the polenta fries from the Ninja Foodi cooker to a plate and serve alongside the chilli-lime mayo as a dipping sauce.

Spinach and Crab Meat Cups

Prep time: 10 minutes | Cook time: 10 minutes | Makes 30 cups

1 (170 g) can crab meat, drained to yield 80 ml meat
60 ml frozen spinach, thawed, drained, and chopped
1 clove garlic, minced
120 ml grated Parmesan cheese
3 tablespoons plain yoghurt
¼ teaspoon lemon juice
½ teaspoon Worcestershire sauce
30 mini frozen filo shells, thawed
Cooking spray

1. Preheat the Ninja Foodi cooker to 200°C. 2. Remove any bits of shell that might remain in the crab meat. 3. Mix the crab meat, spinach, garlic, and cheese together. 4. Stir in the yoghurt, lemon juice, and Worcestershire sauce and mix well. 5. Spoon a teaspoon of filling into each filo shell. 6. Spray the cook & crisp basket with cooking spray and arrange half the shells in the basket. Air crisp for 5 minutes. Repeat with the remaining shells. 7. Serve immediately.

Dark Chocolate and Cranberry Granola Bars

Prep time: 5 minutes | Cook time: 15 minutes | Serves 6

475 ml certified gluten-free quick oats
2 tablespoons sugar-free dark chocolate chunks
2 tablespoons unsweetened dried cranberries
3 tablespoons unsweetened shredded coconut
120 ml raw honey
1 teaspoon ground cinnamon
⅛ teaspoon salt
2 tablespoons olive oil

1. Preheat the Ninja Foodi cooker to 180°C. Line an 8-by-8-inch baking dish with parchment paper that comes up the side so you can lift it out after cooking. 2. In a large bowl, mix together all of the ingredients until well combined. 3. Press the oat mixture into the pan in an even layer. 4. Place the pan into the cook & crisp basket and bake for 15 minutes. 5. Remove the pan from the Ninja Foodi cooker and lift the granola cake out of the pan using the edges of the parchment paper. 6. Allow to cool for 5 minutes before slicing into 6 equal bars. 7. Serve immediately or wrap in plastic wrap and store at room temperature for up to 1 week.

Easy Roasted Chickpeas

Prep time: 5 minutes | Cook time: 15 minutes | Makes about 240 ml

1 (425 g) can chickpeas, drained
2 teaspoons curry powder
¼ teaspoon salt
1 tablespoon olive oil

1. Drain chickpeas thoroughly and spread in a single layer on paper towels. Cover with another paper towel and press gently to remove extra moisture. Don't press too hard or you'll crush the chickpeas. 2. Mix curry powder and salt together. 3. Place chickpeas in a medium bowl and sprinkle with seasonings. Stir well to coat. 4. Add olive oil and stir again to distribute oil. 5. Air crisp at 200°C for 15 minutes, stopping to shake basket about halfway through cooking time. 6. Cool completely and store in airtight container.

Creole Pancetta and Cheese Balls

Prep time: 5 minutes | Cook time: 5 minutes | Serves 6

240 ml water
6 eggs
4 slices pancetta, chopped
80 ml grated Cheddar cheese
60 ml cream cheese
60 ml mayonnaise
1 teaspoon Creole seasonings
Sea salt and ground black pepper, to taste

1. Pour the water into the Ninja Foodi cooker and insert a steamer basket. Place the eggs in the basket. 2. Lock the lid. Set the cooking time for 5 minutes at Low Pressure. 3. When the timer beeps, perform a quick pressure release. Carefully remove the lid. 4. Allow the eggs to cool for 10 to 15 minutes. Peel the eggs and chop them, then transfer to a bowl. Add the remaining ingredients and stir to combine well. 5. Shape the mixture into balls with your hands. Serve chilled.

Bruschetta with Basil Pesto

Prep time: 10 minutes | Cook time: 5 to 11 minutes | Serves 4

8 slices French bread, ½ inch thick
2 tablespoons softened butter
240 ml shredded Mozzarella cheese
120 ml basil pesto
240 ml chopped grape tomatoes
2 spring onions, thinly sliced

1. Preheat the Ninja Foodi cooker to 175ºC. 2. Spread the bread with the butter and place butter-side up in the cook & crisp basket. Bake for 3 to 5 minutes, or until the bread is light golden brown. 3. Remove the bread from the basket and top each piece with some of the cheese. Return to the basket in 2 batches and bake for 1 to 3 minutes, or until the cheese melts. 4. Meanwhile, combine the pesto, tomatoes, and spring onions in a small bowl. 5. When the cheese has melted, remove the bread from the Ninja Foodi cooker and place on a serving plate. Top each slice with some of the pesto mixture and serve.

Egg Roll Pizza Sticks

Prep time: 10 minutes | Cook time: 5 minutes | Serves 4

Olive oil
8 pieces low-fat string cheese
8 egg roll wrappers or spring roll pastry
24 slices turkey pepperoni or salami
Marinara sauce, for dipping (optional)

1. Spray the cook & crisp basket lightly with olive oil. Fill a small bowl with water. 2. Place each egg roll wrapper diagonally on a work surface. It should look like a diamond. 3. Place 3 slices of turkey pepperoni in a vertical line down the centre of the wrapper. 4. Place 1 Mozzarella cheese stick on top of the turkey pepperoni. 5. Fold the top and bottom corners of the egg roll wrapper over the cheese stick. 6. Fold the left corner over the cheese stick and roll the cheese stick up to resemble a spring roll. Dip a finger in the water and seal the edge of the roll 7. Repeat with the rest of the pizza sticks. 8. Place them in the cook & crisp basket in a single layer, making sure to leave a little space between each one. Lightly spray the pizza sticks with oil. You may need to cook these in batches. 9. Air crisp at 190ºC until the pizza sticks are lightly browned and crispy, about 5 minutes. 10. These are best served hot while the cheese is melted. Accompany with a small bowl of marinara sauce, if desired.

Stuffed Fried Mushrooms

Prep time: 20 minutes | Cook time: 10 to 11 minutes | Serves 10

120 ml panko breadcrumbs
½ teaspoon freshly ground black pepper
½ teaspoon onion powder
½ teaspoon cayenne pepper
1 (227 g) package soft white cheese, at room temperature
20 cremini or button mushrooms, stemmed
1 to 2 tablespoons oil

1. In a medium bowl, whisk the breadcrumbs, black pepper, onion powder, and cayenne until blended. 2. Add the soft white cheese and mix until well blended. Fill each mushroom top with 1 teaspoon of the soft white cheese mixture 3. Preheat the Ninja Foodi cooker to 180ºC. Line the cook & crisp basket with a piece of parchment paper. 4. Place the mushrooms on the parchment and spritz with oil. 5. Cook for 5 minutes. Shake the basket and cook for 5 to 6 minutes more until the filling is firm and the mushrooms are soft.

Herbed Prawn

Prep time: 5 minutes | Cook time: 5 minutes | Serves 4

2 tablespoons olive oil
340 g prawn, peeled and deveined
1 teaspoon paprika
1 teaspoon garlic powder
1 teaspoon onion powder
1 teaspoon dried parsley flakes
½ teaspoon dried oregano
½ teaspoon dried thyme
½ teaspoon dried basil
½ teaspoon dried rosemary
¼ teaspoon red pepper flakes
Coarse sea salt and ground black pepper, to taste
240 ml chicken broth

1. Set your Ninja Foodi cooker to Sauté and heat the olive oil. 2. Add the prawn and sauté for 2 to 3 minutes. 3. Add the remaining ingredients to the Ninja Foodi cooker and stir to combine. 4. Secure the lid. Set the cooking time for 2 minutes at Low Pressure. 5. When the timer beeps, perform a quick pressure release. Carefully remove the lid. 6. Transfer the prawn to a plate and serve.

Sesame Mushrooms

Prep time: 2 minutes | Cook time: 10 minutes | Serves 6

3 tablespoons sesame oil
340 g small button mushrooms
1 teaspoon minced garlic
½ teaspoon smoked paprika
½ teaspoon cayenne pepper
Salt and ground black pepper, to taste

1. Set your Ninja Foodi cooker to Sauté and heat the sesame oil. 2. Add the mushrooms and sauté for 4 minutes until just tender, stirring occasionally. 3. Add the remaining ingredients to the Ninja Foodi cooker and stir to mix well. 4. Lock the lid. Set the cooking time for 5 minutes at High Pressure. 5. When the timer beeps, perform a quick pressure release. Carefully remove the lid. 6. Serve warm.

Cabbage and Broccoli Slaw

Prep time: 5 minutes | Cook time: 10 minutes | Serves 6

480 ml broccoli slaw
½ head cabbage, thinly sliced
60 ml chopped kale
4 tablespoons butter
1 teaspoon salt
¼ teaspoon pepper

1. Press the Sauté button and add all ingredients to Ninja Foodi cooker. Stir-fry for 7 to 10 minutes until cabbage softens. Serve warm.

Sweet Potato Fries with Mayonnaise

Prep time: 5 minutes | Cook time: 20 minutes | Serves 2 to 3

1 large sweet potato (about 450 g), scrubbed
1 teaspoon vegetable or rapeseed oil
Salt, to taste
Dipping Sauce:
60 ml light mayonnaise
½ teaspoon sriracha sauce
1 tablespoon spicy brown mustard
1 tablespoon sweet Thai chilli sauce

1. Preheat the Ninja Foodi cooker to 90°C. 2. On a flat work surface, cut the sweet potato into fry-shaped strips about ¼ inch wide and ¼ inch thick. You can use a mandoline to slice the sweet potato quickly and uniformly. 3. In a medium bowl, drizzle the sweet potato strips with the oil and toss well. 4. Transfer to the cook & crisp basket and air crisp for 10 minutes, shaking the basket twice during cooking. 5. Remove the cook & crisp basket and sprinkle with the salt and toss to coat. 6. Increase the Ninja Foodi cooker temperature to 205°C and air crisp for an additional 10 minutes, or until the fries are crispy and tender. Shake the basket a few times during cooking. 7. Meanwhile, whisk together all the ingredients for the sauce in a small bowl. 8. Remove the sweet potato fries from the basket to a plate and serve warm alongside the dipping sauce.

Red Wine Mushrooms

Prep time: 5 minutes | Cook time: 15 minutes | Serves 2

230 g sliced mushrooms
60 ml dry red wine
2 tablespoons beef broth
½ teaspoon garlic powder
¼ teaspoon Worcestershire sauce
Pinch of salt
Pinch of black pepper
¼ teaspoon xanthan gum

1. Add the mushrooms, wine, broth, garlic powder, Worcestershire sauce, salt, and pepper to the pot. 2. Close the lid and seal the vent. Cook on High Pressure for 13 minutes. Quick release the steam. Press Start/Stop. 3. Turn the pot to Sauté mode. Add the xanthan gum and whisk until the juices have thickened, 1 to 2 minutes.

Curried Broccoli Skewers

Prep time: 15 minutes | Cook time: 1 minute | Serves 2

240 ml broccoli florets
½ teaspoon curry paste
2 tablespoons coconut cream
240 ml water, for cooking

1. In the shallow bowl mix up curry paste and coconut cream. 2. Then sprinkle the broccoli florets with curry paste mixture and string on the skewers. 3. Pour water and insert the steamer rack in the Ninja Foodi cooker. 4. Place the broccoli skewers on the rack. Close and seal the lid. 5. Cook the meal on High Pressure for 1 minute. 6. Make a quick pressure release.

Crispy Breaded Beef Cubes

Prep time: 10 minutes | Cook time: 12 to 16 minutes | Serves 4

450 g sirloin tip, cut into 1-inch cubes
240 ml cheese pasta sauce
355 ml soft breadcrumbs
2 tablespoons olive oil
½ teaspoon dried marjoram

1. Preheat the Ninja Foodi cooker to 180°C. 2. In a medium bowl, toss the beef with the pasta sauce to coat. 3. In a shallow bowl, combine the breadcrumbs, oil, and marjoram, and mix well. Drop the beef cubes, one at a time, into the bread crumb mixture to coat thoroughly. 4. Air crisp the beef in two batches for 6 to 8 minutes, shaking the basket once during cooking time, until the beef is at least 63°C and the outside is crisp and brown. 5. Serve hot.

Asparagus with Creamy Dip

Prep time: 5 minutes | Cook time: 1 minute | Serves 6

240 ml water
680 g asparagus spears, trimmed
Dipping Sauce:
120 ml mayonnaise
120 ml sour cream
2 tablespoons chopped scallions
2 tablespoons fresh chervil
1 teaspoon minced garlic
Salt, to taste

1. Pour the water into the Ninja Foodi cooker and insert a steamer basket. Place the asparagus in the basket. 2. Lock the lid. Set the cooking time for 1 minute at High Pressure. 3. When the timer beeps, perform a quick pressure release. Carefully remove the lid. Transfer the asparagus to a plate. 4. Whisk together the remaining ingredients to make your dipping sauce. Serve the asparagus with the dipping sauce on the side.

String Bean Fries

Prep time: 15 minutes | Cook time: 5 to 6 minutes | Serves 4

227 g fresh green beans
2 eggs
4 teaspoons water
120 ml white flour
120 ml breadcrumbs
¼ teaspoon salt
¼ teaspoon ground black pepper
¼ teaspoon mustard powder (optional)
Oil for misting or cooking spray

1. Preheat the Ninja Foodi cooker to 180°C. 2. Trim stem ends from green beans, wash, and pat dry. 3. In a shallow dish, beat eggs and water together until well blended. 4. Place flour in a second shallow dish. 5. In a third shallow dish, stir together the breadcrumbs, salt, pepper, and dry mustard if using. 6. Dip each bean in egg mixture, flour, egg mixture again, then breadcrumbs. 7. When you finish coating all the green beans, open Ninja Foodi cooker and place them in basket. 8. Cook for 3 minutes. 9. Stop and mist green beans with oil or cooking spray. 10. Cook for 2 to 3 more minutes or until green beans are crispy and nicely browned.

Colby Cheese and Pepper Dip

Prep time: 5 minutes | Cook time: 5 minutes | Serves 8

1 tablespoon butter
2 red bell peppers, sliced
480 ml shredded Colby cheese
240 ml cream cheese, room temperature
240 ml chicken broth
2 garlic cloves, minced
1 teaspoon red Aleppo pepper flakes
1 teaspoon sumac
Salt and ground black pepper, to taste

1. Set your Ninja Foodi cooker to Sauté and melt the butter. 2. Add the bell peppers and sauté for about 2 minutes until just tender. 3. Add the remaining ingredients to the Ninja Foodi cooker and gently stir to incorporate. 4. Lock the lid. Set the cooking time for 3 minutes at High Pressure. 5. When the timer beeps, perform a quick pressure release. Carefully remove the lid. 6. Allow to cool for 5 minutes and serve warm.

Lemon-Cheese Cauliflower Bites

Prep time: 5 minutes | Cook time: 8 minutes | Serves 6

240 ml water
450 g cauliflower, broken into florets
Sea salt and ground black pepper, to taste
2 tablespoons extra-virgin olive oil
2 tablespoons lemon juice
240 ml grated Cheddar cheese

1. Pour the water into the Ninja Foodi cooker and insert a steamer basket. Place the cauliflower florets in the basket. 2. Lock the lid. Set the cooking time for 3 minutes at Low Pressure. 3. When the timer beeps, perform a quick pressure release. Carefully remove the lid. 4. Season the cauliflower with salt and pepper. Drizzle with olive oil and lemon juice. Sprinkle the grated cheese all over the cauliflower. 5. Press the Sauté button to heat the Ninja Foodi cooker. Allow to cook for about 5 minutes, or until the cheese melts. Serve warm.

Instant Popcorn

Prep time: 1 minutes | Cook time: 5 minutes | Serves 5

2 tablespoons coconut oil
120 ml popcorn kernels
60 ml margarine spread, melted,
optional
Sea salt to taste

1. Set the Ninja Foodi cooker to Sauté. 2. Melt the coconut oil in the inner pot, then add the popcorn kernels and stir. 3. Press Adjust to bring the temperature up to high. 4. When the corn starts popping, secure the lid on the Ninja Foodi cooker. 5. When you no longer hear popping, turn off the Ninja Foodi cooker, remove the lid, and pour the popcorn into a bowl. 6. Top with the optional melted margarine and season the popcorn with sea salt to your liking.

Brussels Sprouts with Aioli Sauce

Prep time: 5 minutes | Cook time: 7 minutes | Serves 4

1 tablespoon butter
120 ml chopped scallions
340 g Brussels sprouts
Aioli Sauce:
60 ml mayonnaise
1 tablespoon fresh lemon juice
1 garlic clove, minced
½ teaspoon Dijon mustard

1. Set your Ninja Foodi cooker to Sauté and melt the butter. 2. Add the scallions and sauté for 2 minutes until softened. Add the Brussels sprouts and cook for another 1 minute. 3. Lock the lid. Set the cooking time for 4 minutes at High Pressure. 4. Meanwhile, whisk together all the ingredients for the Aioli sauce in a small bowl until well incorporated. 5. When the timer beeps, perform a quick pressure release. Carefully remove the lid. 6. Serve the Brussels sprouts with the Aioli sauce on the side.

Oregano Sausage Balls

Prep time: 10 minutes | Cook time: 16 minutes | Serves 10

425 g ground pork sausage
1 teaspoon dried oregano
110 g Mozzarella, shredded
240 ml coconut flour
1 garlic clove, grated
1 teaspoon coconut oil, melted

1. In the bowl mix up ground pork sausages, dried oregano, shredded Mozzarella, coconut flour, and garlic clove. 2. When the mixture is homogenous, make the balls. 3. After this, pour coconut oil in the Ninja Foodi cooker. 4. Arrange the balls in the Ninja Foodi cooker and cook them on Sauté mode for 8 minutes from each side.

Onion Pakoras

Prep time: 30 minutes | Cook time: 10 minutes per batch | Serves 2

2 medium brown or white onions, sliced (475 ml)
120 ml chopped fresh coriander
2 tablespoons vegetable oil
1 tablespoon chickpea flour
1 tablespoon rice flour, or 2
tablespoons chickpea flour
1 teaspoon ground turmeric
1 teaspoon cumin seeds
1 teaspoon rock salt
½ teaspoon cayenne pepper
Vegetable oil spray

1. In a large bowl, combine the onions, coriander, oil, chickpea flour, rice flour, turmeric, cumin seeds, salt, and cayenne. Stir to combine. Cover and let stand for 30 minutes or up to overnight. (This allows the onions to release moisture, creating a batter.) Mix well before using. 2. Spray the cook & crisp basket generously with vegetable oil spray. Drop half of the batter in 6 heaping tablespoons into the basket. Set the Ninja Foodi cooker to 175°C for 8 minutes. Carefully turn the pakoras over and spray with oil spray. Set the Ninja Foodi cooker for 2 minutes, or until the batter is cooked through and crisp. 3. Repeat with remaining batter to make 6 more pakoras, checking at 6 minutes for doneness. Serve hot.

Cauliflower Fritters with Cheese

Prep time: 10 minutes | Cook time: 8 minutes | Serves 4

240 ml cauliflower, boiled
2 eggs, beaten
2 tablespoons almond flour
60 g Cheddar cheese, shredded
½ teaspoon garlic powder
1 tablespoon avocado oil

1. In a medium bowl, mash the cauliflower. Add the beaten eggs, flour, cheese, and garlic powder and stir until well incorporated. Make the fritters from the cauliflower mixture. 2. Set your Ninja Foodi cooker to Sauté and heat the avocado oil. 3. Add the fritters to the hot oil and cook each side for 3 minutes until golden brown. 4. Serve hot.

Shrimp Pirogues

Prep time: 15 minutes | Cook time: 4 to 5 minutes | Serves 8

340 g small, peeled, and deveined raw shrimp
85 g soft white cheese, room temperature
2 tablespoons natural yoghurt
1 teaspoon lemon juice
1 teaspoon dried dill weed, crushed
Salt, to taste
4 small hothouse cucumbers, each approximately 6 inches long

1. Pour 4 tablespoons water in bottom of Ninja Foodi cooker drawer. 2. Place shrimp in cook & crisp basket in single layer and air crisp at 200ºC for 4 to 5 minutes, just until done. Watch carefully because shrimp cooks quickly, and overcooking makes it tough. 3. Chop shrimp into small pieces, no larger than ½ inch. Refrigerate while mixing the remaining ingredients. 4. With a fork, mash and whip the soft white cheese until smooth. 5. Stir in the yoghurt and beat until smooth. Stir in lemon juice, dill weed, and chopped shrimp. 6. Taste for seasoning. If needed, add ¼ to ½ teaspoon salt to suit your taste. 7. Store in refrigerator until serving time. 8. When ready to serve, wash and dry cucumbers and split them lengthwise. Scoop out the seeds and turn cucumbers upside down on paper towels to drain for 10 minutes. 9. Just before filling, wipe centres of cucumbers dry. Spoon the shrimp mixture into the pirogues and cut in half crosswise. Serve immediately.

Parmesan French Fries

Prep time: 10 minutes | Cook time: 15 minutes per batch | Serves 2

2 to 3 large russet or Maris Piper potatoes, peeled and cut into ½-inch sticks
2 teaspoons vegetable or rapeseed oil
177 ml grated Parmesan cheese
½ teaspoon salt
Freshly ground black pepper, to taste
1 teaspoon fresh chopped parsley

1. Bring a large saucepan of salted water to a boil on the stovetop while you peel and cut the potatoes. Blanch the potatoes in the boiling salted water for 4 minutes while you Preheat the Ninja Foodi cooker to 205ºC. Strain the potatoes and rinse them with cold water. Dry them well with a clean kitchen towel. 2. Toss the dried potato sticks gently with the oil and place them in the cook & crisp basket. Air crisp for 25 minutes, shaking the basket a few times while the fries cook to help them brown evenly. 3. Combine the Parmesan cheese, salt and pepper. With 2 minutes left on the Ninja Foodi cooker cooking time, sprinkle the fries with the Parmesan cheese mixture. Toss the fries to coat them evenly with the cheese mixture and continue to air crisp for the final 2 minutes, until the cheese has melted and just starts to brown. Sprinkle the finished fries with chopped parsley, a little more grated Parmesan cheese if you like, and serve.

Cauliflower Cheese Balls

Prep time: 5 minutes | Cook time: 21 minutes | Serves 8

240 ml water
1 head cauliflower, broken into florets
240 ml shredded Asiago cheese
120 ml grated Parmesan cheese
2 eggs, beaten
2 tablespoons butter
2 tablespoons minced fresh chives
1 garlic clove, minced
½ teaspoon cayenne pepper
Coarse sea salt and white pepper, to taste

1. Pour the water into the Ninja Foodi cooker and insert a steamer basket. Place the cauliflower in the basket. 2. Lock the lid. Set the cooking time for 3 minutes at High Pressure. 3. When the timer beeps, perform a quick pressure release. Carefully remove the lid. 4. Transfer the cauliflower to a food processor, along with the remaining ingredients. Pulse until everything is well combined. 5. Form the mixture into bite-sized balls and place them on a baking sheet. 6. Bake in the preheated oven at 205ºC for 18 minutes until golden brown. Flip the balls halfway through the cooking time. Cool for 5 minutes before serving.

Broccoli with Garlic-Herb Cheese Sauce

Prep time: 5 minutes | Cook time: 3 minutes | Serves 4

120 ml water
450 g broccoli (frozen or fresh)
120 ml double cream
1 tablespoon butter
120 ml shredded Cheddar cheese
3 tablespoons garlic and herb cheese spread
Pinch of salt
Pinch of black pepper

1. Add the water to the pot and place the reversible rack inside. 2. Put the steamer basket on top of the reversible rack. Place the broccoli in the basket. 3. Close the lid and seal the vent. Cook on Low Pressure for 1 minute. Quick release the steam. Press Start/Stop. 4. Carefully remove the steamer basket from the pot and drain the water. If you steamed a full bunch of broccoli, pull the florets off the stem. (Chop the stem into bite-size pieces, it's surprisingly creamy.) 5. Turn the pot to Sauté mode. Add the cream and butter. Stir continuously while the butter melts and the cream warms up. 6. When the cream begins to bubble on the edges, add the Cheddar cheese, cheese spread, salt, and pepper. Whisk continuously until the cheeses are melted and a sauce consistency is reached, 1 to 2 minutes. 7. Top one-fourth of the broccoli with 2 tablespoons cheese sauce.

Crispy Cajun Dill Pickle Chips

Prep time: 5 minutes | Cook time: 10 minutes | Makes 16 slices

60 ml plain flour
120 ml panko breadcrumbs
1 large egg, beaten
2 teaspoons Cajun seasoning
2 large dill pickles, sliced into 8 rounds each
Cooking spray

1. Preheat the Ninja Foodi cooker to 200ºC. 2. Place the plain flour, panko breadcrumbs, and egg into 3 separate shallow bowls, then stir the Cajun seasoning into the flour. 3. Dredge each pickle chip in the flour mixture, then the egg, and finally the breadcrumbs. Shake off any excess, then place each coated pickle chip on a plate. 4. Spritz the cook & crisp basket with cooking spray, then place 8 pickle chips in the basket and air crisp for 5 minutes, or until crispy and golden brown. Repeat this process with the remaining pickle chips. 5. Remove the chips and allow to slightly cool on a wire rack before serving.

Goat Cheese and Garlic Crostini

Prep time: 3 minutes | Cook time: 5 minutes | Serves 4

1 wholemeal baguette
60 ml olive oil
2 garlic cloves, minced
113 g goat cheese
2 tablespoons fresh basil, minced

1. Preheat the Ninja Foodi cooker to 190ºC. 2. Cut the baguette into ½-inch-thick slices. 3. In a small bowl, mix together the olive oil and garlic, then brush it over one side of each slice of bread. 4. Place the olive-oil-coated bread in a single layer in the cook & crisp basket and bake for 5 minutes. 5. Meanwhile, in a small bowl, mix together the goat cheese and basil. 6. Remove the toast from the Ninja Foodi cooker, then spread a thin layer of the goat cheese mixture over the top of each piece and serve.

Crunchy Basil White Beans

Prep time: 2 minutes | Cook time: 19 minutes | Serves 2

1 (425 g) can cooked white beans
2 tablespoons olive oil
1 teaspoon fresh sage, chopped
¼ teaspoon garlic powder
¼ teaspoon salt, divided
1 teaspoon chopped fresh basil

1. Preheat the Ninja Foodi cooker to 190ºC. 2. In a medium bowl, mix together the beans, olive oil, sage, garlic, ⅛ teaspoon salt, and basil. 3. Pour the white beans into the Ninja Foodi cooker and spread them out in a single layer. 4. Bake for 10 minutes. Stir and continue cooking for an additional 5 to 9 minutes, or until they reach your preferred level of crispiness. 5. Toss with the remaining ⅛ teaspoon salt before serving.

Vegetable Pot Stickers

Prep time: 12 minutes | Cook time: 11 to 18 minutes | Makes 12 pot stickers

240 ml shredded red cabbage
60 ml chopped button mushrooms
60 ml grated carrot
2 tablespoons minced onion
2 garlic cloves, minced
2 teaspoons grated fresh ginger
12 gyoza/pot sticker wrappers
2½ teaspoons olive oil, divided

1. In a baking pan, combine the red cabbage, mushrooms, carrot, onion, garlic, and ginger. Add 1 tablespoon of water. Place in the Ninja Foodi cooker and air crisp at 190ºC for 3 to 6 minutes, until the vegetables are crisp-tender. Drain and set aside. 2. Working one at a time, place the pot sticker wrappers on a work surface. Top each wrapper with a scant 1 tablespoon of the filling. Fold half of the wrapper over the other half to form a half circle. Dab one edge with water and press both edges together. 3. To another pan, add 1¼ teaspoons of olive oil. Put half of the pot stickers, seam-side up, in the pan. Air crisp for 5 minutes, or until the bottoms are light golden brown. Add 1 tablespoon of water and return the pan to the Ninja Foodi cooker. 4. Air crisp for 4 to 6 minutes more, or until hot. Repeat with the remaining pot stickers, remaining 1¼ teaspoons of oil, and another tablespoon of water. Serve immediately.

Greek Potato Skins with Olives and Feta

Prep time: 5 minutes | Cook time: 45 minutes | Serves 4

2 russet or Maris Piper potatoes
3 tablespoons olive oil, divided, plus more for drizzling (optional)
1 teaspoon rock salt, divided
¼ teaspoon black pepper
2 tablespoons fresh coriander, chopped, plus more for serving
60 ml Kalamata olives, diced
60 ml crumbled feta
Chopped fresh parsley, for garnish (optional)

1. Preheat the Ninja Foodi cooker to 190ºC. 2. Using a fork, poke 2 to 3 holes in the potatoes, then coat each with about ½ tablespoon olive oil and ½ teaspoon salt. 3. Place the potatoes into the cook & crisp basket and bake for 30 minutes. 4. Remove the potatoes from the Ninja Foodi cooker, and slice in half. Using a spoon, scoop out the flesh of the potatoes, leaving a ½-inch layer of potato inside the skins, and set the skins aside. 5. In a medium bowl, combine the scooped potato middles with the remaining 2 tablespoons of olive oil, ½ teaspoon of salt, black pepper, and coriander. Mix until well combined. 6. Divide the potato filling into the now-empty potato skins, spreading it evenly over them. Top each potato with a tablespoon each of the olives and feta. 7. Place the loaded potato skins back into the Ninja Foodi cooker and bake for 15 minutes. 8. Serve with additional chopped coriander or parsley and a drizzle of olive oil, if desired.

Chapter 7 Vegetables and Sides

Seeds

Prep time: 10 minutes | Cook time: 2 minutes | Serves 4

450 g Brussels sprouts
2 tablespoons avocado oil, divided
240 ml vegetable broth or chicken bone broth
1 tablespoon minced garlic
½ teaspoon rock salt
Freshly ground black pepper, to taste
½ medium lemon
½ tablespoon poppy seeds

1. Trim the Brussels sprouts by cutting off the stem ends and removing any loose outer leaves. Cut each in half lengthwise (through the stem). 2. Set the electric pressure cooker to the Sauté. When the pot is hot, pour in 1 tablespoon of the avocado oil. 3. Add half of the Brussels sprouts to the pot, cut-side down, and let them brown for 3 to 5 minutes without disturbing. Transfer to a bowl and add the remaining tablespoon of avocado oil and the remaining Brussels sprouts to the pot. Hit Start/Stop and return all of the Brussels sprouts to the pot. 4. Add the broth, garlic, salt, and a few grinds of pepper. Stir to distribute the seasonings. 5. Close and lock the lid of the pressure cooker. Set the valve to sealing. 6. Cook on high pressure for 2 minutes. 7. While the Brussels sprouts are cooking, zest the lemon, then cut it into quarters. 8. When the cooking is complete, hit Start/Stop and quick release the pressure. 9. Once the pin drops, unlock and remove the lid. 10. Using a slotted spoon, transfer the Brussels sprouts to a serving bowl. Toss with the lemon zest, a squeeze of lemon juice, and the poppy seeds. Serve immediately.

Broccoli and Mushroom Bake

Prep time: 10 minutes | Cook time: 3 minutes | Serves 4

120 ml sunflower seeds, soaked overnight
2 tablespoons sesame seeds
240 ml water
240 ml unsweetened almond milk
¼ teaspoon grated nutmeg
½ teaspoon sea salt
1 tablespoon nutritional yeast
2 tablespoons rice vinegar
450 g broccoli, broken into florets
120 ml chopped spring onions
280 g white fresh mushrooms, sliced
Sea salt and white pepper, to taste
1 tablespoon cayenne pepper
¼ teaspoon dried dill
¼ teaspoon ground bay leaf

1. Add sunflower seeds, sesame seeds, water, milk, nutmeg, ½ teaspoon of sea salt, nutritional yeast, and vinegar to your blender. 2. Blend until smooth and uniform. 3. Spritz a casserole dish with a nonstick cooking spray. Add broccoli, spring onions and mushrooms. 4. Sprinkle with salt, white pepper, cayenne pepper, dill, and ground bay leaf. Pour the prepared vegan béchamel over your casserole. 5. Add 240 ml of water and a metal rack to your Ninja Foodi cooker. Place the dish on the rack. 6. Secure the lid. Choose High Pressure; cook for 3 minutes. Once cooking is complete, use a quick pressure release; carefully remove the lid. 7. Allow the dish to stand for 5 to 10 minutes before slicing and serving. Bon appétit!

Spiced Honey-Walnut Carrots

Prep time: 5 minutes | Cook time: 12 minutes | Serves 6

450 g baby carrots
2 tablespoons olive oil
80 g raw honey
¼ teaspoon ground cinnamon
25 g black walnuts, chopped

1. Preheat the Ninja Foodi cooker to 180°C. 2. In a large bowl, toss the baby carrots with olive oil, honey, and cinnamon until well coated. 3. Pour into the Ninja Foodi cooker and roast for 6 minutes. Shake the basket, sprinkle the walnuts on top, and roast for 6 minutes more. 4. Remove the carrots from the Ninja Foodi cooker and serve.

Braised Fennel with radicchio, Pear, and Pecorino

Prep time: 20 minutes | Cook time: 12 minutes | Serves 4

6 tablespoons extra-virgin olive oil, divided
2 fennel bulbs (340 g each), 2 tablespoons fronds chopped, stalks discarded, bulbs halved, each half cut into 1-inch-thick wedges
¾ teaspoon table salt, divided
½ teaspoon grated lemon zest plus 4 teaspoons juice
142 g baby rocket
1 small head radicchio (170 g), shredded
1 Bosc or Bartlett pear, quartered, cored, and sliced thin
60 ml whole almonds, toasted and chopped
Shaved Pecorino Romano cheese

1. Using highest sauté function, heat 2 tablespoons oil in Ninja Foodi cooker for 5 minutes (or until just smoking). Brown half of fennel, about 3 minutes per side; transfer to plate. Repeat with 1 tablespoon oil and remaining fennel; do not remove from pot. 2. Return first batch of fennel to pot along with 120 ml water and ½ teaspoon salt. Lock lid in place and close pressure release valve. Select high pressure and cook for 2 minutes. Turn off Ninja Foodi cooker and quick-release pressure. Carefully remove lid, allowing steam to escape away from you. Using slotted spoon, transfer fennel to plate; discard cooking liquid. 3. Whisk remaining 3 tablespoons oil, lemon zest and juice, and remaining ¼ teaspoon salt together in large bowl. Add rocket, radicchio, and pear and toss to coat. Transfer rocket mixture to serving dish and arrange fennel wedges on top. Sprinkle with almonds, fennel fronds, and Pecorino. Serve.

Satarash with Eggs

Prep time: 10 minutes | Cook time: 5 minutes | Serves 4

2 tablespoons olive oil
1 white onion, chopped
2 cloves garlic
2 ripe tomatoes, puréed
1 green bell pepper, deseeded and sliced
1 red bell pepper, deseeded and sliced
1 teaspoon paprika
½ teaspoon dried oregano
½ teaspoon turmeric
Rock salt and ground black pepper, to taste
240 ml water
4 large eggs, lightly whisked

1. Press the Sauté button on the Ninja Foodi cooker and heat the olive oil. Add the onion and garlic to the pot and sauté for 2 minutes, or until fragrant. Stir in the remaining ingredients, except for the eggs. 2. Lock the lid. Set the cooking time for 3 minutes on High Pressure. When the timer goes off, perform a quick pressure release. Carefully open the lid. 3. Fold in the eggs and stir to combine. Lock the lid and let it sit in the residual heat for 5 minutes. Serve warm.

Asparagus and Mushroom Soup

Prep time: 10 minutes | Cook time: 7 minutes | Serves 4

2 tablespoons coconut oil
120 ml chopped shallots
2 cloves garlic, minced
450 g asparagus, washed, trimmed, and chopped
110 g button mushrooms, sliced
1 L vegetable broth
2 tablespoons balsamic vinegar
Himalayan salt, to taste
¼ teaspoon ground black pepper
¼ teaspoon paprika
60 ml vegan sour cream

1. Press the Sauté button to heat up your Ninja Foodi cooker. Heat the oil and cook the shallots and garlic for 2 to 3 minutes. 2. Add the remaining ingredients, except for sour cream, to the Ninja Foodi cooker. 3. Secure the lid. Choose High Pressure; cook for 4 minutes. Once cooking is complete, use a quick pressure release; carefully remove the lid. 4. Spoon into four soup bowls; add a dollop of sour cream to each serving and serve immediately. Bon appétit!

Thyme Cabbage

Prep time: 10 minutes | Cook time: 5 minutes | Serves 4

450 g white cabbage
2 tablespoons butter
1 teaspoon dried thyme
½ teaspoon salt
240 ml water

1. Cut the white cabbage on medium size petals and sprinkle with the butter, dried thyme and salt. Place the cabbage petals in the Ninja Foodi cooker pan. 2. Pour the water and insert the reversible rack in the Ninja Foodi cooker. Put the pan on the reversible rack. 3. Set the lid in place. Set the cooking time for 5 minutes on High Pressure. When the timer goes off, do a quick pressure release. Carefully open the lid. 4. Serve immediately.

Mashed Sweet Potato Tots

Prep time: 10 minutes | Cook time: 12 to 13 minutes per batch | Makes 18 to 24 tots

210 g cooked mashed sweet potatoes
1 egg white, beaten
⅛ teaspoon ground cinnamon
1 dash nutmeg
2 tablespoons chopped pecans
1½ teaspoons honey
Salt, to taste
50 g panko bread crumbs
Oil for misting or cooking spray

1. Preheat the Ninja Foodi cooker to 200ºC. 2. In a large bowl, mix together the potatoes, egg white, cinnamon, nutmeg, pecans, honey, and salt to taste. 3. Place panko crumbs on a sheet of wax paper. 4. For each tot, use about 2 teaspoons of sweet potato mixture. To shape, drop the measure of potato mixture onto panko crumbs and push crumbs up and around potatoes to coat edges. Then turn tot over to coat other side with crumbs. 5. Mist tots with oil or cooking spray and place in cook & crisp basket in single layer. 6. Air crisp at 200ºC for 12 to 13 minutes, until browned and crispy. 7. Repeat steps 5 and 6 to cook remaining tots.

Turnip Fries

Prep time: 10 minutes | Cook time: 20 to 30 minutes | Serves 4

900 g turnip, peeled and cut into ¼ to ½-inch fries
2 tablespoons olive oil
Salt and freshly ground black pepper, to taste

1. Preheat the Ninja Foodi cooker to 200ºC. 2. In a large bowl, combine the turnip and olive oil. Season to taste with salt and black pepper. Toss gently until thoroughly coated. 3. Working in batches if necessary, spread the turnip in a single layer in the cook & crisp basket. Pausing halfway through the cooking time to shake the basket, air crisp for 20 to 30 minutes until the fries are lightly browned and crunchy.

Fig, Chickpea, and Rocket Salad

Prep time: 15 minutes | Cook time: 20 minutes | Serves 4

8 fresh figs, halved
250 g cooked chickpeas
1 teaspoon crushed roasted cumin seeds
4 tablespoons balsamic vinegar
2 tablespoons extra-virgin olive oil, plus more for greasing
Salt and ground black pepper, to taste
40 g rocket, washed and dried

1. Preheat the Ninja Foodi cooker to 190ºC. 2. Cover the cook & crisp basket with aluminum foil and grease lightly with oil. Put the figs in the cook & crisp basket and air crisp for 10 minutes. 3. In a bowl, combine the chickpeas and cumin seeds. 4. Remove the air fried figs from the Ninja Foodi cooker and replace with the chickpeas. Air crisp for 10 minutes. Leave to cool. 5. In the meantime, prepare the dressing. Mix the balsamic vinegar, olive oil, salt and pepper. 6. In a salad bowl, combine the rocket with the cooled figs and chickpeas. 7. Toss with the sauce and serve.

Falafel and Lettuce Salad

Prep time: 10 minutes | Cook time: 6 to 8 minutes | Serves 4

240 ml shredded cauliflower
80 ml coconut flour
1 teaspoon grated lemon zest
1 egg, beaten
2 tablespoons coconut oil
480 ml chopped lettuce
1 cucumber, chopped
1 tablespoon olive oil
1 teaspoon lemon juice
½ teaspoon cayenne pepper

1. In a bowl, combine the cauliflower, coconut flour, grated lemon zest and egg. Form the mixture into small balls. 2. Set the Ninja Foodi cooker to the Sauté mode and melt the coconut oil. Place the balls in the pot in a single layer. Cook for 3 to 4 minutes per side, or until they are golden brown. 3. In a separate bowl, stir together the remaining ingredients. 4. Place the cooked balls on top and serve.

Roasted Salsa

Prep time: 15 minutes | Cook time: 30 minutes | Makes 500 g

2 large San Marzano tomatoes, cored and cut into large chunks
½ medium white onion, peeled and large-diced
½ medium jalapeño, seeded and large-diced
2 cloves garlic, peeled and diced
½ teaspoon salt
1 tablespoon coconut oil
65 ml fresh lime juice

1. Place tomatoes, onion, and jalapeño into an ungreased round nonstick baking dish. Add garlic, then sprinkle with salt and drizzle with coconut oil. 2. Place dish into cook & crisp basket. Adjust the temperature to 150°C and bake for 30 minutes. Vegetables will be dark brown around the edges and tender when done. 3. Pour mixture into a food processor or blender. Add lime juice. Process on low speed 30 seconds until only a few chunks remain. 4. Transfer salsa to a sealable container and refrigerate at least 1 hour. Serve chilled.

Wild Rice Salad with Cranberries and Almonds

Prep time: 10 minutes | Cook time: 25 minutes | Serves 18

For the rice
480 ml wild rice blend, rinsed
1 teaspoon rock salt
600 ml Vegetable Broth or Chicken Bone Broth
For the dressing
60 ml extra-virgin olive oil
60 ml white wine vinegar
1½ teaspoons grated orange zest
Juice of 1 medium orange (about 60 ml)
1 teaspoon honey or pure maple syrup
For the salad
180 ml unsweetened dried cranberries
120 ml sliced almonds, toasted
Freshly ground black pepper

Make the Rice 1. In the electric pressure cooker, combine the rice, salt, and broth. 2. Close and lock the lid. Set the valve to sealing. 3. Cook on high pressure for 25 minutes. 4. When the cooking is complete, hit Start/Stop and allow the pressure to release naturally for 15 minutes, then quick release any remaining pressure. 5. Once the pin drops, unlock and remove the lid. 6. Let the rice cool briefly, then fluff it with a fork. Make the Dressing 7. While the rice cooks, make the dressing: In a small jar with a screw-top lid, combine the olive oil, vinegar, zest, juice, and honey. (If you don't have a jar, whisk the ingredients together in a small bowl.) Shake to combine. Make the Salad 8. In a large bowl, combine the rice, cranberries, and almonds. 9. Add the dressing and season with pepper. 10. Serve warm or refrigerate.

Courgette Balls

Prep time: 5 minutes | Cook time: 10 minutes | Serves 4

4 courgettes
1 egg
45 g grated Parmesan cheese
1 tablespoon Italian herbs
75 g grated coconut

1. Thinly grate the courgettes and dry with a cheesecloth, ensuring to remove all the moisture. 2. In a bowl, combine the courgettes with the egg, Parmesan, Italian herbs, and grated coconut, mixing well to incorporate everything. Using the hands, mold the mixture into balls. 3. Preheat the Ninja Foodi cooker to 200°C. 4. Lay the courgette balls in the cook & crisp basket and air crisp for 10 minutes. 5. Serve hot.

Buttery Mushrooms

Prep time: 10 minutes | Cook time: 10 minutes | Serves 4

230 g shitake mushrooms, halved
2 tablespoons salted butter,
melted
¼ teaspoon salt
¼ teaspoon ground black pepper

1. In a medium bowl, toss mushrooms with butter, then sprinkle with salt and pepper. Place into ungreased cook & crisp basket. Adjust the temperature to 200°C and air crisp for 10 minutes, shaking the basket halfway through cooking. Mushrooms will be tender when done. Serve warm.

Sweet and Crispy Roasted Pearl Onions

Prep time: 5 minutes | Cook time: 18 minutes | Serves 3

1 (410 g) package frozen pearl onions (do not thaw)
2 tablespoons extra-virgin olive oil
2 tablespoons balsamic vinegar
2 teaspoons finely chopped fresh rosemary
½ teaspoon coarse sea salt
¼ teaspoon black pepper

1. In a medium bowl, combine the onions, olive oil, vinegar, rosemary, salt, and pepper until well coated. 2. Transfer the onions to the cook & crisp basket. Set the Ninja Foodi cooker to 200°C for 18 minutes, or until the onions are tender and lightly charred, stirring once or twice during the cooking time.

Gobi Masala

Prep time: 5 minutes | Cook time: 4 to 5 minutes | Serves 4 to 6

1 tablespoon olive oil	1 tablespoon ground coriander
1 teaspoon cumin seeds	1 teaspoon ground cumin
1 white onion, diced	½ teaspoon garam masala
1 garlic clove, minced	½ teaspoon salt
1 head cauliflower, chopped	240 ml water

1. Set the Ninja Foodi cooker to the Sauté mode and heat the olive oil. Add the cumin seeds to the pot and sauté for 30 seconds, stirring constantly. Add the onion and sauté for 2 to 3 minutes, stirring constantly. Add the garlic and sauté for 30 seconds, stirring frequently. 2. Stir in the remaining ingredients. 3. Lock the lid. Set the cooking time for 1 minute on High Pressure. When the timer goes off, perform a quick pressure release. Carefully open the lid. 4. Serve immediately.

Mediterranean Courgette Boats

Prep time: 5 minutes | Cook time: 10 minutes | Serves 4

1 large courgette, ends removed, halved lengthwise	65 g feta cheese
6 grape tomatoes, quartered	1 tablespoon balsamic vinegar
¼ teaspoon salt	1 tablespoon olive oil

1. Use a spoon to scoop out 2 tablespoons from centre of each courgette half, making just enough space to fill with tomatoes and feta. 2. Place tomatoes evenly in centres of courgette halves and sprinkle with salt. Place into ungreased cook & crisp basket. Adjust the temperature to 180°C and roast for 10 minutes. When done, courgette will be tender. 3. Transfer boats to a serving tray and sprinkle with feta, then drizzle with vinegar and olive oil. Serve warm.

Lemon-Garlic Mushrooms

Prep time: 10 minutes | Cook time: 10 to 15 minutes | Serves 6

340 g sliced mushrooms	1 teaspoon freshly squeezed lemon juice
1 tablespoon avocado oil	½ teaspoon red pepper flakes
Sea salt and freshly ground black pepper, to taste	2 tablespoons chopped fresh parsley
3 tablespoons unsalted butter	
1 teaspoon minced garlic	

1. Place the mushrooms in a medium bowl and toss with the oil. Season to taste with salt and pepper. 2. Place the mushrooms in a single layer in the cook & crisp basket. Set your Ninja Foodi cooker to 190°C and roast for 10 to 15 minutes, until the mushrooms are tender. 3. While the mushrooms cook, melt the butter in a small pot or skillet over medium-low heat. Stir in the garlic and cook for 30 seconds. Remove the pot from the heat and stir in the lemon juice and red pepper flakes. 4. Toss the mushrooms with the lemon-garlic butter and garnish with the parsley before serving.

Cauliflower Rice Curry

Prep time: 5 minutes | Cook time: 2 minutes | Serves 4

1 (255 g) head cauliflower, chopped	½ teaspoon ground turmeric
½ teaspoon garlic powder	½ teaspoon curry powder
½ teaspoon freshly ground black pepper	½ teaspoon rock salt
	½ teaspoon fresh paprika
	¼ small onion, thinly sliced

1. Pour 240 ml of filtered water into the inner pot of the Ninja Foodi cooker, then insert the reversible rack. In a well-greased, Ninja Foodi cooker-friendly dish, add the cauliflower. Sprinkle the garlic powder, black pepper, turmeric, curry powder, salt, paprika, and onion over top. 2. Place the dish onto the reversible rack, and cover loosely with aluminium foil. Close the lid, set the Ninja Foodi cooker to 2 minutes on High Pressure, and let cook. 3. Once cooked, perform a quick release. 4. Open the Ninja Foodi cooker, and remove the dish. Serve, and enjoy!

Rosemary-Roasted Red Potatoes

Prep time: 5 minutes | Cook time: 20 minutes | Serves 6

450 g red potatoes, quartered	¼ teaspoon black pepper
65 ml olive oil	1 garlic clove, minced
½ teaspoon coarse sea salt	4 rosemary sprigs

1. Preheat the Ninja Foodi cooker to 180°C. 2. In a large bowl, toss the potatoes with the olive oil, salt, pepper, and garlic until well coated. 3. Pour the potatoes into the cook & crisp basket and top with the sprigs of rosemary. 4. Roast for 10 minutes, then stir or toss the potatoes and roast for 10 minutes more. 5. Remove the rosemary sprigs and serve the potatoes. Season with additional salt and pepper, if needed.

Spicy Roasted Bok Choy

Prep time: 10 minutes | Cook time: 7 to 10 minutes | Serves 4

2 tablespoons olive oil	2 cloves garlic, minced
2 tablespoons reduced-sodium coconut aminos	1 head (about 450 g) bok choy, sliced lengthwise into quarters
2 teaspoons sesame oil	2 teaspoons black sesame seeds
2 teaspoons chili-garlic sauce	

1. Preheat the Ninja Foodi cooker to 200°C. 2. In a large bowl, combine the olive oil, coconut aminos, sesame oil, chili-garlic sauce, and garlic. Add the bok choy and toss, massaging the leaves with your hands if necessary, until thoroughly coated. 3. Arrange the bok choy in the basket of the Ninja Foodi cooker. Pausing about halfway through the cooking time to shake the basket, air crisp for 7 to 10 minutes until the bok choy is tender and the tips of the leaves begin to crisp. 4. Remove from the basket and let cool for a few minutes before coarsely chopping. Serve sprinkled with the sesame seeds.

Lemony Broccoli

Prep time: 10 minutes | Cook time: 9 to 14 minutes per batch | Serves 4

1 large head broccoli, rinsed and patted dry	1 tablespoon freshly squeezed lemon juice
2 teaspoons extra-virgin olive oil	Olive oil spray

1. Cut off the broccoli florets and separate them. You can use the stems, too; peel the stems and cut them into 1-inch chunks. 2. Insert the crisper plate into the basket and the basket into the unit. Preheat the unit by selecting AIR ROAST, setting the temperature to 200ºC, and setting the time to 3 minutes. Select START/STOP to begin. 3. In a large bowl, toss together the broccoli, olive oil, and lemon juice until coated. 4. Once the unit is preheated, spray the crisper plate with olive oil. Working in batches, place half the broccoli into the basket. 5. Select AIR ROAST, set the temperature to 200ºC, and set the time to 14 minutes. Select START/STOP to begin. 6. After 5 minutes, remove the basket and shake the broccoli. Reinsert the basket to resume cooking. Check the broccoli after 5 minutes. If it is crisp-tender and slightly brown around the edges, it is done. If not, resume cooking. 7. When the cooking is complete, transfer the broccoli to a serving bowl. Repeat steps 5 and 6 with the remaining broccoli. Serve immediately.

Ninja Foodi cooker Courgette Sticks

Prep time: 5 minutes | Cook time: 8 minutes | Serves 2

2 courgettes, trimmed and cut into sticks	½ teaspoon white pepper
2 teaspoons olive oil	½ teaspoon salt
	240 ml water

1. Place the courgette sticks in the Ninja Foodi cooker pan and sprinkle with the olive oil, white pepper and salt. 2. Pour the water and put the reversible rack in the pot. Place the pan on the reversible rack. 3. Lock the lid. Set the cooking time for 8 minutes at High Pressure. Once the timer goes off, use a quick pressure release. Carefully open the lid. 4. Remove the courgettes from the pot and serve.

Garlic Cauliflower with Tahini

Prep time: 10 minutes | Cook time: 20 minutes | Serves 4

Cauliflower:	½ teaspoon coarse sea salt
500 g cauliflower florets (about 1 large head)	Sauce:
6 garlic cloves, smashed and cut into thirds	2 tablespoons tahini (sesame paste)
3 tablespoons vegetable oil	2 tablespoons hot water
½ teaspoon ground cumin	1 tablespoon fresh lemon juice
½ teaspoon ground coriander	1 teaspoon minced garlic
	½ teaspoon coarse sea salt

1. For the cauliflower: In a large bowl, combine the cauliflower florets and garlic. Drizzle with the vegetable oil. Sprinkle with the cumin, coriander, and salt. Toss until well coated. 2. Place the cauliflower in the cook & crisp basket. Set the Ninja Foodi cooker to 200ºC for 20 minutes, turning the cauliflower halfway through the cooking time. 3. Meanwhile, for the sauce: In a small bowl, combine the tahini, water, lemon juice, garlic, and salt. (The sauce will appear curdled at first, but keep stirring until you have a thick, creamy, smooth mixture.) 4. Transfer the cauliflower to a large serving bowl. Pour the sauce over and toss gently to coat. Serve immediately.

Cauliflower Steaks Gratin

Prep time: 10 minutes | Cook time: 13 minutes | Serves 2

1 head cauliflower	thyme leaves
1 tablespoon olive oil	3 tablespoons grated Parmigiano-Reggiano cheese
Salt and freshly ground black pepper, to taste	2 tablespoons panko bread crumbs
½ teaspoon chopped fresh	

1. Preheat the Ninja Foodi cooker to 190ºC. 2. Cut two steaks out of the centre of the cauliflower. To do this, cut the cauliflower in half and then cut one slice about 1-inch thick off each half. The rest of the cauliflower will fall apart into florets, which you can roast on their own or save for another meal. 3. Brush both sides of the cauliflower steaks with olive oil and season with salt, freshly ground black pepper and fresh thyme. Place the cauliflower steaks into the cook & crisp basket and air crisp for 6 minutes. Turn the steaks over and air crisp for another 4 minutes. Combine the Parmesan cheese and panko bread crumbs and sprinkle the mixture over the tops of both steaks and air crisp for another 3 minutes until the cheese has melted and the bread crumbs have browned. Serve this with some sautéed bitter greens and air-fried blistered tomatoes.

Lemony Brussels Sprouts with Poppy Lemon Cabbage and Tempeh

Prep time: 8 minutes | Cook time: 10 minutes | Serves 3

2 tablespoons sesame oil	2 garlic cloves, minced
120 ml chopped scallions	1 tablespoon lemon juice
480 ml shredded cabbage	Salt and pepper, to taste
170 g tempeh, cubed	¼ teaspoon paprika
1 tablespoon coconut aminos	60 ml roughly chopped fresh coriander
240 ml vegetable stock	

1. Press the Sauté button to heat up your Ninja Foodi cooker. Heat the sesame oil and sauté the scallions until tender and fragrant. 2. Then, add the cabbage, tempeh, coconut aminos, vegetable stock, garlic, lemon juice, salt, pepper, and paprika. 3. Secure the lid. Choose Low Pressure; cook for 3 minutes. Once cooking is complete, use a quick pressure release; carefully remove the lid. 4. Press the Sauté button to thicken the sauce if desired. Divide between serving bowls, garnish with fresh coriander, and serve warm. Bon appétit!

Spicy Cauliflower Head

Prep time: 5 minutes | Cook time: 7 minutes | Serves 4

370 g cauliflower head
240 ml water
1 tablespoon coconut cream
1 tablespoon avocado oil
1 teaspoon ground paprika
1 teaspoon ground turmeric
½ teaspoon ground cumin
½ teaspoon salt

1. Pour the water in the Ninja Foodi cooker and insert the reversible rack. 2. In the mixing bowl, stir together the coconut cream, avocado oil, paprika, turmeric, cumin and salt. 3. Carefully brush the cauliflower head with the coconut cream mixture. Sprinkle the remaining coconut cream mixture over the cauliflower. 4. Transfer the cauliflower head onto the reversible rack. 5. Lock the lid. Set the cooking time for 7 minutes at High Pressure. When the timer goes off, use a natural pressure release for 10 minutes, then release any remaining pressure. Carefully open the lid. 6. Serve immediately.

Savoury and Rich Creamed Kale

Prep time: 10 minutes | Cook time: 5 minutes | Serves 4

2 tablespoons extra-virgin olive oil
2 cloves garlic, crushed
1 small onion, chopped
340 g kale, finely chopped
120 ml chicken broth
1 teaspoon Herbes de Provence
110 g cream cheese
120 ml full-fat double cream
1 teaspoon dried tarragon

1. Press the Sauté button on the Ninja Foodi cooker and heat the olive oil. Add the garlic and onion to the pot and sauté for 2 minutes, or until the onion is soft. Stir in the kale, chicken broth and Herbes de Provence. 2. Lock the lid. Set the cooking time for 3 minutes at High Pressure. When the timer goes off, perform a quick pressure release. Carefully open the lid. 3. Stir in the cream cheese, double cream and tarragon. Stir well to thicken the dish. Serve immediately.

Potatoes with Parsley

Prep time: 10 minutes | Cook time: 5 minutes | Serves 4

3 tablespoons margarine, divided
900 g medium red potatoes (about 60 g each), halved lengthwise
1 clove garlic, minced
½ teaspoon salt
120 ml chicken broth
2 tablespoons chopped fresh parsley

1. Place 1 tablespoon margarine in the inner pot of the Ninja Foodi cooker and select Sauté. 2. After margarine is melted, add potatoes, garlic, and salt, stirring well. 3. Sauté 4 minutes, stirring frequently. 4. Add chicken broth and stir well. 5. Seal lid, make sure vent is on sealing, then cook for 5 minutes on high pressure. 6. When cooking time is up, manually release the pressure. 7. Strain potatoes, toss with remaining 2 tablespoons margarine and chopped parsley, and serve immediately.

Saltine Wax Beans

Prep time: 10 minutes | Cook time: 7 minutes | Serves 4

60 g flour
1 teaspoon smoky chipotle powder
½ teaspoon ground black pepper
1 teaspoon sea salt flakes
2 eggs, beaten
55 g crushed cream crackers
285 g wax beans
Cooking spray

1. Preheat the Ninja Foodi cooker to 180°C. 2. Combine the flour, chipotle powder, black pepper, and salt in a bowl. Put the eggs in a second bowl. Put the crushed cream crackers in a third bowl. 3. Wash the beans with cold water and discard any tough strings. 4. Coat the beans with the flour mixture, before dipping them into the beaten egg. Cover them with the crushed cream crackers. 5. Spritz the beans with cooking spray. 6. Air crisp for 4 minutes. Give the cook & crisp basket a good shake and continue to air crisp for 3 minutes. Serve hot.

Asparagus Fries

Prep time: 15 minutes | Cook time: 5 to 7 minutes per batch | Serves 4

340 g fresh asparagus spears with tough ends trimmed off
2 egg whites
60 ml water
80 g panko bread crumbs
25 g grated Parmesan cheese, plus 2 tablespoons
¼ teaspoon salt
Oil for misting or cooking spray

1. Preheat the Ninja Foodi cooker to 200°C. 2. In a shallow dish, beat egg whites and water until slightly foamy. 3. In another shallow dish, combine panko, Parmesan, and salt. 4. Dip asparagus spears in egg, then roll in crumbs. Spray with oil or cooking spray. 5. Place a layer of asparagus in cook & crisp basket, leaving just a little space in between each spear. Stack another layer on top, crosswise. Air crisp at 200°C for 5 to 7 minutes, until crispy and golden brown. 6. Repeat to cook remaining asparagus.

Air Fried Potatoes with Olives

Prep time: 15 minutes | Cook time: 40 minutes | Serves 1

1 medium Maris Piper potatoes, scrubbed and peeled
1 teaspoon olive oil
¼ teaspoon onion powder
⅛ teaspoon salt
Dollop of butter
Dollop of cream cheese
1 tablespoon Kalamata olives
1 tablespoon chopped chives

1. Preheat the Ninja Foodi cooker to 200°C. 2. In a bowl, coat the potatoes with the onion powder, salt, olive oil, and butter. 3. Transfer to the Ninja Foodi cooker and air crisp for 40 minutes, turning the potatoes over at the halfway point. 4. Take care when removing the potatoes from the Ninja Foodi cooker and serve with the cream cheese, Kalamata olives and chives on top.

Garlicky Broccoli with Roasted Almonds

Prep time: 10 minutes | Cook time: 4 minutes | Serves 4 to 6

1.5 L broccoli florets
240 ml water
1½ tablespoons olive oil
8 garlic cloves, thinly sliced
2 shallots, thinly sliced
½ teaspoon crushed red pepper flakes
Grated zest and juice of 1 medium lemon
½ teaspoon rock salt
Freshly ground black pepper, to taste
60 ml chopped roasted almonds
60 ml finely slivered fresh basil

1. Pour the water into the Ninja Foodi cooker. Place the broccoli florets in a steamer basket and lower into the pot. 2. Close and secure the lid. Select the Steam setting and set the cooking time for 2 minutes at Low Pressure. Once the timer goes off, use a quick pressure release. Carefully open the lid. 3. Transfer the broccoli to a large bowl filled with cold water and ice. Once cooled, drain the broccoli and pat dry. 4. Select the Sauté mode on the Ninja Foodi cooker and heat the olive oil. Add the garlic to the pot and sauté for 30 seconds, tossing constantly. Add the shallots and pepper flakes to the pot and sauté for 1 minute. 5. Stir in the cooked broccoli, lemon juice, salt and black pepper. Toss the ingredients together and cook for 1 minute. 6. Transfer the broccoli to a serving platter and sprinkle with the chopped almonds, lemon zest and basil. Serve immediately.

Buttery Green Beans

Prep time: 5 minutes | Cook time: 8 to 10 minutes | Serves 6

450 g green beans, trimmed
1 tablespoon avocado oil
1 teaspoon garlic powder
Sea salt and freshly ground black pepper, to taste
4 tablespoons unsalted butter, melted
20 g freshly grated Parmesan cheese

1. In a large bowl, toss together the green beans, avocado oil, and garlic powder and season with salt and pepper. 2. Set the Ninja Foodi cooker to 200°C. Arrange the green beans in a single layer in the cook & crisp basket. Air crisp for 8 to 10 minutes, tossing halfway through. 3. Transfer the beans to a large bowl and toss with the melted butter. Top with the Parmesan cheese and serve warm.

Roasted Radishes with Sea Salt

Prep time: 5 minutes | Cook time: 18 minutes | Serves 4

450 g radishes, ends trimmed if needed
2 tablespoons olive oil
½ teaspoon sea salt

1. Preheat the Ninja Foodi cooker to 180°C. 2. In a large bowl, combine the radishes with olive oil and sea salt. 3. Pour the radishes into the Ninja Foodi cooker and roast for 10 minutes. Stir or turn the radishes over and roast for 8 minutes more, then serve.

Spaghetti Squash

Prep time: 5 minutes | Cook time: 7 minutes | Serves 4

1 spaghetti squash (about 900 g)

1. Cut the spaghetti squash in half crosswise and use a large spoon to remove the seeds. 2. Pour 240 ml of water into the electric pressure cooker and insert a wire rack or reversible rack. 3. Place the squash halves on the rack, cut-side up. 4. Close and lock the lid of the pressure cooker. Set the valve to sealing. 5. Cook on high pressure for 7 minutes. 6. When the cooking is complete, hit Start/Stop and quick release the pressure. 7. Once the pin drops, unlock and remove the lid. 8. With tongs, remove the squash from the pot and transfer it to a plate. When it is cool enough to handle, scrape the squash with the tines of a fork to remove the strands. Discard the skin.

Parmesan Courgette Noodles

Prep time: 5 minutes | Cook time: 5 minutes | Serves 2

1 large courgette, trimmed and spiralized
1 tablespoon butter
1 garlic clove, diced
½ teaspoon chili flakes
85 g Parmesan cheese, grated

1. Set the Ninja Foodi cooker on the Sauté mode and melt the butter. Add the garlic and chili flakes to the pot. Sauté for 2 minutes, or until fragrant. 2. Stir in the courgette spirals and sauté for 2 minutes, or until tender. 3. Add the grated Parmesan cheese to the pot and stir well. Continue to cook it for 1 minute, or until the cheese melts. 4. Transfer to a plate and serve immediately

Chanterelle Mushrooms with Cheddar Cheese

Prep time: 10 minutes | Cook time: 5 minutes | Serves 4

1 tablespoon olive oil
2 cloves garlic, minced
1 (1-inch) ginger root, grated
450 g Chanterelle mushrooms, brushed clean and sliced
120 ml unsweetened tomato purée
120 ml water
2 tablespoons dry white wine
1 teaspoon dried basil
½ teaspoon dried thyme
½ teaspoon dried dill weed
⅓ teaspoon freshly ground black pepper
Rock salt, to taste
240 ml shredded Cheddar cheese

1. Press the Sauté button on the Ninja Foodi cooker and heat the olive oil. Add the garlic and grated ginger to the pot and sauté for 1 minute, or until fragrant. Stir in the remaining ingredients, except for the cheese. 2. Lock the lid. Set the cooking time for 5 minutes on Low Pressure. When the timer goes off, perform a quick pressure release. Carefully open the lid.. 3. Serve topped with the shredded cheese.

Braised Radishes with Sugar Snap Peas and Dukkah

Prep time: 20 minutes | Cook time: 5 minutes | Serves 4

60 ml extra-virgin olive oil, divided
1 shallot, sliced thin
3 garlic cloves, sliced thin
680 g radishes, 480 ml greens reserved, radishes trimmed and halved if small or quartered if large
120 ml water
½ teaspoon table salt
230 g sugar snap peas, strings removed, sliced thin on bias
230 g cremini mushrooms, trimmed and sliced thin
2 teaspoons grated lemon zest plus 1 teaspoon juice
240 ml plain Greek yoghurt
120 ml fresh coriander leaves
3 tablespoons dukkah

1. Using highest sauté function, heat 2 tablespoons oil in Ninja Foodi cooker until shimmering. Add shallot and cook until softened, about 2 minutes. Stir in garlic and cook until fragrant, about 30 seconds. Stir in radishes, water, and salt. Lock lid in place and close pressure release valve. Select high pressure and cook for 1 minute. 2. Turn off Ninja Foodi cooker and quick-release pressure. Carefully remove lid, allowing steam to escape away from you. Stir in snap peas, cover, and let sit until heated through, about 3 minutes. Add radish greens, mushrooms, lemon zest and juice, and remaining 2 tablespoons oil and gently toss to combine. Season with salt and pepper to taste. 3. Spread 60 ml yoghurt over bottom of 4 individual serving plates. Using slotted spoon, arrange vegetable mixture on top and sprinkle with coriander and dukkah. Serve.

Green Peas with Mint

Prep time: 5 minutes | Cook time: 5 minutes | Serves 4

75 g shredded lettuce
1 (280 g) package frozen green peas, thawed
1 tablespoon fresh mint, shredded
1 teaspoon melted butter

1. Lay the shredded lettuce in the cook & crisp basket. 2. Toss together the peas, mint, and melted butter and spoon over the lettuce. 3. Air crisp at 180ºC for 5 minutes, until peas are warm and lettuce wilts.

Fried Brussels Sprouts

Prep time: 10 minutes | Cook time: 18 minutes | Serves 4

1 teaspoon plus 1 tablespoon extra-virgin olive oil, divided
2 teaspoons minced garlic
2 tablespoons honey
1 tablespoon sugar
2 tablespoons freshly squeezed lemon juice
2 tablespoons rice vinegar
2 tablespoons sriracha
450 g Brussels sprouts, stems trimmed and any tough leaves removed, rinsed, halved lengthwise, and dried
½ teaspoon salt
Cooking oil spray

1. In a small saucepan over low heat, combine 1 teaspoon of olive oil, the garlic, honey, sugar, lemon juice, vinegar, and sriracha. Cook for 2 to 3 minutes, or until slightly thickened. Remove the pan from the heat, cover, and set aside. 2. Place the Brussels sprouts in a resealable bag or small bowl. Add the remaining olive oil and the salt, and toss to coat. 3. Insert the crisper plate into the basket and the basket into the unit. Preheat the unit by selecting AIR FRY, setting the temperature to 200ºC, and setting the time to 3 minutes. Select START/STOP to begin. 4. Once the unit is preheated, spray the crisper plate with cooking oil. Add the Brussels sprouts to the basket. 5. Select AIR FRY, set the temperature to 200ºC, and set the time to 15 minutes. Select START/STOP to begin. 6. After 7 or 8 minutes, remove the basket and shake it to toss the sprouts. Reinsert the basket to resume cooking. 7. When the cooking is complete, the leaves should be crispy and light brown and the sprout centres tender. 8. Place the sprouts in a medium serving bowl and drizzle the sauce over the top. Toss to coat, and serve immediately.

Crispy Courgette Sticks

Prep time: 5 minutes | Cook time: 14 minutes | Serves 4

2 small courgette, cut into 2-inch × ½-inch sticks
3 tablespoons chickpea flour
2 teaspoons arrowroot (or cornflour)
½ teaspoon garlic granules
¼ teaspoon sea salt
⅛ teaspoon freshly ground black pepper
1 tablespoon water
Cooking spray

1. Preheat the Ninja Foodi cooker to 200ºC. 2. Combine the courgette sticks with the chickpea flour, arrowroot, garlic granules, salt, and pepper in a medium bowl and toss to coat. Add the water and stir to mix well. 3. Spritz the cook & crisp basket with cooking spray and spread out the courgette sticks in the basket. Mist the courgette sticks with cooking spray. 4. Air crisp for 14 minutes, shaking the basket halfway through, or until the courgette sticks are crispy and nicely browned. 5. Serve warm.

Herbed Shiitake Mushrooms

Prep time: 10 minutes | Cook time: 5 minutes | Serves 4

230 g shiitake mushrooms, stems removed and caps roughly chopped
1 tablespoon olive oil
½ teaspoon salt
Freshly ground black pepper, to taste
1 teaspoon chopped fresh thyme leaves
1 teaspoon chopped fresh oregano
1 tablespoon chopped fresh parsley

1. Preheat the Ninja Foodi cooker to 200ºC. 2. Toss the mushrooms with the olive oil, salt, pepper, thyme and oregano. Air crisp for 5 minutes, shaking the basket once or twice during the cooking process. The mushrooms will still be somewhat chewy with a meaty texture. If you'd like them a little more tender, add a couple of minutes to this cooking time. 3. Once cooked, add the parsley to the mushrooms and toss. Season again to taste and serve.

Corn on the Cob

Prep time: 5 minutes | Cook time: 12 to 15 minutes | Serves 4

2 large ears fresh corn
Olive oil for misting
Salt, to taste (optional)

1. Shuck corn, remove silks, and wash. 2. Cut or break each ear in half crosswise. 3. Spray corn with olive oil. 4. Air fry at 200ºC for 12 to 15 minutes or until browned as much as you like. 5. Serve plain or with coarsely ground salt.

Lemony Asparagus with Gremolata

Prep time: 15 minutes | Cook time: 2 minutes | Serves 2 to 4

Gremolata:
240 ml finely chopped fresh Italian flat-leaf parsley leaves
3 garlic cloves, peeled and grated
Zest of 2 small lemons
Asparagus:
680 g asparagus, trimmed
240 ml water
Lemony Vinaigrette:
1½ tablespoons fresh lemon juice
1 teaspoon granulated sweetener
1 teaspoon Dijon mustard
2 tablespoons extra-virgin olive oil
Rock salt and freshly ground black pepper, to taste
Garnish:
3 tablespoons slivered almonds

1. In a small bowl, stir together all the ingredients for the gremolata. 2. Pour the water into the Ninja Foodi cooker. Arrange the asparagus in a steamer basket. Lower the steamer basket into the pot. 3. Lock the lid. Select the Steam mode and set the cooking time for 2 minutes on Low Pressure. 4. Meanwhile, prepare the lemony vinaigrette: In a bowl, combine the lemon juice, granulated sweetener and mustard and whisk to combine. Slowly drizzle in the olive oil and continue to whisk. Season generously with salt and pepper. 5. When the timer goes off, perform a quick pressure release. Carefully open the lid. Remove the steamer basket from the Ninja Foodi cooker. 6. Transfer the asparagus to a serving platter. Drizzle with the vinaigrette and sprinkle with the gremolata. Serve the asparagus topped with the slivered almonds.

Steamed Tomato with Halloumi Cheese

Prep time: 5 minutes | Cook time: 3 minutes | Serves 4

8 tomatoes, sliced
240 ml water
120 ml crumbled Halloumi cheese
2 tablespoons extra-virgin olive
oil
2 tablespoons snipped fresh basil
2 garlic cloves, smashed

1. Pour the water into the Ninja Foodi cooker and put the reversible rack in the pot. Place the tomatoes in the reversible rack. 2. Lock the lid. Set the cooking time for 3 minutes on High Pressure. When the timer goes off, perform a quick pressure release. Carefully open the lid. 3. Toss the tomatoes with the remaining ingredients and serve.

Perfect Sweet Potatoes

Prep time: 5 minutes | Cook time: 15 minutes | Serves 4 to 6

4–6 medium sweet potatoes
240 ml of water

1. Scrub skin of sweet potatoes with a brush until clean. Pour water into inner pot of the Ninja Foodi cooker. Place steamer basket in the bottom of the inner pot. Place sweet potatoes on top of steamer basket. 2. Secure the lid and turn valve to seal. 3. Set to Pressure on high for 15 minutes. 4. Allow pressure to release naturally (about 10 minutes). 5. Once the pressure valve lowers, remove lid and serve immediately.

Dinner Rolls

Prep time: 10 minutes | Cook time: 12 minutes | Serves 6

225 g shredded Mozzarella cheese
30 g full-fat cream cheese
95 g blanched finely ground almond flour
40 g ground flaxseed
½ teaspoon baking powder
1 large egg

1. Place Mozzarella, cream cheese, and almond flour in a large microwave-safe bowl. Microwave for 1 minute. Mix until smooth. 2. Add flaxseed, baking powder, and egg until fully combined and smooth. Microwave an additional 15 seconds if it becomes too firm. 3. Separate the dough into six pieces and roll into balls. Place the balls into the cook & crisp basket. 4. Adjust the temperature to 160ºC and air crisp for 12 minutes. 5. Allow rolls to cool completely before serving.

Broccoli-Cheddar Twice-Baked Potatoes

Prep time: 10 minutes | Cook time: 46 minutes | Serves 4

Oil, for spraying
2 medium Maris Piper potatoes
1 tablespoon olive oil
30 g broccoli florets
1 tablespoon sour cream
1 teaspoon garlic powder
1 teaspoon onion powder
60 g shredded Cheddar cheese

1. Line the cook & crisp basket with parchment and spray lightly with oil. 2. Rinse the potatoes and pat dry with paper towels. Rub the outside of the potatoes with the olive oil and place them in the prepared basket. 3. Air crisp at 200ºC for 40 minutes, or until easily pierced with a fork. Let cool just enough to handle, then cut the potatoes in half lengthwise. 4. Meanwhile, place the broccoli in a microwave-safe bowl, cover with water, and microwave on high for 5 to 8 minutes. Drain and set aside. 5. Scoop out most of the potato flesh and transfer to a medium bowl. 6. Add the sour cream, garlic, and onion powder and stir until the potatoes are mashed. 7. Spoon the potato mixture back into the hollowed potato skins, mounding it to fit, if necessary. Top with the broccoli and cheese. Return the potatoes to the basket. You may need to work in batches, depending on the size of your Ninja Foodi cooker. 8. Air crisp at 200ºC for 3 to 6 minutes, or until the cheese has melted. Serve immediately.

Dijon Roast Cabbage

Prep time: 10 minutes | Cook time: 10 minutes | Serves 4

1 small head cabbage, cored and sliced into 1-inch-thick slices
2 tablespoons olive oil, divided
½ teaspoon salt
1 tablespoon Dijon mustard
1 teaspoon apple cider vinegar
1 teaspoon granular erythritol

1. Drizzle each cabbage slice with 1 tablespoon olive oil, then sprinkle with salt. Place slices into ungreased cook & crisp basket, working in batches if needed. Adjust the temperature to 180°C and air crisp for 10 minutes. Cabbage will be tender and edges will begin to brown when done. 2. In a small bowl, whisk remaining olive oil with mustard, vinegar, and erythritol. Drizzle over cabbage in a large serving dish. Serve warm.

Chermoula-Roasted Beetroots

Prep time: 15 minutes | Cook time: 25 minutes | Serves 4

Chermoula:
30 g packed fresh coriander leaves
15 g packed fresh parsley leaves
6 cloves garlic, peeled
2 teaspoons smoked paprika
2 teaspoons ground cumin
1 teaspoon ground coriander
½ to 1 teaspoon cayenne pepper
Pinch crushed saffron (optional)
115 ml extra-virgin olive oil
coarse sea salt, to taste
Beetroots:
3 medium beetroots, trimmed, peeled, and cut into 1-inch chunks
2 tablespoons chopped fresh coriander
2 tablespoons chopped fresh parsley

1. For the chermoula: In a food processor, combine the fresh coriander, parsley, garlic, paprika, cumin, ground coriander, and cayenne. Pulse until coarsely chopped. Add the saffron, if using, and process until combined. With the food processor running, slowly add the olive oil in a steady stream; process until the sauce is uniform. Season to taste with salt. 2. For the beetroots: In a large bowl, drizzle the beetroots with ½ cup of the chermoula, or enough to coat. Arrange the beetroots in the cook & crisp basket. Set the Ninja Foodi cooker to 190°C for 25 to minutes, or until the beetroots are tender. 3. Transfer the beetroots to a serving platter. Sprinkle with chopped coriander and parsley and serve.

Parmesan-Thyme Butternut Squash

Prep time: 15 minutes | Cook time: 20 minutes | Serves 4

350 g butternut squash, cubed into 1-inch pieces (approximately 1 medium)
2 tablespoons olive oil
¼ teaspoon salt
¼ teaspoon garlic powder
¼ teaspoon black pepper
1 tablespoon fresh thyme
20 g grated Parmesan

1. Preheat the Ninja Foodi cooker to 180°C. 2. In a large bowl, combine the cubed squash with the olive oil, salt, garlic powder, pepper, and thyme until the squash is well coated. 3. Pour this mixture into the cook & crisp basket, and roast for 10 minutes. Stir and roast another 8 to 10 minutes more. 4. Remove the squash from the Ninja Foodi cooker and toss with freshly grated Parmesan before serving.

Parmesan-Topped Acorn Squash

Prep time: 10 minutes | Cook time: 20 minutes | Serves 4

1 acorn squash (about 450 g)
1 tablespoon extra-virgin olive oil
1 teaspoon dried sage leaves, crumbled
¼ teaspoon freshly grated nutmeg
⅛ teaspoon rock salt
⅛ teaspoon freshly ground black pepper
2 tablespoons freshly grated Parmesan cheese

1. Cut the acorn squash in half lengthwise and remove the seeds. Cut each half in half for a total of 4 wedges. Snap off the stem if it's easy to do. 2. In a small bowl, combine the olive oil, sage, nutmeg, salt, and pepper. Brush the cut sides of the squash with the olive oil mixture. 3. Pour 240 ml of water into the electric pressure cooker and insert a wire rack or reversible rack. 4. Place the squash on the reversible rack in a single layer, skin-side down. 5. Close and lock the lid of the pressure cooker. Set the valve to sealing. 6. Cook on high pressure for 20 minutes. 7. When the cooking is complete, hit Start/Stop and quick release the pressure. 8. Once the pin drops, unlock and remove the lid. 9. Carefully remove the squash from the pot, sprinkle with the Parmesan, and serve.

Cauliflower Rice Balls

Prep time: 10 minutes | Cook time: 8 minutes | Serves 4

1 (280 g) steamer bag cauliflower rice, cooked according to package instructions
110 g shredded Mozzarella cheese
1 large egg
60 g plain pork scratchings, finely crushed
¼ teaspoon salt
½ teaspoon Italian seasoning

1. Place cauliflower into a large bowl and mix with Mozzarella. 2. Whisk egg in a separate medium bowl. Place pork scratchings into another large bowl with salt and Italian seasoning. 3. Separate cauliflower mixture into four equal sections and form each into a ball. Carefully dip a ball into whisked egg, then roll in pork scratchings. Repeat with remaining balls. 4. Place cauliflower balls into ungreased cook & crisp basket. Adjust the temperature to 200°C and air crisp for 8 minutes. Rice balls will be golden when done. 5. Use a spatula to carefully move cauliflower balls to a large dish for serving. Serve warm.

Chapter 8 Desserts

Vanilla Cookies with Hazelnuts

Prep time: 20 minutes | Cook time: 10 minutes | Serves 6

110 g almond flour
55 g coconut flour
1 teaspoon baking soda
1 teaspoon fine sea salt
110 g unsalted butter
120 g powdered sweetener
2 teaspoons vanilla
2 eggs, at room temperature
130 g hazelnuts, coarsely chopped

1. Preheat the Ninja Foodi cooker to 175ºC. 2. Mix the flour with the baking soda, and sea salt. 3. In the bowl of an electric mixer, beat the butter, sweetener, and vanilla until creamy. Fold in the eggs, one at a time, and mix until well combined. 4. Slowly and gradually, stir in the flour mixture. Finally, fold in the coarsely chopped hazelnuts. 5. Divide the dough into small balls using a large cookie scoop; drop onto the prepared cookie sheets. Bake for 10 minutes or until golden brown, rotating the pan once or twice through the cooking time. 6. Work in batches and cool for a couple of minutes before removing to wire racks. Enjoy!

Lemon Poppy Seed Macaroons

Prep time: 10 minutes | Cook time: 14 minutes | Makes 1 dozen

cookies
2 large egg whites, room temperature
35 g powdered sweetener
2 tablespoons grated lemon zest, plus more for garnish if desired
2 teaspoons poppy seeds
1 teaspoon lemon extract
¼ teaspoon fine sea salt
190 g desiccated unsweetened coconut
Lemon Icing:
25 g sweetener
1 tablespoon lemon juice

1. Preheat the Ninja Foodi cooker to 165ºC. Line a pie pan or a casserole dish that will fit inside your Ninja Foodi cooker with baking paper. 2. Place the egg whites in a medium-sized bowl and use a hand mixer on high to beat the whites until stiff peaks form. Add the sweetener, lemon zest, poppy seeds, lemon extract, and salt. Mix on low until combined. Gently fold in the coconut with a rubber spatula. 3. Use a 1-inch cookie scoop to place the cookies on the baking paper, spacing them about ¼ inch apart. Place the pan in the Ninja Foodi cooker and bake for 12 to 14 minutes, until the cookies are golden, and a toothpick inserted into the center comes out clean. 4. While the cookies bake, make the lemon icing: Place the sweetener in a small bowl. Add the lemon juice and stir well. If the icing is too thin, add a little more sweetener. If the icing is too thick, add a little more lemon juice. 5. Remove the cookies from the Ninja Foodi cooker and allow to cool for about 10 minutes, then drizzle with the icing. Garnish with lemon zest, if desired. Store leftovers in an airtight container in the fridge for up to 5 days or in the freezer for up to a month.

Pumpkin Pie Spice Pots De Crème

Prep time: 5 minutes | Cook time: 7 minutes | Serves 4

480 ml double cream (or full-fat coconut milk for dairy-free)
4 large egg yolks
60 ml granulated sweetener, or more to taste
2 teaspoons pumpkin pie spice
1 teaspoon vanilla extract
Pinch of fine sea salt
240 ml cold water

1. Heat the cream in a pan over medium-high heat until hot, about 2 minutes. 2. Place the remaining ingredients except the water in a medium bowl and stir until smooth. 3. Slowly pour in the hot cream while stirring. Taste and adjust the sweetness to your liking. Scoop the mixture into four ramekins with a spatula. Cover the ramekins with aluminium foil. 4. Place a reversible rack in the Ninja Foodi cooker and pour in the water. Place the ramekins on the reversible rack. 5. Lock the lid. Set the cooking time for 5 minutes at High Pressure. 6. When the timer beeps, use a quick pressure release. Carefully remove the lid. 7. Remove the foil and set the foil aside. Let the pots de crème cool for 15 minutes. Cover the ramekins with the foil again and place in the refrigerator to chill completely, about 2 hours. 8. Serve.

Southern Almond Pie

Prep time: 10 minutes | Cook time: 35 minutes | Serves 12

480 ml almond flour
360 ml granulated sweetener
1 teaspoon baking powder
Pinch of salt
120 ml sour cream
4 tablespoons butter, melted
1 egg
1 teaspoon vanilla extract
Cooking spray
1½ teaspoons ground cinnamon
1½ teaspoons granulated sweetener
240 ml water

1. In a large bowl, whisk together the almond flour, granulated sweetener, baking powder, and salt. 2. Add the sour cream, butter, egg, and vanilla and whisk until well combined. The batter will be very thick, almost like cookie dough. 3. Grease the baking dish with cooking spray. Line with baking paper, if desired. 4. Transfer the batter to the dish and level with an offset spatula. 5. In a small bowl, combine the cinnamon and granulated sweetener. Sprinkle over the top of the batter. 6. Cover the dish tightly with aluminium foil. Add the water to the pot. Set the dish on the reversible rack and carefully lower it into the pot. 7. Set the lid in place. Set the cooking time for 35 minutes on High Pressure. When the timer goes off, do a quick pressure release. Carefully open the lid. 8. Remove the reversible rack and pie from the pot. Remove the foil from the pan. The pie should be set but soft, and the top should be slightly cracked. 9. Cool completely before cutting.

Breaded Bananas with Chocolate Topping

Prep time: 10 minutes | Cook time: 10 minutes | Serves 6

40 g cornflour	3 bananas, halved crosswise
25 g plain breadcrumbs	Cooking spray
1 large egg, beaten	Chocolate sauce, for serving

1. Preheat the Ninja Foodi cooker to 175°C. 2. Place the cornflour, breadcrumbs, and egg in three separate bowls. 3. Roll the bananas in the cornstarch, then in the beaten egg, and finally in the breadcrumbs to coat well. 4. Spritz the cook & crisp basket with the cooking spray. 5. Arrange the banana halves in the basket and mist them with the cooking spray. Air crisp for 5 minutes. Flip the bananas and continue to air crisp for another 2 minutes. 6. Remove the bananas from the basket to a serving plate. Serve with the chocolate sauce drizzled over the top.

Courgette Nut Muffins

Prep time: 15 minutes | Cook time: 15 minutes | Serves 4

60 ml vegetable oil, plus more for greasing	¼ teaspoon baking soda
90 g plain flour	¼ teaspoon baking powder
¾ teaspoon ground cinnamon	2 large eggs
¼ teaspoon kosher, or coarse sea salt	100 g granulated sugar
	90 g grated courgette
	35 g chopped walnuts

1. Generously grease four ramekins or a baking pan with vegetable oil. 2. In a medium bowl, sift together the flour, cinnamon, salt, baking soda, and baking powder. 3. In a separate medium bowl, beat together the eggs, sugar, and vegetable oil. Add the dry ingredients to the wet ingredients. Add the courgette and nuts and stir gently until well combined. Transfer the batter to the prepared ramekins or baking pan. 4. Place the ramekins or pan in the cook & crisp basket. Set the Ninja Foodi cooker to 165°C, and cook for 15 minutes, or until a cake tester or toothpick inserted into the center comes out clean. If it doesn't, cook for 3 to 5 minutes more and test again. 5. Let cool in the ramekins or pan on a wire rack for 10 minutes. Carefully remove from the ramekins or pan and let cool completely on the rack before serving.

Chocolate Peppermint Cheesecake

Prep time: 5 minutes | Cook time: 18 minutes | Serves 6

Crust:	110 g unsweetened cooking chocolate
110 g butter, melted	180 g mascarpone cheese, at room temperature
55 g coconut flour	1 teaspoon vanilla extract
2 tablespoons granulated sweetener	2 drops peppermint extract
Cooking spray	
Topping:	

1. Preheat the Ninja Foodi cooker to 175°C. Lightly coat a baking pan with cooking spray. 2. In a mixing bowl, whisk together the butter, flour, and sweetener until well combined. Transfer the mixture to the prepared baking pan. 3. Place the baking pan in the Ninja Foodi cooker and bake for 18 minutes until a toothpick inserted in the center comes out clean. 4. Remove the crust from the Ninja Foodi cooker to a wire rack to cool. 5. Once cooled completely, place it in the freezer for 20 minutes. 6. When ready, combine all the ingredients for the topping in a small bowl and stir to incorporate. 7. Spread this topping over the crust and let it sit for another 15 minutes in the freezer. 8. Serve chilled.

Double Chocolate Brownies

Prep time: 5 minutes | Cook time: 15 to 20 minutes | Serves 8

110 g almond flour	and cooled
50 g unsweetened cocoa powder	3 eggs
½ teaspoon baking powder	1 teaspoon vanilla extract
35 g powdered sweetener	2 tablespoons mini semisweet chocolate chips
¼ teaspoon salt	
110 g unsalted butter, melted	

1. Preheat the Ninja Foodi cooker to 175°C. Line a cake pan with baking paper and brush with oil. 2. In a large bowl, combine the almond flour, cocoa powder, baking powder, sweetener, and salt. Add the butter, eggs, and vanilla. Stir until thoroughly combined (the batter will be thick.) Spread the batter into the prepared pan and scatter the chocolate chips on top. 3. Air crisp for 15 to 20 minutes until the edges are set (the center should still appear slightly undercooked.) Let cool completely before slicing. To store, cover and refrigerate the brownies for up to 3 days.

Hearty Crème Brûlée

Prep time: 5 minutes | Cook time: 30 minutes | Serves 4

5 egg yolks	360 ml double cream
5 tablespoons granulated sweetener	2 teaspoons vanilla extract
	480 ml water

1. In a small bowl, use a fork to break up the egg yolks. Stir in the sweetener. 2. Pour the cream into a small saucepan over medium-low heat and let it warm up for 3 to 4 minutes. Remove the saucepan from the heat. 3. Temper the egg yolks by slowly adding a small spoonful of the warm cream, keep whisking. Do this three times to make sure the egg yolks are fully tempered. 4. Slowly add the tempered eggs to the cream, whisking the whole time. Add the vanilla and whisk again. 5. Pour the cream mixture into the ramekins. Each ramekin should have 120 ml liquid. Cover each with aluminium foil. 6. Place the reversible rack inside the Ninja Foodi cooker. Add the water. Carefully place the ramekins on top of the reversible rack. 7. Close the lid. Set cooking time for 11 minutes on High Pressure. 8. When timer beeps, use a natural release for 15 minutes, then release any remaining pressure. Open the lid. 9. Carefully remove a ramekin from the pot. Remove the foil and check for doneness. The custard should be mostly set with a slightly jiggly centre. 10. Place all the ramekins in the fridge for 2 hours to chill and set. Serve chilled.

Pecan Bars

Prep time: 5 minutes | Cook time: 40 minutes | Serves 12

220 g coconut flour
5 tablespoons granulated sweetener
4 tablespoons coconut oil, softened
60 ml heavy cream
1 egg, beaten
4 pecans, chopped

1. Mix coconut flour, sweetener, coconut oil, heavy cream, and egg. 2. Pour the batter in the cook & crisp basket and flatten well. 3. Top the mixture with pecans and cook the meal at 175ºC for 40 minutes. 4. Cut the cooked meal into the bars.

Egg Custard Tarts

Prep time: 10 minutes | Cook time: 20 minutes | Serves 2

60 ml almond flour
1 tablespoon coconut oil
2 egg yolks
60 ml coconut milk
1 tablespoon sweetener
1 teaspoon vanilla extract
240 ml water, for cooking

1. Make the dough: Mix up almond flour and coconut oil. 2. Then place the dough into 2 mini tart molds and flatten well in the shape of cups. 3. Pour water in the Ninja Foodi cooker. Insert the steamer rack. 4. Place the tart mold in the Ninja Foodi cooker. Close and seal the lid. 5. Cook them for 3 minutes on High Pressure. Make a quick pressure release. 6. Then whisk together vanilla extract, sweetener, coconut milk, and egg yolks. 7. Pour the liquid in the tart molds and close the lid. 8. Cook the dessert for 7 minutes on High Pressure. 9. Then allow the natural pressure release for 10 minutes more.

Cinnamon Cupcakes with Cream Cheese Frosting

Prep time: 10 minutes | Cook time: 20 to 25 minutes | Serves 6

50 g almond flour, plus 2 tablespoons
2 tablespoons low-carb vanilla protein powder
⅛ teaspoon salt
1 teaspoon baking powder
¼ teaspoon ground cinnamon
55 g unsalted butter
25 g powdered sweetener
2 eggs
½ teaspoon vanilla extract
2 tablespoons heavy cream
Cream Cheese Frosting:
110 g cream cheese, softened
2 tablespoons unsalted butter, softened
½ teaspoon vanilla extract
2 tablespoons powdered sweetener
1 to 2 tablespoons heavy cream

1. Preheat the Ninja Foodi cooker to 160ºC. Lightly coat 6 silicone muffin cups with oil and set aside. 2. In a medium bowl, combine the almond flour, protein powder, salt, baking powder, and cinnamon; set aside. 3. In a stand mixer fitted with a paddle attachment, beat the butter and sweetener until creamy. Add the eggs, vanilla, and heavy cream, and beat again until thoroughly combined. Add half the flour mixture at a time to the butter mixture, mixing after each addition, until you have a smooth, creamy batter. 4. Divide the batter evenly among the muffin cups, filling each one about three-fourths full. Arrange the muffin cups in the Ninja Foodi cooker and air crisp for 20 to 25 minutes, or until a toothpick inserted into the center of a cupcake comes out clean. Transfer the cupcakes to a rack and let cool completely. 5. To make the cream cheese frosting: In a stand mixer fitted with a paddle attachment, beat the cream cheese, butter, and vanilla until fluffy. Add the sweetener and mix again until thoroughly combined. With the mixer running, add the heavy cream a tablespoon at a time until the frosting is smooth and creamy. Frost the cupcakes as desired.

Chocolate Macadamia Bark

Prep time: 5 minutes | Cook time: 20 minutes | Serves 20

450 g raw dark chocolate
3 tablespoons raw coconut butter
2 tablespoons coconut oil
480 ml chopped macadamia nuts
1 tablespoon almond butter
½ teaspoon salt
80 ml granulated sweetener, or more to taste

1. In a large bowl, mix together the chocolate, coconut butter, coconut oil, macadamia nuts, almond butter, salt, and granulated sweetener. Combine them very thoroughly, until a perfectly even mixture is obtained. 2. Pour 240 ml of filtered water into the Ninja Foodi cooker, and insert the reversible rack. Transfer the mixture from the bowl into a well-greased, Ninja Foodi cooker-friendly dish. 3. Place the dish onto the reversible rack, and cover loosely with aluminium foil. Close the lid, set the Ninja Foodi cooker to 20 minutes on High Pressure, and let cook. 4. Once cooked, let the pressure naturally disperse from the Ninja Foodi cooker for about 10 minutes, then carefully switch the pressure release to Venting. 5. Open the Ninja Foodi cooker and remove the dish. Cool in the refrigerator until set. Break into pieces, serve, and enjoy! Store remaining bark in the refrigerator or freezer.

Strawberry Cheesecake

Prep time: 20 minutes | Cook time: 10 minutes | Serves 2

1 tablespoon gelatin
4 tablespoon water (for gelatin)
4 tablespoon cream cheese
1 strawberry, chopped
60 ml coconut milk
1 tablespoon granulated sweetener

1. Mix up gelatin and water and leave the mixture for 10 minutes. 2. Meanwhile, pour coconut milk in the Ninja Foodi cooker. 3. Bring it to boil on Sauté mode, about 10 minutes. 4. Meanwhile, mash the strawberry and mix it up with cream cheese. 5. Add the mixture in the hot coconut milk and stir until smooth. 6. Cool the liquid for 10 minutes and add gelatin. Whisk it until gelatin is melted. 7. Then pour the cheesecake in the mold and freeze in the freezer for 3 hours.

Simple Apple Turnovers

Prep time: 10 minutes | Cook time: 10 minutes | Serves 4

1 apple, peeled, quartered, and thinly sliced	1 tablespoon granulated sugar
½ teaspoons pumpkin pie spice	Pinch of kosher, or coarse sea salt
Juice of ½ lemon	6 sheets filo pastry

1. Preheat the Ninja Foodi cooker to 165°C. 2. In a medium bowl, combine the apple, pumpkin pie spice, lemon juice, granulated sugar, and kosher salt. 3. Cut the filo pastry sheets into 4 equal pieces and place individual tablespoons of apple filling in the center of each piece, then fold in both sides and roll from front to back. 4. Spray the cook & crisp basket with nonstick cooking spray, then place the turnovers in the basket and bake for 10 minutes or until golden brown. 5. Remove the turnovers from the Ninja Foodi cooker and allow to cool on a wire rack for 10 minutes before serving.

Almond Butter Cookie Balls

Prep time: 5 minutes | Cook time: 10 minutes | Makes 10 balls

70 g almond butter	25 g desiccated unsweetened coconut
1 large egg	40 g low-carb, sugar-free chocolate chips
1 teaspoon vanilla extract	½ teaspoon ground cinnamon
30 g low-carb protein powder	
30 g powdered sweetener	

1. In a large bowl, mix almond butter and egg. Add in vanilla, protein powder, and sweetener. 2. Fold in coconut, chocolate chips, and cinnamon. Roll into 1-inch balls. Place balls into a round baking pan and put into the cook & crisp basket. 3. Adjust the temperature to 160°C and bake for 10 minutes. 4. Allow to cool completely. Store in an airtight container in the refrigerator up to 4 days.

Crispy Pineapple Rings

Prep time: 5 minutes | Cook time: 6 to 8 minutes | Serves 6

240 ml rice milk	½ teaspoon vanilla essence
85 g plain flour	½ teaspoon ground cinnamon
120 ml water	¼ teaspoon ground star anise
25 g unsweetened flaked coconut	Pinch of kosher, or coarse sea salt
4 tablespoons granulated sugar	1 medium pineapple, peeled and sliced
½ teaspoon baking soda	
½ teaspoon baking powder	

1. Preheat the Ninja Foodi cooker to 190°C. 2. In a large bowl, stir together all the ingredients except the pineapple. 3. Dip each pineapple slice into the batter until evenly coated. 4. Arrange the pineapple slices in the basket and air crisp for 6 to 8 minutes until golden brown. 5. Remove from the basket to a plate and cool for 5 minutes before serving warm

Spiced Pear Applesauce

Prep time: 15 minutes | Cook time: 5 minutes | Makes: 850 ml

450 g pears, peeled, cored, and sliced	cinnamon
2 teaspoons apple pie spice or	Pinch rock salt
	Juice of ½ small lemon

1. In the electric pressure cooker, combine the apples, pears, apple pie spice, salt, lemon juice, and 60 ml of water. 2. Close and lock the lid of the pressure cooker. Set the valve to sealing. 3. Cook on high pressure for 5 minutes. 4. When the cooking is complete, hit Start/Stop and let the pressure release naturally. 5. Once the pin drops, unlock and remove the lid. 6. Mash the apples and pears with a potato masher to the consistency you like. 7. Serve warm, or cool to room temperature and refrigerate.

Old-Fashioned Fudge Pie

Prep time: 15 minutes | Cook time: 25 to 30 minutes | Serves 8

300 g granulated sugar	melted
40 g unsweetened cocoa powder	1½ teaspoons vanilla extract
70 g self-raising flour	1 (9-inch) unbaked piecrust
3 large eggs, unbeaten	30 g icing sugar (optional)
12 tablespoons unsalted butter,	

1. In a medium bowl, stir together the sugar, cocoa powder, and flour. Stir in the eggs and melted butter. Stir in the vanilla. 2. Preheat the Ninja Foodi cooker to 175°C. 3. Pour the chocolate filing into the crust. 4. Cook for 25 to 30 minutes, stirring every 10 minutes, until a knife inserted into the middle comes out clean. Let sit for 5 minutes before dusting with icing sugar (if using) to serve.

Pine Nut Mousse

Prep time: 5 minutes | Cook time: 35 minutes | Serves 8

1 tablespoon butter	240 ml granulated sweetener, reserve 1 tablespoon
300 ml pine nuts	1 c water
300 ml full-fat double cream	240 ml full-fat heavy whipping cream
2 large eggs	
1 teaspoon vanilla extract	

1. Butter the bottom and the side of a pie pan and set aside. 2. In a food processor, blend the pine nuts and double cream. Add the eggs, vanilla extract and granulated sweetener and pulse a few times to incorporate. 3. Pour the batter into the pan and loosely cover with aluminium foil. Pour the water in the Ninja Foodi cooker and place the reversible rack inside. Place the pan on top of the reversible rack. 4. Close the lid. Set the timer for 35 minutes on High pressure. 5. In a small mixing bowl, whisk the heavy whipping cream and 1 tablespoon of granulated sweetener until a soft peak forms. 6. When timer beeps, use a natural pressure release for 15 minutes, then release any remaining pressure and open the lid. 7. Serve immediately with whipped cream on top.

Chocolate Chip Brownies

Prep time: 10 minutes | Cook time: 33 minutes | Serves 8

360 ml almond flour
80 ml unsweetened cocoa powder
180 ml granulated sweetener
1 teaspoon baking powder
2 eggs
1 tablespoon vanilla extract
5 tablespoons butter, melted
60 ml sugar-free chocolate chips
120 ml water

1. In a large bowl, add the almond flour, cocoa powder, sweetener, and baking powder. Use a hand mixer on low speed to combine and smooth out any lumps. 2. Add the eggs and vanilla and mix until well combined. 3. Add the butter and mix on low speed until well combined. Scrape the bottom and sides of the bowl and mix again if needed. Fold in the chocolate chips. 4. Grease a baking dish with cooking spray. Pour the batter into the dish and smooth with a spatula. Cover tightly with aluminium foil. 5. Pour the water into the pot. Place the reversible rack in the pot and carefully lower the baking dish onto the reversible rack. 6. Close the lid. Set cooking time for 33 minutes on High Pressure. 7. When timer beeps, use a quick pressure release and open the lid. 8. Use the handles to carefully remove the reversible rack from the pot. Remove the foil from the dish. 9. Let the brownies cool for 10 minutes before turning out onto a plate.

Chocolate Croissants

Prep time: 5 minutes | Cook time: 24 minutes | Serves 8

1 sheet frozen puff pastry, thawed
100 g chocolate-hazelnut spread
1 large egg, beaten

1. On a lightly floured surface, roll puff pastry into a 14-inch square. Cut pastry into quarters to form 4 squares. Cut each square diagonally to form 8 triangles. 2. Spread 2 teaspoons chocolate-hazelnut spread on each triangle; from wider end, roll up pastry. Brush egg on top of each roll. 3. Preheat the Ninja Foodi cooker to 190ºC. Air crisp rolls in batches, 3 or 4 at a time, 8 minutes per batch, or until pastry is golden brown. 4. Cool on a wire rack; serve while warm or at room temperature.

Fried Oreos

Prep time: 7 minutes | Cook time: 6 minutes per batch | Makes 12 cookies

Coconut, or avocado oil for misting, or nonstick spray
120 g ready-made pancake mix
1 teaspoon vanilla extract
120 ml water, plus 2 tablespoons
12 Oreos or other chocolate sandwich biscuits
1 tablespoon icing sugar

1. Spray baking pan with oil or nonstick spray and place in basket. 2. Preheat the Ninja Foodi cooker to 200ºC. 3. In a medium bowl, mix together the pancake mix, vanilla, and water. 4. Dip 4 cookies in batter and place in baking pan. 5. Cook for 6 minutes, until browned. 6. Repeat steps 4 and 5 for the remaining cookies. 7. Sift icing sugar over warm cookies.

Vanilla Cream Pie

Prep time: 20 minutes | Cook time: 35 minutes | Serves 12

240 ml double cream
3 eggs, beaten
1 teaspoon vanilla extract
60 ml sweetener
240 ml coconut flour
1 tablespoon butter, melted
240 ml water, for cooking

1. In the mixing bowl, mix up coconut flour, sweetener, vanilla extract, eggs, and double cream. 2. Grease the baking pan with melted butter. 3. Pour the coconut mixture in the baking pan. 4. Pour water and insert the steamer rack in the Ninja Foodi cooker. 5. Place the pie on the rack. Close and seal the lid. 6. Cook the pie on High Pressure for 35 minutes. 7. Allow the natural pressure release for 10 minutes.

Almond Butter Keto Fat Bombs

Prep time: 3 minutes | Cook time: 3 minutes | Serves 6

60 ml coconut oil
60 ml no-sugar-added almond butter
2 tablespoons cacao powder
60 ml granulated sweetener

1. Press the Sauté button and add coconut oil to Ninja Foodi cooker. Let coconut oil melt completely and press the Start/Stop button. Stir in remaining ingredients. Mixture will be liquid. 2. Pour into 6 silicone molds and place into freezer for 30 minutes until set. Store in fridge.

Cocoa Custard

Prep time: 5 minutes | Cook time: 7 minutes | Serves 4

480 ml double cream (or full-fat coconut milk for dairy-free)
4 large egg yolks
60 ml granulated sweetener, or more to taste
1 tablespoon plus 1 teaspoon unsweetened cocoa powder, or more to taste
½ teaspoon almond extract
Pinch of fine sea salt
240 ml cold water

1. Heat the cream in a pan over medium-high heat until hot, about 2 minutes. 2. Place the remaining ingredients except the water in a blender and blend until smooth. 3. While the blender is running, slowly pour in the hot cream. Taste and adjust the sweetness to your liking. Add more cocoa powder, if desired. 4. Scoop the custard mixture into four ramekins with a spatula. Cover the ramekins with aluminium foil. 5. Place a reversible rack in the Ninja Foodi cooker and pour in the water. Place the ramekins on the reversible rack. 6. Lock the lid. Set the cooking time for 5 minutes at High Pressure. 7. When the timer beeps, use a quick pressure release. Carefully remove the lid. 8. Remove the foil and set the foil aside. Let the custard cool for 15 minutes. Cover the ramekins with the foil again and place in the refrigerator to chill completely, about 2 hours. 9. Serve.

Hazelnut Butter Cookies

Prep time: 30 minutes | Cook time: 20 minutes | Serves 10

4 tablespoons liquid monk fruit, or agave syrup
65 g hazelnuts, ground
110 g unsalted butter, room temperature
190 g almond flour
110 g coconut flour
55 g granulated sweetener
2 teaspoons ground cinnamon

1. Firstly, cream liquid monk fruit with butter until the mixture becomes fluffy. Sift in both types of flour. 2. Now, stir in the hazelnuts. Now, knead the mixture to form a dough; place in the refrigerator for about 35 minutes. 3. To finish, shape the prepared dough into the bite-sized balls; arrange them on a baking dish; flatten the balls using the back of a spoon. 4. Mix granulated sweetener with ground cinnamon. Press your cookies in the cinnamon mixture until they are completely covered. 5. Bake the cookies for 20 minutes at 155°C. 6. Leave them to cool for about 10 minutes before transferring them to a wire rack. Bon appétit!

Grilled Peaches

Prep time: 5 minutes | Cook time: 10 minutes | Serves 4

Coconut, or avocado oil, for spraying
25 g crushed digestive biscuits
50 g packed light brown sugar
8 tablespoons unsalted butter
¼ teaspoon cinnamon
2 peaches, pitted and cut into quarters
4 scoops vanilla ice cream

1. Line the cook & crisp basket with baking paper, and spray lightly with oil. 2. In a small bowl, mix together the crushed biscuits, brown sugar, butter, and cinnamon with a fork until crumbly. 3. Place the peach wedges in the prepared basket, skin-side up. You may need to work in batches, depending on the size of your Ninja Foodi cooker. 4. Air crisp at 175°C for 5 minutes, flip, and sprinkle with a spoonful of the biscuit mixture. Cook for another 5 minutes, or until tender and caramelized. 5. Top with a scoop of vanilla ice cream and any remaining crumble mixture. Serve immediately.

Apple Wedges with Apricots

Prep time: 5 minutes | Cook time: 15 to 18 minutes | Serves 4

4 large apples, peeled and sliced into 8 wedges
2 tablespoons light olive oil
95 g dried apricots, chopped
1 to 2 tablespoons granulated sugar
½ teaspoon ground cinnamon

1. Preheat the Ninja Foodi cooker to 180°C. 2. Toss the apple wedges with the olive oil in a mixing bowl until well coated. 3. Place the apple wedges in the cook & crisp basket and air crisp for 12 to 15 minutes. 4. Sprinkle with the dried apricots and air crisp for another 3 minutes. 5. Meanwhile, thoroughly combine the sugar and cinnamon in a small bowl. 6. Remove the apple wedges from the basket to a plate. Serve sprinkled with the sugar mixture.

Baked Peaches with Yogurt and Blueberries

Prep time: 10 minutes | Cook time: 7 to 11 minutes | Serves 6

3 peaches, peeled, halved, and pitted
2 tablespoons packed brown sugar
285 g plain Greek yogurt
¼ teaspoon ground cinnamon
1 teaspoon pure vanilla extract
190 g fresh blueberries

1. Preheat the Ninja Foodi cooker to 190°C. 2. Arrange the peaches in the cook & crisp basket, cut side up. Top with a generous sprinkle of brown sugar. 3. Bake in the preheated Ninja Foodi cooker for 7 to 11 minutes, or until the peaches are lightly browned and caramelized. 4. Meanwhile, whisk together the yogurt, cinnamon, and vanilla in a small bowl until smooth. 5. Remove the peaches from the basket to a plate. Serve topped with the yogurt mixture and fresh blueberries.

Cocoa Cookies

Prep time: 15 minutes | Cook time: 25 minutes | Serves 4

120 ml coconut flour
3 tablespoons cream cheese
1 teaspoon cocoa powder
1 tablespoon sweetener
¼ teaspoon baking powder
1 teaspoon apple cider vinegar
1 tablespoon butter
240 ml water, for cooking

1. Make the dough: Mix up coconut flour, cream cheese, cocoa powder, sweetener, baking powder, apple cider vinegar, and butter. Knead the dough, 2. Then transfer the dough in the baking pan and flatten it in the shape of a cookie. 3. Pour water and insert the steamer rack in the Ninja Foodi cooker. 4. Put the pan with a cookie in the Ninja Foodi cooker. Close and seal the lid. 5. Cook the cookie on High Pressure for 25 minutes. Make a quick pressure release. Cool the cookie well.

Almond Pie with Coconut

Prep time: 5 minutes | Cook time: 41 minutes | Serves 8

240 ml almond flour
120 ml coconut milk
1 teaspoon vanilla extract
2 tablespoons butter, softened
1 tablespoon Truvia
60 ml desiccated coconut
240 ml water

1. In the mixing bowl, mix up almond flour, coconut milk, vanilla extract, butter, Truvia, and desiccated coconut. 2. When the mixture is smooth, transfer it in the baking pan and flatten. 3. Pour water and insert the reversible rack in the Ninja Foodi cooker. 4. Put the baking pan with cake on the reversible rack. 5. Lock the lid. Set the cooking time for 41 minutes on High Pressure. Once the timer goes off, perform a natural pressure release for 10 minutes, then release any remaining pressure. Carefully open the lid. 6. Serve immediately.

Daikon and Almond Cake

Prep time: 10 minutes | Cook time: 45 minutes | Serves 12

5 eggs, beaten
120 ml double cream
240 ml almond flour
1 daikon, diced
1 teaspoon ground cinnamon
2 tablespoon sweetener
1 tablespoon butter, melted
240 ml water

1. In the mixing bowl, mix up eggs, double cream, almond flour, ground cinnamon, and sweetener. 2. When the mixture is smooth, add daikon and stir it carefully with the help of the spatula. 3. Pour the mixture in the cake pan. 4. Then pour water and insert the reversible rack in the Ninja Foodi cooker. 5. Place the cake in the Ninja Foodi cooker. 6. Set the lid in place. Set the cooking time for 45 minutes on High Pressure. When the timer goes off, do a quick pressure release. Carefully open the lid. 7. Serve immediately.

Fried Cheesecake Bites

Prep time: 30 minutes | Cook time: 2 minutes | Makes 16 bites

225 g cream cheese, softened
50 g powdered sweetener, plus 2 tablespoons, divided
4 tablespoons heavy cream, divided
½ teaspoon vanilla extract
50 g almond flour

1. In a stand mixer fitted with a paddle attachment, beat the cream cheese, 50 g of the sweetener, 2 tablespoons of the heavy cream, and the vanilla until smooth. Using a small ice-cream scoop, divide the mixture into 16 balls and arrange them on a rimmed baking sheet lined with baking paper. Freeze for 45 minutes until firm. 2. Line the cook & crisp basket with baking paper and Preheat the Ninja Foodi cooker to 175°C. 3. In a small shallow bowl, combine the almond flour with the remaining 2 tablespoons of sweetener. 4. In another small shallow bowl, place the remaining 2 tablespoons cream. 5. One at a time, dip the frozen cheesecake balls into the cream and then roll in the almond flour mixture, pressing lightly to form an even coating. Arrange the balls in a single layer in the cook & crisp basket, leaving room between them. Air crisp for 2 minutes until the coating is lightly browned.

Maple-Pecan Tart with Sea Salt

Prep time: 15 minutes | Cook time: 25 minutes | Serves 8

Tart Crust:
Vegetable oil spray
75 g unsalted butter, softened
50 g firmly packed brown sugar
125 g plain flour
¼ teaspoon kosher, or coarse sea salt
Filling:
4 tablespoons unsalted butter, diced
95 g packed brown sugar
60 ml pure maple syrup
60 ml whole milk
¼ teaspoon pure vanilla extract
190 g finely chopped pecans
¼ teaspoon flaked sea salt

1. For the crust: Line a baking pan with foil, leaving a couple of inches of overhang. Spray the foil with vegetable oil spray. 2. In a medium bowl, combine the butter and brown sugar. Beat with an electric mixer on medium-low speed until light and fluffy. Add the flour and kosher salt and beat until the ingredients are well blended. Transfer the mixture (it will be crumbly) to the prepared pan. Press it evenly into the bottom of the pan. 3. Place the pan in the cook & crisp basket. Set the Ninja Foodi cooker to 175°C and cook for 13 minutes. When the crust has 5 minutes left to cook, start the filling. 4. For the filling: In a medium saucepan, combine the butter, brown sugar, maple syrup, and milk. Bring to a simmer, stirring occasionally. When it begins simmering, cook for 1 minute. Remove from the heat and stir in the vanilla and pecans. 5. Carefully pour the filling evenly over the crust, gently spreading with a rubber spatula so the nuts and liquid are evenly distributed. Keep the Ninja Foodi cooker at 175°C and cook for 12 minutes, or until mixture is bubbling. (The center should still be slightly jiggly; it will thicken as it cools.) 6. Remove the pan from the Ninja Foodi cooker and sprinkle the tart with the sea salt. Cool completely on a wire rack until room temperature. 7. Transfer the pan to the refrigerator to chill. When cold (the tart will be easier to cut), use the foil overhang to remove the tart from the pan and cut into 8 wedges. Serve at room temperature.

Grilled Pineapple Dessert

Prep time: 5 minutes | Cook time: 12 minutes | Serves 4

Coconut, or avocado oil for misting, or cooking spray
4 ½-inch-thick slices fresh pineapple, core removed
1 tablespoon honey
¼ teaspoon brandy, or apple juice
2 tablespoons slivered almonds, toasted
Vanilla frozen yogurt, coconut sorbet, or ice cream

1. Spray both sides of pineapple slices with oil or cooking spray. Place into cook & crisp basket. 2. Air crisp at 200°C for 6 minutes. Turn slices over and cook for an additional 6 minutes. 3. Mix together the honey and brandy. 4. Remove cooked pineapple slices from Ninja Foodi cooker, sprinkle with toasted almonds, and drizzle with honey mixture. 5. Serve with a scoop of frozen yogurt or sorbet on the side.

Pecan Brownies

Prep time: 10 minutes | Cook time: 20 minutes | Serves 6

50 g blanched finely ground almond flour
55 g powdered sweetener
2 tablespoons unsweetened cocoa powder
½ teaspoon baking powder
55 g unsalted butter, softened
1 large egg
35 g chopped pecans
40 g low-carb, sugar-free chocolate chips

1. In a large bowl, mix almond flour, sweetener, cocoa powder, and baking powder. Stir in butter and egg. 2. Fold in pecans and chocolate chips. Scoop mixture into a round baking pan. Place pan into the cook & crisp basket. 3. Adjust the temperature to 150°C and bake for 20 minutes. 4. When fully cooked a toothpick inserted in center will come out clean. Allow 20 minutes to fully cool and firm up.

Goat Cheese–Stuffed Pears

Prep time: 6 minutes | Cook time: 2 minutes | Serves 4

60 g goat cheese, at room temperature
2 teaspoons pure maple syrup
2 ripe, firm pears, halved lengthwise and cored
2 tablespoons chopped pistachios, toasted

1. Pour 240 ml of water into the electric pressure cooker and insert a wire rack or reversible rack. 2. In a small bowl, combine the goat cheese and maple syrup. 3. Spoon the goat cheese mixture into the cored pear halves. Place the pears on the rack inside the pot, cut-side up. 4. Close and lock the lid of the pressure cooker. Set the valve to sealing. 5. Cook on high pressure for 2 minutes. 6. When the cooking is complete, hit Start/Stop and quick release the pressure. 7. Once the pin drops, unlock and remove the lid. 8. Using tongs, carefully transfer the pears to serving plates. 9. Sprinkle with pistachios and serve immediately.

Flourless Chocolate Tortes

Prep time: 7 minutes | Cook time: 10 minutes | Serves 8

200 g unsweetened baking chocolate, finely chopped
180 ml plus 2 tablespoons unsalted butter (or butter-flavored coconut oil for dairy-free)
300 ml granulated sweetener, or more to taste
5 large eggs
1 tablespoon coconut flour
2 teaspoons ground cinnamon
Seeds scraped from 1 vanilla bean (about 8 inches long), or 2 teaspoons vanilla extract
Pinch of fine sea salt

1. Grease 8 ramekins. Place the chocolate and butter in a pan over medium heat and stir until the chocolate is completely melted, about 3 minutes. 2. Remove the pan from the heat, then add the remaining ingredients and stir until smooth. Taste and adjust the sweetness to your liking. Pour the batter into the greased ramekins. 3. Place a reversible rack in the bottom of the Ninja Foodi cooker and pour in 240 ml of cold water. Place four of the ramekins on the reversible rack. 4. Lock the lid. Set the cooking time for 7 minutes at High Pressure. 5. When the timer beeps, use a quick pressure release. Carefully remove the lid. 6. Use tongs to remove the ramekins. Repeat with the remaining ramekins. 7. Serve the tortes warm or chilled.

Candied Mixed Nuts

Prep time: 5 minutes | Cook time: 15 minutes | Serves 8

240 ml pecan halves
240 ml chopped walnuts
80 ml granulated sweetener, or more to taste
80 ml grass-fed butter
1 teaspoon ground cinnamon

1. Preheat your oven to 180°C, and line a baking sheet with aluminium foil. 2. While your oven is warming, pour 120 ml of filtered water into the inner pot of the Ninja Foodi cooker, followed by the pecans, walnuts, granulated sweetener, butter, and cinnamon. Stir nut mixture, close the lid, and then set the pressure valve to Sealing. Cook at High Pressure, for 5 minutes. 3. Once cooked, perform a quick release by carefully switching the pressure valve to Venting, and strain the nuts. Pour the nuts onto the baking sheet, spreading them out in an even layer. Place in the oven for 5 to 10 minutes (or until crisp, being careful not to overcook). Cool before serving. Store leftovers in the refrigerator or freezer.

New York Cheesecake

Prep time: 1 hour | Cook time: 37 minutes | Serves 8

170 g almond flour
85 g powdered sweetener
55 g unsalted butter, melted
565 g full-fat cream cheese
120 ml heavy cream
340 g granulated sweetener
3 eggs, at room temperature
1 tablespoon vanilla essence
1 teaspoon grated lemon zest

1. Coat the sides and bottom of a baking pan with a little flour. 2. In a mixing bowl, combine the almond flour and powdered sweetener. Add the melted butter and mix until your mixture looks like breadcrumbs. 3. Press the mixture into the bottom of the prepared pan to form an even layer. Bake at 165°C for 7 minutes until golden brown. Allow it to cool completely on a wire rack. 4. Meanwhile, in a mixer fitted with the paddle attachment, prepare the filling by mixing the soft cheese, heavy cream, and granulated sweetener; beat until creamy and fluffy. 5. Crack the eggs into the mixing bowl, one at a time; add the vanilla and lemon zest and continue to mix until fully combined. 6. Pour the prepared topping over the cooled crust and spread evenly. 7. Bake in the preheated Ninja Foodi cooker at 165°C for 25 to 30 minutes; leave it in the Ninja Foodi cooker to keep warm for another 30 minutes. 8. Cover your cheesecake with plastic wrap. Place in your refrigerator and allow it to cool at least 6 hours or overnight. Serve well chilled.

Butter Flax Cookies

Prep time: 25 minutes | Cook time: 20 minutes | Serves 4

225 g almond meal
2 tablespoons flaxseed meal
30 g monk fruit, or equivalent sweetener
1 teaspoon baking powder
A pinch of grated nutmeg
A pinch of coarse salt
1 large egg, room temperature.
110 g unsalted butter, room temperature
1 teaspoon vanilla extract

1. Mix the almond meal, flaxseed meal, monk fruit, baking powder, grated nutmeg, and salt in a bowl. 2. In a separate bowl, whisk the egg, butter, and vanilla extract. 3. Stir the egg mixture into dry mixture; mix to combine well or until it forms a nice, soft dough. 4. Roll your dough out and cut out with a cookie cutter of your choice. Bake in the preheated Ninja Foodi cooker at 175°C for 10 minutes. Decrease the temperature to 165°C and cook for 10 minutes longer. Bon appétit!

Pumpkin Pudding with Vanilla Wafers

Prep time: 10 minutes | Cook time: 12 to 17 minutes | Serves 4

250 g canned no-salt-added pumpkin purée (not pumpkin pie filling)
50 g packed brown sugar
3 tablespoons plain flour
1 egg, whisked
2 tablespoons milk
1 tablespoon unsalted butter, melted
1 teaspoon pure vanilla extract
4 low-fat vanilla, or plain wafers, crumbled
Nonstick cooking spray

1. Preheat the Ninja Foodi cooker to 175°C. Coat a baking pan with nonstick cooking spray. Set aside. 2. Mix the pumpkin purée, brown sugar, flour, whisked egg, milk, melted butter, and vanilla in a medium bowl and whisk to combine. Transfer the mixture to the baking pan. 3. Place the baking pan in the cook & crisp basket and bake for 12 to 17 minutes until set. 4. Remove the pudding from the basket to a wire rack to cool. 5. Divide the pudding into four bowls and serve with the vanilla wafers sprinkled on top.

Thai Pandan Coconut Custard

Prep time: 10 minutes | Cook time: 30 minutes | Serves 4
Nonstick cooking spray
240 ml unsweetened coconut milk
3 eggs
80 ml granulated sweetener
3 to 4 drops pandan extract, or use vanilla extract if you must

1. Grease a 6-inch heatproof bowl with the cooking spray. 2. In a large bowl, whisk together the coconut milk, eggs, granulated sweetener, and pandan extract. Pour the mixture into the prepared bowl and cover it with aluminium foil. 3. Pour 480 ml of water into the inner cooking pot of the Ninja Foodi cooker, then place a reversible rack in the pot. Place the bowl on the reversible rack. 4. Lock the lid into place. Adjust the pressure to High. Cook for 30 minutes. When the cooking is complete, let the pressure release naturally. Unlock the lid. 5. Remove the bowl from the pot and remove the foil. A knife inserted into the custard should come out clean. Cool in the refrigerator for 6 to 8 hours, or until the custard is set.

Pumpkin Pie Pudding

Prep time: 10 minutes | Cook time: 20 minutes | Serves 6

Nonstick cooking spray
2 eggs
120 ml heavy (whipping) cream or almond milk (for dairy-free)
180 ml granulated sweetener
1 (425 g) can pumpkin purée
1 teaspoon pumpkin pie spice
1 teaspoon vanilla extract
For Serving:
120 ml heavy (whipping) cream

1. Grease a 6-by-3-inch pan extremely well with the cooking spray, making sure it gets into all the nooks and crannies. 2. In a medium bowl, whisk the eggs. Add the cream, granulated sweetener, pumpkin purée, pumpkin pie spice, and vanilla, and stir to mix thoroughly. 3. Pour the mixture into the prepared pan and cover it with a silicone lid or aluminium foil. 4. Pour 480 ml of water into the inner cooking pot of the Ninja Foodi cooker, then place a reversible rack in the pot. Place the covered pan on the reversible rack. 5. Lock the lid into place. Adjust the pressure to High. Cook for 20 minutes. When the cooking is complete, let the pressure release naturally for 10 minutes, then quick-release any remaining pressure. Unlock the lid. 6. Remove the pan and place it in the refrigerator. Chill for 6 to 8 hours. 8. When ready to serve, finish by making the whipped cream. Using a hand mixer, beat the double cream until it forms soft peaks. Do not overbeat and turn it to butter. Serve each pudding with a dollop of whipped cream.

Vanilla Crème Brûlée

Prep time: 7 minutes | Cook time: 9 minutes | Serves 4

240 ml double cream (or full-fat coconut milk for dairy-free)
2 large egg yolks
2 tablespoons granulated sweetener, or more to taste
Seeds scraped from ½ vanilla
bean (about 8 inches long), or 1 teaspoon vanilla extract
240 ml cold water
4 teaspoons granulated sweetener, for topping

1. Heat the cream in a pan over medium-high heat until hot, about 2 minutes. 2. Place the egg yolks, granulated sweetener, and vanilla seeds in a blender and blend until smooth. 3. While the blender is running, slowly pour in the hot cream. Taste and adjust the sweetness to your liking. 4. Scoop the mixture into four ramekins with a spatula. Cover the ramekins with aluminium foil. 5. Add the water to the Ninja Foodi cooker and insert a reversible rack. Place the ramekins on the reversible rack. 6. Lock the lid. Set the cooking time for 7 minutes at High Pressure. 7. When the timer beeps, perform a quick pressure release. Carefully remove the lid. 8. Keep the ramekins covered with the foil and place in the refrigerator for about 2 hours until completely chilled. 9. Sprinkle 1 teaspoon of granulated sweetener on top of each crème brûlée. Use the oven broiler to melt the sweetener. 10. Allow the topping to cool in the fridge for 5 minutes before serving.

Blackberry Cobbler

Prep time: 15 minutes | Cook time: 25 to 30 minutes | Serves 6

330 g fresh or frozen blackberries
350 g granulated sugar, divided into 200 g and 150 g
1 teaspoon vanilla extract
8 tablespoons butter, melted
125 g self-raising flour
1 to 2 tablespoons oil

1. In a medium bowl, stir together the blackberries, 200 g of sugar, and vanilla. 2. In another medium bowl, stir together the melted butter, remaining 150 g of sugar, and flour until a dough forms. 3. Spritz a baking pan with oil. Add the blackberry mixture. Crumble the flour mixture over the fruit. Cover the pan with aluminum foil. 4. Preheat the Ninja Foodi cooker to 175°C. 5. Place the covered pan in the cook & crisp basket. Cook for 20 to 25 minutes until the filling is thickened. 6. Uncover the pan and cook for 5 minutes more, depending on how juicy and browned you like your cobbler. Let sit for 5 minutes before serving.

Coconut Lemon Squares

Prep time: 5 minutes | Cook time: 40 minutes | Serves 5 to 6

3 eggs
2 tablespoons grass-fed butter, softened
120 ml full-fat coconut milk
½ teaspoon baking powder
½ teaspoon vanilla extract
120 ml granulated sweetener, or more to taste
60 ml lemon juice
240 ml blanched almond flour

1. In a large bowl, mix together the eggs, butter, coconut milk, baking powder, vanilla, granulated sweetener, lemon juice, and flour. Stir thoroughly, until a perfectly even mixture is obtained. 2. Next, pour 240 ml filtered water into the Ninja Foodi cooker, and insert the reversible rack. Transfer the mixture from the bowl into a well-greased, Ninja Foodi cooker-friendly pan (or dish). 3. Using a sling if desired, place the dish onto the reversible rack, and cover loosely with aluminium foil. Close the lid, set the Ninja Foodi cooker to 40 minutes on High Pressure, and let cook. 4. Once cooked, let the pressure naturally disperse from the Ninja Foodi cooker for about 10 minutes, then carefully switch the pressure release to Venting. 5. Open the Ninja Foodi cooker, and remove the dish. Let cool, cut into 6 squares, serve, and enjoy!

Cardamom Rolls with Cream Cheese

Prep time: 20 minutes | Cook time: 18 minutes | Serves 5

120 ml coconut flour
1 tablespoon ground cardamom
2 tablespoon granulated sweetener
1 egg, whisked
60 ml almond milk
1 tablespoon butter, softened
1 tablespoon cream cheese
80 ml water

1. Combine together coconut flour, almond milk, and softened butter. 2. Knead the smooth dough. 3. Roll up the dough with the help of the rolling pin. 4. Then combine together granulated sweetener and ground cardamom. 5. Sprinkle the surface of the dough with the ground cardamom mixture. 6. Roll the dough into one big roll and cut them into servings. 7. Place the rolls into the Ninja Foodi cooker round mold. 8. Pour water in the Ninja Foodi cooker (80 ml) and insert the mold inside. 9. Cook on High Pressure for 18 minutes. 10. Then use the natural pressure release method for 15 minutes. 11. Chill the rolls to the room temperature and spread with cream cheese.

Apple Fries

Prep time: 10 minutes | Cook time: 7 minutes | Serves 8

Coconut, or avocado oil, for spraying
110 g plain flour
3 large eggs, beaten
100 g crushed digestive biscuits
55 g granulated sugar
1 teaspoon ground cinnamon
3 large Gala apples, peeled, cored and cut into wedges
240 ml caramel sauce, warmed

1. Preheat the Ninja Foodi cooker to 190ºC. Line the cook & crisp basket with baking paper and spray lightly with oil. 2. Place the flour and beaten eggs in separate bowls and set aside. In another bowl, mix together the crushed biscuits, sugar and cinnamon. 3. Working one at a time, coat the apple wedges in the flour, dip in the egg and then dredge in the biscuit mix until evenly coated. 4. Place the apples in the prepared basket, taking care not to overlap, and spray lightly with oil. You may need to work in batches, depending on the size of your Ninja Foodi cooker. 5. Cook for 5 minutes, flip, spray with oil, and cook for another 2 minutes, or until crunchy and golden brown. 6. Drizzle the caramel sauce over the top and serve.

Chocolate Fondue

Prep time: 5 minutes | Cook time: 2 minutes | Serves 4

60 g unsweetened baking chocolate, finely chopped, divided
240 ml double cream, divided
80 ml granulated sweetener, divided
Fine sea salt
240 ml cold water
Special Equipment:
Set of fondue forks or wooden skewers

1. Divide the chocolate, cream, and sweetener evenly among four ramekins. Add a pinch of salt to each one and stir well. Cover the ramekins with aluminium foil. 2. Place a reversible rack in the bottom of your Ninja Foodi cooker and pour in the water. Place the ramekins on the reversible rack. 3. Lock the lid. Set the cooking time for 2 minutes at High Pressure. 4. When the timer beeps, perform a natural pressure release for 10 minutes. Carefully remove the lid. 5. Use tongs to remove the ramekins from the pot. Use a fork to stir the fondue until smooth. 6. Use immediately.

Indian Toast and Milk

Prep time: 10 minutes | Cook time: 20 minutes | Serves 4

305 g sweetened, condensed milk
240 ml evaporated milk
240 ml single cream
1 teaspoon ground cardamom, plus additional for garnish
1 pinch saffron threads
4 slices white bread
2 to 3 tablespoons ghee or butter, softened
2 tablespoons crushed pistachios, for garnish (optional)

1. In a baking pan, combine the condensed milk, evaporated milk, half-and-half, cardamom, and saffron. Stir until well combined. 2. Place the pan in the cook & crisp basket. Set the Ninja Foodi cooker to 175ºC for 15 minutes, stirring halfway through the cooking time. Remove the sweetened milk from the Ninja Foodi cooker and set aside. 3. Cut each slice of bread into two triangles. Brush each side with ghee. Place the bread in the cook & crisp basket. Keeping the Ninja Foodi cooker on 175ºC cook for 5 minutes or until golden brown and toasty. 4. Remove the bread from the Ninja Foodi cooker. Arrange two triangles in each of four wide, shallow bowls. Pour the hot milk mixture on top of the bread and let soak for 30 minutes. 5. Garnish with pistachios if using, and sprinkle with additional cardamom.

Nutmeg Cupcakes

Prep time: 5 minutes | Cook time: 30 minutes | Serves 7

Cake:
- 480 ml blanched almond flour
- 2 tablespoons grass-fed butter, softened
- 2 eggs
- 120 ml unsweetened almond milk
- 120 ml granulated sweetener, or more to taste
- ½ teaspoon ground nutmeg
- ½ teaspoon baking powder

Frosting:
- 110 g full-fat cream cheese, softened
- 4 tablespoons grass-fed butter, softened
- 480 ml heavy whipping cream
- 1 teaspoon vanilla extract
- 120 ml granulated sweetener, or more to taste
- 6 tablespoons sugar-free chocolate chips (optional)

1. Pour 240 ml of filtered water into the inner pot of the Ninja Foodi cooker, then insert the reversible rack. In a large bowl, combine the flour, butter, eggs, almond milk, granulated sweetener, nutmeg, and baking powder. Mix thoroughly. Working in batches if needed, transfer this mixture into a well-greased, Ninja Foodi cooker-friendly muffin (or egg bites) mold. 2. Place the molds onto the reversible rack, and cover loosely with aluminium foil. Close the lid, set the Ninja Foodi cooker to 30 minutes on High Pressure, and let cook. 3. While you wait, in a large bowl, combine the cream cheese, butter, whipping cream, vanilla, granulated sweetener, and chocolate chips. Use an electric hand mixer until you achieve a light and fluffy texture. Place frosting in refrigerator. 4. Once the cupcakes are cooked, let the pressure release naturally, for about 10 minutes. Then, switch the pressure release to Venting. Open the Ninja Foodi cooker, and remove the food. Let cool, top each cupcake evenly with a scoop of frosting.

Printed in Great Britain
by Amazon

14073495R00050